T0300597

U.S. HISTORY

Workman Kids
Workman Publishing
Hachette Book Group, Inc.
1290 Avenue of the Americas
New York, NY 10104
workman.com

Workman Kids is an imprint of Workman Publishing, a division of Hachette Book Group, Inc. BRAIN QUEST, BIG FAT NOTE-BOOK, and the Workman name and logo are registered trademarks of Hachette Book Group, Inc.

Originally published as *Everything You Need to Ace American History in One Big Fat Notebook*, © 2016 by Workman Publishing

Writer: Lily Rothman   Contributor: Ella-Kari Loftfield
Illustrators: Tim Hall and Chris Pearce   Designers: Tim Hall and Abby Dening
Concept by Raquel Jaramillo

The publisher is not responsible for websites (or their content) that are not owned by the publisher.

Workman books may be purchased in bulk for business, educational, or promotional use. For information, please contact your local bookseller or the Hachette Book Group Special Markets Department at special.markets@hbgusa.com.

Library of Congress Cataloging-in-Publication Data is available.

Print ISBN 978-1-5235-1594-3

Ebook ISBNs 978-1-5235-2084-8, 978-1-5235-2076-3, 978-1-5235-2080-0

Second Edition March 2023 IVIV

Distributed in Europe by Hachette Livre, 58 rue Jean Bleuzen, 92 178 Vanves Cedex, France.
Distributed in the United Kingdom by Hachette Book Group, UK, Carmelite House,
50 Victoria Embankment, London EC4Y 0DZ.

Printed in Rawang, Malaysia, on responsibly sourced paper.

10 9 8 7 6 5 4 3

THE **COMPLETE** MIDDLE SCHOOL STUDY GUIDE

EVERYTHING YOU NEED TO ACE

U.S.

HISTORY

IN ONE BIG FAT NOTEBOOK

Borrowed from the smartest kid in class
Double-checked by Philip Bigler

WORKMAN PUBLISHING
NEW YORK

HI!

These are the notes from my U.S. history class. Oh, who am I? Well, some people said I was the smartest kid in class.

I wrote everything you need to ace **U.S. HISTORY**, from the ICE AGE to the INTERNET AGE, and only the really important stuff in between—you know, the stuff that's usually on the test!

I tried to keep everything organized, so I almost always

- highlight vocabulary words in **YELLOW**.
- color in definitions in green highlighter.
- use BLUE PEN for important people, places, dates, and terms.
- doodle a pretty sweet Eleanor Roosevelt and whatnot to visually show the big ideas.

AGREED!

If you're not loving your textbook and you're not so great at taking notes in class, this notebook will help. It hits all the major points. (But if your teacher spends a whole class talking about something that's not covered, go ahead and write that down for yourself.)

zzz...WHAT?

Now that I've aced U.S. history, this notebook is **YOURS**. I'm done with it, so this notebook's purpose in life is to help **YOU** learn and remember just what you need to ace **YOUR** U.S. history class.

EVERYTHING YOU NEED TO ACE U.S. HISTORY IN ONE BIG FAT NOTEBOOK, 2ND EDITION has been updated to present a more accurate, inclusive recounting of historical events. Conscious language is used throughout to ensure a respectful tone when referring to people and their experiences. And Unit 10 has been updated to include the most recent key historical events!

CONTENTS

THIS ONE IS A DOOZIE!

BCE = BEFORE the COMMON ERA
(or before the year 1)

CE = the COMMON ERA
(or the year 1 and after)

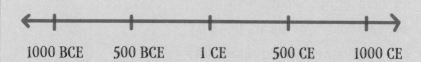

| 1000 BCE | 500 BCE | 1 CE | 500 CE | 1000 CE |

BCE dates sorta work like negative numbers.
For example, 1000 BCE is further in the past than 500 BCE.

YEAR VS. CENTURY

1300s = 14th century	1700s = 18th century
1400s = 15th century	1800s = 19th century
1500s = 16th century	1900s = 20th century
1600s = 17th century	2000s = 21st century

Unit 1

Prehistory— Early 1600s

The United States is technically only about 250 years old. But if you really want to understand all of what makes this nation unique, you have to travel much further back in time. Who lived on these lands first? How did they live? How did the first Europeans get here, and how did they treat the Indigenous people of the continent? How was Africa swept into the nation's history? What kinds of conflicts were stirred up? Why is English the dominant language here? With so many questions, it is important to set the stage. . . .

The very beginning is a very good place to start.

Chapter 1

EARLY PEOPLE IN AMERICA

MIGRATION

People have been living in the Americas much longer than scientists used to think. The first people started arriving around 38,000 BCE (BEFORE the COMMON ERA—which starts with the year 1!), 40,000 years ago.

They were **NOMADIC HUNTER-GATHERERS**. They followed herds of the animals they hunted and ate the plants they found. Like the rest of humankind, they started out in Africa, but after thousands of years they made their way east and north across Asia. When a group moves from one place to another, it's called a **MIGRATION**.

> **NOMADIC HUNTER-GATHERERS**
> communities of people who move from place to place, relying on plants and animals found in the wild for food

> **MIGRATION**
> the movement of a number of people (or animals), often to establish a new homeland

The ICE AGE and the BERING LAND BRIDGE

These nomadic hunter-gatherers *TOOK PLACE DURING THE MOST RECENT GLACIAL PERIOD* lived during the ICE AGE, when much of the earth was covered in ice and snow and entire oceans were frozen over. When seawater is frozen solid, the ocean level gets lower, exposing whole stretches of land that are underwater during warmer climates. The land connecting the northeast tip of Asia and present-day Alaska, called the BERING LAND BRIDGE (or BERINGIA), emerged. According to the LAND BRIDGE THEORY, nomadic hunter-gatherers crossed on this land bridge from Asia into North America (what is now Alaska), most likely in search of food. The Americas were filled with woolly mammoths, mastodons, and other huge creatures. Just one could feed an entire nomad group for months. The Land Bridge Theory is one of many theories. Scientists are still uncertain about this.

ASIA

WOO-HOO!!!

BERING LAND BRIDGE

NORTH AMERICA

SOUTH AMERICA

HEY!

EAT THIS GUY!

The theory says that people kept crossing until around 10,500 BCE, when the Ice Age, which had lasted about 100,000 years, finally ended. The oceans rose and covered the Bering Land Bridge, cutting off further migrations from Asia. Ice Age animals died off or were hunted into extinction. These animals were replaced by smaller animals that could thrive in warmer weather, changing people's diets and lifestyles.

3

MESOAMERICAN CIVILIZATIONS

MESOAMERICA
the area now called
Central America

NORTH AMERICA

SOUTH AMERICA

Gulf of Mexico

Mexico

TENOCHTITLÁN ★

Caribbean Sea

Belize

Honduras

Guatemala

El Salvador

Nicaragua

Costa Rica

Panama

Pacific Ocean

Colombia

OLMEC
Mesoamerica,
1200–400 BCE

MAYA
Mesoamerica,
300 BCE–900 CE

Ecuador

Peru

Brazil

AZTEC
Mexico, 1110–1521 CE,
capital: Tenochtitlán

CUZCO ★

Bolivia

INCA
South America, 1100–
1533 CE, capital: Cuzco

Chile

MAYA PYRAMID

Some nomad **SOCIETIES** stayed in Alaska, while others continued south through Central and South America and the rest of North America. As societies spread, they developed individual **CULTURES** and traditions, and sometimes different physical traits.

SETTLING DOWN

When agriculture developed, many societies stopped being nomadic. They changed their focus to planting seeds and farming foods like beans, squash,

> **SOCIETY**
> a group of people living together as a group
>
> **CULTURE**
> the way a society behaves and its system of beliefs, laws, and customs

and MAIZE (an early form of corn). These societies cultivated diverse strains of corn, beans, and squash, and created enough food to nourish the entire continent. They settled down, built permanent homes, formed villages, and invented advanced technologies, like irrigation systems and canals, that helped make their daily lives more productive.

One of the first great **CIVILIZATIONS** was the OLMEC society, which flourished around 1200 BCE on the coast

> **CIVILIZATION**
> an advanced and complicated society

of **MESOAMERICA** when small groups began to band together. The Olmecs were skilled people with an extensive knowledge of the land. Their expertise enabled them to grow enough food to feed thousands of people. They were also known for harnessing the skills of their large population to create giant stone sculptures and pyramids.

Around 400 BCE, the Olmecs disappeared. No one knows why—famine, war, and natural disaster are all possibilities.

Around this time, the **MAYA** civilization developed in the Mesoamerican rain forest. As the Olmecs disappeared, Maya cities grew. The Maya were also skilled in farming and building, raising crops, and constructing huge pyramids and temples. They had a **THEOCRACY**; worshipped the sun, stars, and moon; and developed a 365-day calendar. They built canals and a large trade network, which helped them grow into a powerful civilization. Mayans used forced labor to achieve much of their greatness. By around 900 CE, their power and influence had greatly diminished and they ultimately fell because of rebellions from the enslaved and the working class.

> **THEOCRACY**
> rule by god(s);
> government where the
> priests are in charge

The **AZTECS**, who began as warriors and hunters, conquered what is now Central Mexico around 1100 CE. In 1325, they founded their capital, TENOCHTITLÁN, on an island in the middle of Lake Texcoco. They used advanced engineering skills to build bridges to connect their capital to the mainland, making Tenochtitlán one of the largest cities in the world. The Aztecs continued to conquer, using some of their prisoners as human sacrifices. By 1500, they were a powerful **EMPIRE**.

> **EMPIRE**
> a powerful political
> unit made up of a
> number of territories
> under a single rule

The **INCAS** started as small groups in the Andes Mountains. Around 1100 CE, they founded their capital, CUZCO, in what is now Peru. A powerful government united them into a population of about 12 million people, all speaking the common language of QUECHUA (which today is the most commonly spoken Indigenous language in the Americas, with speakers throughout the Andes, Colombia, Ecuador, and elsewhere).

The Incas' innovations included terraced farming, a network of roads, and the use of knotted strings (QUIPU) for record-keeping. They built cities such as MACHU PICCHU for their religious ceremonies.

Remember the order in which these first empires rose and fell with this mnemonic device:

OH OLMEC
MY! MAYA
AMERICA'S AZTEC
INTERESTING! INCA

In the 1500s, the Aztec and Inca civilizations were invaded and colonized by Spanish Conquistadors, which led to their downfall.

CHECK YOUR KNOWLEDGE

1. What is the Land Bridge Theory?

2. What effect did the end of the Ice Age have on the Americas?

3. How might migration affect a society's culture?

4. What is a nomadic hunter-gatherer society?

5. How did innovations in farming affect societies?

6. What is one invention of the Maya people?

7. What is a theocracy?

STILL FRIENDS?

8. What was the capital of the Aztec Empire? When was it founded?

9. What was the language of the Inca Empire?

10. How did knowledge of engineering help establish the Mesoamerican civilizations?

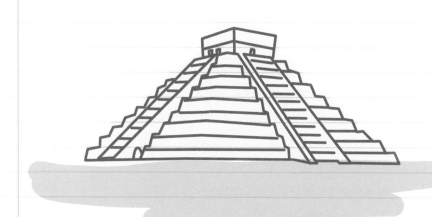

1. The Land Bridge Theory is one of many theories that tries to explain the early period of migration. It says that nomadic hunter-gatherers crossed a stretch of land called the Bering Land Bridge (or Beringia), which connected northeast Asia and present-day Alaska, in search of food.

2. The end of the Ice Age meant that Ice Age animals died off and were replaced with smaller animals that could live in the warmer climate. This changed the way people lived and ate.

3. As people are separated from their roots, they develop new traditions.

4. People who move regularly, and hunt and gather for food

5. Populations and wealth grew immensely. Sedentary living became the standard. Few nomadic groups remained after agriculture was developed.

6. A calendar, canals

7. A government controlled by priests

8. Tenochtitlán, founded 1325 CE

9. Quechua

10. The Olmecs created giant stone sculptures and pyramids; the Mayas built pyramids, temples, and canals; and the Aztecs built bridges that connected their capital to the mainland.

☆ Chapter 2 ☆

INDIGENOUS PEOPLES
★ ★ ☆ ★ ★ ★ IN ★ ★ ★ ★ ★ ★
NORTH AMERICA

The millions of people who formed complex communities and who originally settled the land that is now the U.S. and Canada are called INDIGENOUS PEOPLES.

> **INDIGENOUS**
> native to an area

EARLY INDIGENOUS PEOPLES

Around 1200 BCE, the ANCESTRAL PUEBLO PEOPLE (called the Anasazi people by Anglo-American historians), settled in the FOUR CORNERS area. Their first homes were PIT HOUSES,

THE MAP IS ON THE NEXT PAGE.

dwellings dug partly into the ground. By about 750 CE they were building PUEBLOS: multistoried, apartment-like buildings made from **ADOBE** and other local materials. The Pueblo people were also known for CLIFF DWELLINGS built along cliff walls and mountainsides. For religious rites, they created cavelike underground ceremonial chambers called KIVAS. The Pueblo people

> **ADOBE**
> a kind of clay still used for building in the Southwest

FOUR CORNERS
THE PLACE WHERE UTAH, COLORADO, ARIZONA, AND NEW MEXICO MEET

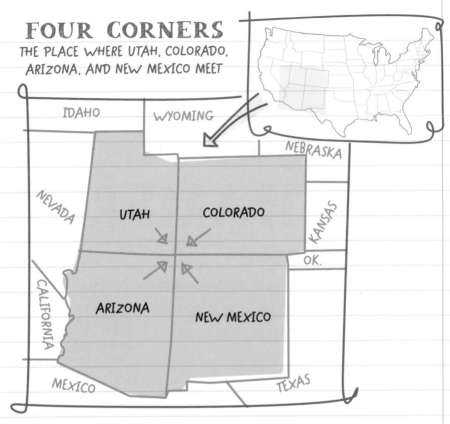

were astute farmers. Since the Four Corners area was relatively dry, they devised irrigation techniques to grow crops, especially maize. The Pueblo people inhabited the area until around 1300 CE, when they split into hundreds of smaller city-states along the Rio Grande that traded with each other, some of them becoming major trade centers. There was prosperity, and their descendants still live in the region and practice the culture. Historians still don't know why they split up.

The HUGUGAM, also known as Hohokam, lived in present-day Arizona. They arrived from Mexico around the year 300 CE and stayed for about a millennium. The Hugugam had the most extensive and advanced irrigation system in the world at the time. And their community connected North and Central America, making it a major trading crossroads in the Americas.

The MOUND BUILDER societies created huge earthen mounds as temples and burial sites that can still be seen in the central United States. The first were built around 1000 BCE and echo the look of Mesoamerican pyramids. It's a clue that Mound Builders may have come from Mesoamerica.

The Mound Builders were the ADENA, HOPEWELL, and MISSISSIPPIAN peoples. The ADENA hunter-gatherers thrived around 800 BCE. The HOPEWELL were farmers and traders at their height around 200–500 BCE. When the Hopewell population declined around the year 700 CE, the MISSISSIPPIAN people became more widespread. Around 900 CE, they formed their largest settlement, CAHOKIA. Located in present-day Illinois, Cahokia was home to tens of thousands of people and was the site of the Mississippian people's largest mound, **MONKS MOUND**.

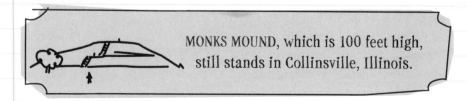

MONKS MOUND, which is 100 feet high, still stands in Collinsville, Illinois.

DIFFERENT SOCIETIES

THE NORTH, in present-day Alaska, was so cold that the INUITS and ALEUTS who settled there built **IGLOOS** to protect themselves from the harsh weather. They relied on hunting and fishing. They were likely originally from Siberia and may have been the last migrants to cross the Bering Land Bridge.

THE NORTHWEST had so many forests and such easy access to the ocean that the TLINGIT, HAIDA, and CHINOOK who settled there used wood to build their houses and make **TOTEM POLES** with religious significance. Fish, especially salmon, became their major food source.

THE WEST had such fertile land that the UTE and SHOSHONE tribes could live off abundant crops. These tribes formed small clans rather than large villages.

THE SOUTHWEST was home to descendants of the Ancestral Pueblo people (the HOPI, the ACOMA, and the ZUNI), who continued to build with adobe and grow maize. Around the 1500s, two nomadic hunter-gatherer societies arrived—the APACHE and the NAVAJO (also called the DINÉ). Within a century they had built villages, too.

THE GREAT PLAINS were filled with herds of buffalo, or **BISON**, so the peoples there became nomads and hunters. The BLACKFEET and the APACHE lived in **TEPEES** (conical tents) that were easy to pack up to follow the bison. Starting in the 1500s, some tribes, like the COMANCHE and DAKOTA, used horses that had escaped from Spanish explorers, and became famous for their equestrian skills.

THE SOUTHEAST had rich soil from its rivers and mountains, and the CREEK, CHICKASAW, SEMINOLE, and TSALAGI (called the CHEROKEE by Anglo-American historians) farmed and built permanent villages around their fields.

Many Indigenous groups maintain their cultural traditions today.

DIFFERENT ENVIRONMENTS

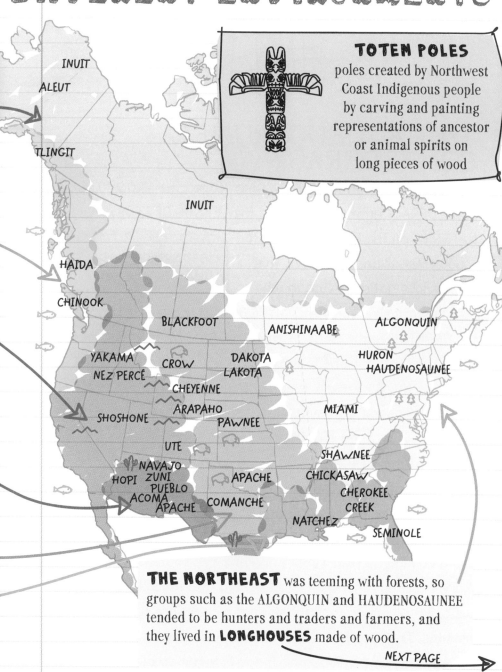

TOTEM POLES
poles created by Northwest Coast Indigenous people by carving and painting representations of ancestor or animal spirits on long pieces of wood

INUIT
ALEUT
TLINGIT
INUIT
HAIDA
CHINOOK
BLACKFOOT
ANISHINAABE
ALGONQUIN
YAKAMA
NEZ PERCÉ
CROW
DAKOTA
LAKOTA
HURON
HAUDENOSAUNEE
CHEYENNE
ARAPAHO
PAWNEE
MIAMI
SHOSHONE
UTE
SHAWNEE
NAVAJO
HOPI ZUNI
PUEBLO
ACOMA
APACHE
APACHE
COMANCHE
CHICKASAW
CHEROKEE
CREEK
NATCHEZ
SEMINOLE

THE NORTHEAST was teeming with forests, so groups such as the ALGONQUIN and HAUDENOSAUNEE tended to be hunters and traders and farmers, and they lived in **LONGHOUSES** made of wood.

NEXT PAGE

HAUDENOSAUNEE MEANS "PEOPLE OF THE LONGHOUSE."

The HAUDENOSAUNEE CONFEDERACY

The HAUDENOSAUNEE CONFEDERACY (called the IROQUOIS CONFEDERACY by the French and the LEAGUE OF FIVE NATIONS by the English) refers to a powerful alliance between five Indigenous nations living in what's now upstate New York: the CAYUGA, the ONONDAGA, the SENECA, the MOHAWK, and the ONEIDA. Each nation of the Confederacy had a distinct language and culture, but they were governed together by the GREAT LAW OF PEACE, ← INSPIRED THE U.S. CONSTITUTION!

> Use this mnemonic device to remember the five original nations of the Haudenosaunee Confederacy:
>
> **C**AYUGA
> **O**NONDAGA
> **S**ENECA
> **M**OHAWK
> **O**NEIDA

a set of rules that all nations followed. Representatives from each nation formed the GRAND COUNCIL, which governed and settled disputes. They had a communal food supply and ensured that crops were shared equally among all people. They also used discussions (we call it diplomacy today) instead of warfare to settle disputes. In 1722, the TUSCARORA people joined, and the Haudenosaunee Confederacy today is made up of six nations.

CHECK YOUR KNOWLEDGE

1. Name three types of homes that the Ancestral Pueblo people created.

2. How did the Mound Builders use mounds?

3. What was Cahokia?

4. What was a major factor in the differences between Indigenous cultures?

5. What is an example of a nomadic Indigenous society?

6. What is the Haudenosaunee Confederacy?

7. What did nations of the Haudenosaunee Confederacy share? What about them remained distinct?

ANSWERS

CHECK YOUR ANSWERS

1. Pit houses, pueblos, and cliff dwellings
2. To be used as temples and tombs
3. The largest settlement of the Mississippian people
4. Where they lived: climate, geography, and resources
5. The Blackfoot, Apache, Comanche, Dakota, Cheyenne, Kiowa, Ojibwe, and Navajo are all examples of Indigenous societies that were nomadic.
6. An alliance between six (previously five) Indigenous nations in upstate New York
7. The Haudenosaunee shared a set of laws called the Great Law of Peace, and leaders, called the Great Council. Their languages and cultures remained distinct.

☆ Chapter 3 ☆

THE PRICE OF EXPANSION

CONTACT, CONFLICT, CONQUEST, and COLONIZATION

Some call this period the Age of Exploration, and there was a lot of exploring going on. But this exploration by people living in Europe also led to the exploitation of the original inhabitants of the other three continents bordering the Atlantic Ocean: North America, South America, and Africa. The "Age of Exploration" led the four continents that frame the Atlantic Ocean into contact, conflict, conquest, and **COLONIZATION**.

COLONIZATION
the process of settling and establishing control over land and the Indigenous people settled on that land

WHAT ABOUT THE VIKINGS?
The Vikings, seafaring people from Scandinavia, were the first Europeans to explore North America. ERIK THE RED discovered Greenland, and his son LEIF ERIKSSON reached present-day Canada in the year 1000 CE. Eriksson named the land "Vinland," but since the Vikings didn't stay, future explorers were credited with being the first Europeans.

MOTIVE and MEANS to TRAVEL and TRADE

What does trading have to do with U.S. history? A lot, it turns out. Europeans fell in love with trade goods from Asia after **THE CRUSADES** of the 12th century and the travels of MARCO POLO in the 13th century. These

events introduced Europeans to the four **S**'s (spices, silk, scents, and precious stones). Traders used caravan routes and the SILK ROAD, a network of trading routes that linked China and the West, to move goods. Trade over land was difficult, and after the fall of Constantinople in 1453, the Ottoman Empire cut off access to those essential trade routes.

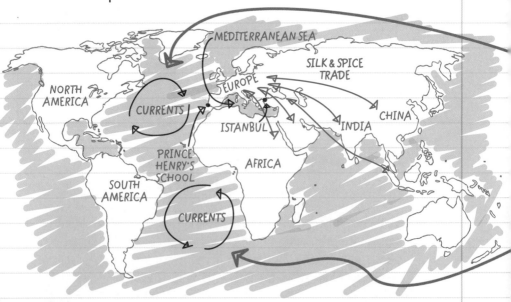

20

This appetite for Asian goods was the motivation for Europeans to find other ways to get the items they wanted. So, Europeans worked on the means to get to Asia by sailing!

NICE RIDE!

The Portuguese took the lead in sailing the seas, mostly because of PRINCE HENRY THE NAVIGATOR. He built a school of navigation in the 1400s. This school used Arab boats as a model to develop the CARAVEL, a speedy and maneuverable ship that could sail into the wind, making it easier to explore coastlines. MAGNETIC COMPASSES, invented in China, improved the safety and efficiency of ocean travel.

ASTROLABES allowed sailors to figure out their location in the ocean by measuring the distance of the sun and stars, like an ancient GPS.

Sailors figured out that the NORTH ATLANTIC CURRENT moves clockwise between Europe and the Caribbean, and the SOUTH ATLANTIC CURRENT travels counterclockwise between Africa and South America. This saved them from being randomly swept out to sea (sometimes that's how they discovered new places; sometimes that's how they disappeared forever).

The Portuguese used this knowledge to explore the west coast of Africa (called the Gold Coast), where they traded with Arab and African merchants for gold, ivory, and enslaved people.

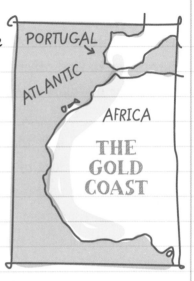

PORTUGAL

ATLANTIC

AFRICA

THE GOLD COAST

The WEST AFRICAN SLAVE TRADE GROWS

By the 1400s, West Africa's largest kingdoms had fractured into many small kingdoms that warred over land and trade. Enslaving captured enemies was an established practice, and a slave trade was a big, and terrible, part of the West African economy. When the Portuguese and other Europeans arrived in the 1480s, they saw Western Africa as a source of enslaved labor that they could profit from and utilize in their new colonies. Europeans established ports along the African coast and raided towns, capturing as many African adults and children as they could. The more Europeans explored and colonized, the bigger the slave trade grew.

EUROPEAN EXPEDITIONS

1487 A storm and winds accidentally took BARTOLOMEU DIAS to the southern tip of Africa. Dias named the land the CAPE OF GOOD HOPE, in the hope that it would lead to a route to India.

1492 CHRISTOPHER COLUMBUS thought he could reach India faster if he sailed west.

1497 VASCO DA GAMA sailed around the Cape of Good Hope and reached India in May 1498. The Portuguese made this a regular trade route, and LISBON (the capital of Portugal) became a major trade city, which made Portugal VERY RICH.

1497 JOHN CABOT (aka Giovanni Caboto) was an Italian navigator who explored the North Atlantic for England's Henry VII. He brought back stirring reports of fishing grounds where the fish practically jumped into their boat!

1497 A Portuguese fleet led by PEDRO ALVARES CABRAL ended up in present-day Brazil while on the way to Africa, so Cabral claimed the land for Portugal.

1502 AMERIGO VESPUCCI sailed along the coast of South America. He was one of the first Europeans to realize for sure that these lands were not in Asia. A German mapmaker labeled these new lands "America" in his honor.

1513 PONCE DE LEON was the first European to set foot in Florida . . . looking for the Fountain of Youth.

1513 VASCO NÚÑEZ DE BALBOA crossed Panama and was the first European to see the Pacific Ocean from the west.

⤋——COINED THE NAME "PACIFIC OCEAN" FROM "PEACEFUL SEA"

1519 FERDINAND MAGELLAN, sailing on behalf of Spain, reached the tip of South America. He was killed in battle in the Philippines, but his ships and sailors who returned to Spain in 1522 were the first Europeans to **CIRCUMNAVIGATE** the earth.

1519 HERNÁN CORTÉS explored Mexico.

> **CIRCUMNAVIGATE**
> sail around ("circum-"—
> think, "circle")

1522 FRANCISCO PIZARRO explored the Andes.

1524 GIOVANNI DA VERRAZZANO (an Italian sent by the French) explored Nova Scotia, Canada.

1528 ÁLVAR NÚÑEZ CABEZA DE VACA was stranded on an island off the coast of what is now Texas. He and three other survivors (two Spanish sailors and an enslaved African) made their way to Spanish settlements in northern Mexico. Cabeza de Vaca came to respect the many Indigenous societies he met along the way.

1535 JACQUES CARTIER (a Frenchman) explored the St. Lawrence River and claimed what is now Canada for France.

1539 HERNANDO DE SOTO explored North America and in 1541 crossed the Mississippi River.

1540 FRANCISCO CORONADO traveled overland seeking the "Seven Cities of Gold" in modern-day New Mexico.

ARE WE THERE YET?

CONFLICT BETWEEN COUNTRIES: DRAWING the LINE of DEMARCATION

Immediately, there was conflict between Spain and Portugal over their claims to lands. In 1493, they asked Pope Alexander VI to settle their argument. On a map of the world, the pope drew a LINE OF DEMARCATION from the top to the bottom, declaring that everything to the west "belonged" to Spain and everything to the east "belonged" to Portugal. (They didn't acknowledge that the land already "belonged" to the millions of people who had lived on it for centuries.) A year later the two countries agreed to move the line about 1,175 miles west in the TREATY OF TORDESILLAS. Spain was given almost all of the American continents except Brazil (which is why Portuguese, not Spanish, is spoken in Brazil now) and some islands in the Atlantic.

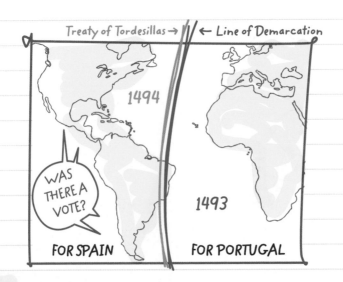

Treaty of Tordesillas → ← Line of Demarcation

1494

WAS THERE A VOTE?

1493

FOR SPAIN

FOR PORTUGAL

CONQUEST and COLONIZATION: The CONQUISTADORES

During the 16th century, the Spanish and the Portuguese came into contact and conflict with Indigenous populations. But the Spanish created a system of conquest and colonization that proved very effective. It was so effective, they even had a special name for the men who did this work: CONQUISTADORES.

The Conquistadores were given permission from the king and queen to settle in the Americas in return for 20 percent of any treasure they seized in the area. This was known as "the king's fifth." (The Spanish had already learned that these lands were rich in mineral resources, and they were preparing to take as much as they could manage.)

THE KING'S FIFTH ⟶

The Conquistadores wanted to

convert people to Christianity

trade for goods

FIND LOTS OF GOLD

CHRISTOPHER COLUMBUS

Christopher Columbus sailed for Spain and set the stage for
the Spanish Conquistadors. On August 3, 1492, Columbus set out
with three ships (the *NIÑA* and the *PINTA*—both caravels—
and the flagship *SANTA MARIA*). Two months later, Columbus's
team landed on the Bahamian Island of Guanahani, inhabited
by the Taíno people. Columbus claimed the island for Spain,
and called it San Salvador.

Though the Taíno people were friendly to Columbus and his
crew, the European settlers were more interested in gold
and tobacco than in friendship. In general, they treated the
Indigenous people they encountered with extreme cruelty,
enslaving them, forcing them to mine for gold, attacking
and even killing them, and kidnapping around 1,500 people to
enslave and sell in Europe.

Columbus made three more voyages to the Caribbean. He
explored Hispaniola (the island of present-day Haiti and the
Dominican Republic), Cuba, and Jamaica, claiming the land

COLUMBUS SAILED THE OCEAN BLUE IN 1492

Columbus and his crew thought they were
in the Indies in Asia, and this is why the
Caribbean islands are called the WEST Indies,
and why Indigenous Americans were called Indians.

AT LAST, INDIA!   UH...

for Spain. Once these Caribbean islands had been colonized, they were used as bases for the invasions of the nearby continents.

FROM the ISLANDS to the INLAND EMPIRES

In 1518, Governor Diego Velázquez of the now settled colonial island of Cuba granted Conquistador HERNÁN CORTÉS permission (and several ships) to explore the Yucatán Peninsula, 120 miles west of Cuba. Landing in the Yucatán, Cortés saw the Maya pyramids for himself, and met Geronimo de Aguilar, a Spaniard who'd been shipwrecked there for seven years. Aguilar, fluent in Mayan and Spanish, became Cortes's translator. After a show of force at Potonchan, the Indigenous people there gave the Spanish gifts, including 20 enslaved women. Among the enslaved was a young woman, MALINTZIN (aka La Malinche), who spoke Mayan and Nahuatl (a language spoken in central Mexico). These translators provided Cortés with a big advantage.

By April 1519 Cortés met with a messenger of MONTEZUMA, emperor of the MEXICA EMPIRE (formerly called the Aztec Empire). Cortés showed off his horses, cannons, and guns while the messenger told him about Mexica's capital city, TENOCHTITLÁN.

THE COLUMBIAN EXCHANGE

There had been no mixing of plants and animals between the Americas and the rest of the world for more than 10,000 years. Corn and potatoes found only in the Americas proved an absolute nutritional boon to Europe, whose population skyrocketed as a result. Europeans brought wheat, barley, grapes, and onions, as well as cattle, pigs, and horses to the Americas. The horse provided such an advantage that it was illegal to give or sell a horse to an Indigenous person, but these laws failed to stop the spread of horses and horsemanship to many Indigenous civilizations whose cultures were transformed by this new tool. European cows and pigs, however, were responsible for the destruction of many Indigenous farm fields and often led to conflict.

But hitchhikers also crossed the Atlantic. Dandelions and other weeds came in the sacks of seeds for planting, and germs came ashore on the backs of Europeans. Diseases such as smallpox, measles, and the flu were common in Europe, but since people there had developed some **IMMUNITY** to them, they were increasingly less deadly to Europeans. But the Indigenous peoples of the Americas had no such immunities. Soon these diseases were spreading through Indigenous contact. Villages were wiped out by smallpox. It is estimated that as much as 90 percent of the Indigenous population of the Americas may have died as a result of these diseases.

This mixing of plants, animals, viruses, and bacteria is known as the COLUMBIAN EXCHANGE or the GREAT BIOLOGICAL EXCHANGE.

> **IMMUNITY**
> resistance to a disease or sickness, particularly due to previous exposure to the germs

Cortés decided to attack the Mexica. He knew that many local tribes resented the Mexica, and he invited them to join the attack. If they resisted, he used violence to force them to work with him. When Cortés and his men got to Tenochtitlán, Montezuma offered the Spaniards treasures and hoped they'd leave. Instead, Cortés and his crew captured Montezuma, and tension grew. On June 30, 1520, LA NOCHE TRISTE ("the sad night," so named by the Spanish), the people of Tenochtitlán drove the Spanish and their allies from the city; Montezuma was killed in the fighting, along with numerous Spanish soldiers. But in May 1521, as smallpox ravaged the city, Cortés returned with more Spanish troops, and this time Tenochtitlán was destroyed, and the Spanish built Mexico City on top of the rubble.

Disease also helped the Spanish conquer the Inca Empire (in modern-day Peru). In 1528, Conquistador FRANCISCO PIZARRO sailed down the western coast of South America. He was gathering information about the wealth and strength of the Inca Empire. Returning to Spain with samples of Incan wealth, he received funding for an army to conquer the Incas. When Pizarro returned to the area in 1532 (with 62 horsemen and 102 foot soldiers under his command) the Incan Empire was in the midst of a terrible civil war. Emperor Huayna Capac had contracted smallpox and died shortly after Pizarro's first visit. His sons ATAHUALPA and HUÁSCAR fought over who would command the empire.

Atahualpa welcomed Pizarro, but Pizarro took him prisoner.

Atahualpa offered the Spaniards gold in exchange for his freedom. Pizarro tried him for treason and executed him. Pizarro and his troops marched into the capital, Cuzco. By 1534, they had conquered the entire 2,000-mile-long territory that made up the Inca Empire.

Why did these powerful Mesoamerican empires fall to the Spanish?

The Spaniards' weapons, armor, and especially their horses were unfamiliar to the Mesoamericans, giving them a **MILITARY EDGE**.

The Spanish took advantage of **LOCAL RIVALRIES**, encouraging or forcing Indigenous tribes to fight each other.

BIG REASON! European **DISEASES LIKE SMALLPOX** devastated the Indigenous populations by as much as 90 percent, weakening their ability to defend themselves.

SPANISH SOCIETY in the AMERICAS

The Spanish colonies were under the control of the Spanish monarchs. They had two main missions:

→ Convert the Indigenous population to Catholicism

→ Enrich the Spanish monarchy

Through the COUNCIL OF THE INDIES (formed in 1524), the Spanish monarchs appointed two VICEROYS. Each was in charge of a VICEROYALTY, one in "New Spain" (Central America and its surroundings) and one in Peru. The monarchs got men to travel to the Americas by rewarding the settlers with **ENCOMIENDAS**. (Remember that the king or queen got 20 percent of all profits earned.)

> **ENCOMIENDA**
> a royal grant of land that gave settlers the right to tax and enslave Indigenous inhabitants

Most of the Spanish colonists were men, and it was common for them to form families with Indigenous women, who by this time had been converted to Catholicism. The social hierarchy depended on race and birthplace:

Land and positions of influence belonged to the PENINSULARES from the peninsula of Spain. Although they were the smallest population, they held almost all the power.

CREOLES (the first generation born to Spanish parents) ranked below the peninsulares.

MESTIZOS (of mixed European and Indigenous parentage) were next.

Indigenous people

Enslaved Africans

There were three main kinds of settlements:

→ **PUEBLOS,** WHICH WERE TOWNS AND TRADING CENTERS

→ **MISSIONS,** WHICH FOCUSED ON CONVERTING PEOPLE TO CHRISTIANITY

→ **PRESIDIOS,** WHICH WERE MILITARY FORTS

EL CAMINO REAL, the royal road from Mexico City to Santa Fe, connected many of these settlements. In and around the towns, HACIENDAS (large estates) and PLANTATIONS (large farms raising **CASH CROPS**) grew coffee, cotton, tobacco, and sugar. Settlers also mined the abundance of mineral resources in the area,

> **CASH CROP**
> a plant that farmers grow to make money

including gold and even more silver. These huge farm and mining operations required a lot of hard labor, and settlers used enslaved Indigenous and African laborers to run them.

Sugar, and later tobacco, became very profitable exports to Europe. Sugar was called "white gold" because it was so valuable.

The Spanish got their foothold in central Mexico and the Andes, but they spread from there. In 1598, JUAN DE OÑATE established the Province of New Mexico. He brought cows and horses and hundreds of settlers. The colony founded its capital city, Santa Fe, in 1607. Though the area was not as rich in resources as other areas, the same system of conversion, social hierarchies, and forced labor continued.

SLAVERY in the EARLY AMERICAS

Sugar and tobacco plantations in South America and the Caribbean were highly profitable because colonizers used unpaid, enslaved laborers. At first, the Spanish and Portuguese plantation owners primarily enslaved Indigenous people. But, because they had never been exposed to European diseases before, Indigenous people died at very high rates. And because they were indigenous to the land, when they ran away, they often successfully hid in the terrain.

MOST SUGAR PLANTATIONS WERE IN THE CARIBBEAN. AT THE TIME EUROPEANS CALLED IT THE WEST INDIES.

Plantation owners decided they needed a different source of forced labor and began importing enslaved people from West Africa. Captive Africans were considered a better source of labor because they had a harder time running away (they were unfamiliar with the terrain), and they already had immunity to many diseases that killed Indigenous people. Even so, the terrible working conditions meant mortality rates were still high—kidnapped Africans who landed in the Caribbean lived an average of only three years there.

TRIANGLE TRADE

High death rates of enslaved workers meant that Spanish and Portuguese colonies (and later, English colonies along the east coast of North America) imported enslaved people all the time, and in huge numbers, leading to the growth of the West African slave trade. The slave trade was part of THE TRIANGULAR TRADE, a trade route with three Atlantic stops: the West African coast, the sugar islands of the West Indies, and the east coast of North America.

NORTH AMERICA

SUGAR & MOLASSES

RUM & IRON

WEST AFRICA

WEST INDIES

ENSLAVED PEOPLE & GOLD

37

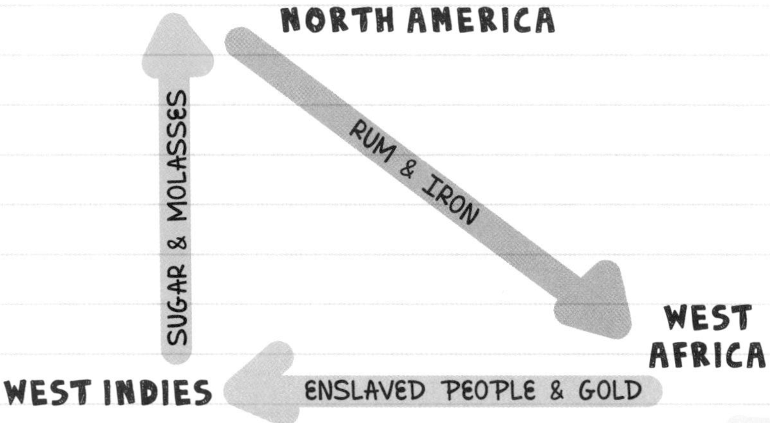

The Triangular Trade was just one part of a larger exchange of goods and enslaved people that included Europe.

FOR EXAMPLE:

Europeans strictly controlled manufactured goods (like glass, and weapons) to trade for raw materials (like furs and sugar).

African societies that wanted to maintain power over their neighbors needed manufactured weapons from Europe, which they paid for with captured Africans.

Colonists in the West Indies and North America needed endless labor to fuel their plantations and bought it with rum and iron.

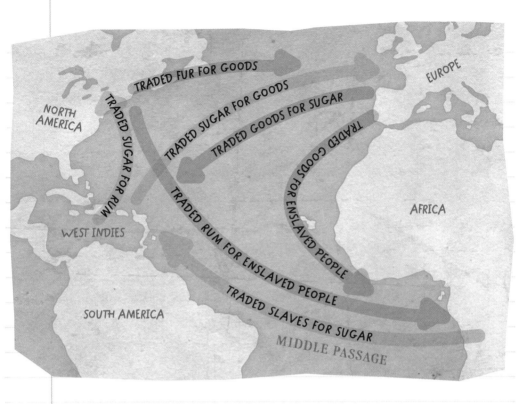

On the map:
TRADED FUR FOR GOODS
TRADED SUGAR FOR GOODS
TRADED GOODS FOR SUGAR
TRADED GOODS FOR ENSLAVED PEOPLE
TRADED SUGAR FOR RUM
TRADED RUM FOR ENSLAVED PEOPLE
TRADED SLAVES FOR SUGAR
MIDDLE PASSAGE

NORTH AMERICA
EUROPE
AFRICA
WEST INDIES
SOUTH AMERICA

The MIDDLE PASSAGE

The middle leg of the Triangular Trade, when ships left Africa filled with people whom they had either kidnapped or bought from kidnappers, was the MIDDLE PASSAGE. Because the purpose was to make a profit, the owners and captains of slave ships packed the Africans tightly together, like cargo, and provided little food for them. These conditions led to rampant disease. About 15 percent out of an estimated 9 to 12 million captive Africans died during the Middle Passage en route to the colonies.

Although enslavers used this time to try to reshape independent people into submissive servants, Africans considered this passage a period of "in-betweenness." Despite the enslavers deliberately filling ships with diverse peoples who did not speak the same languages, organized resistance often occurred. The captives used their voices, bodies, and even the ships' hulls to create music—a language that their captors did not understand. Uprisings were staged on about 10 percent of the voyages from Africa, often coordinated across tribal lines using this new language. Jumping overboard was another common act of defiance. This form of escape by which enslaved people would meet their ancestors in the afterlife was so common that many slave ships were equipped with nets to prevent it.

Each European colonial power managed the resources and the labor within their empires, making the rules by which these newly established societies would operate successfully. Life in this new Atlantic world wasn't easy for anyone, but it proved devastating for Indigenous peoples and Africans, whom the colonizing powers would continue to exploit for centuries.

CHECK YOUR KNOWLEDGE

1. What is colonization?

2. How did Colombus and his crew treat the Indigenous people they met?

3. Why is Portuguese spoken in Brazil?

4. What does it mean to "circumnavigate" something?

5. What was the Columbian Exchange?

6. How did the Conquistadores conquer entire empires with only a few hundred soldiers?

7. What were the three kinds of Spanish settlements in the Americas?

8. How did captive Africans demonstrate resistance and defiance during the middle passage?

9. What is the legacy of European exploration in the Americas?

ANSWERS

CHECK YOUR ANSWERS

1. The process of one country settling and establishing control over land and the Indigenous people living on that land
2. With extreme cruelty. They abused and enslaved Indigenous people and forced them to mine for gold.
3. Portugal colonized Brazil and established Portuguese as the official language.
4. To sail around it
5. The exchange of plants, animals, and germs between the two hemispheres
6. They had the support of oppressed locals and technology, and they brought diseases with them that killed large parts of the populations they were conquering.
7. Pueblos, missions, and presidios
8. They created a shared language through music, staged organized revolts, and jumped overboard.
9. European nations established powerful and long-lasting civilizations in the Americas, but at the expense, exploitation, and destruction of Indigenous and African people and societies.

☆ Chapter 4 ☆

THE ATLANTIC WORLD
★ ★ ★ ★ ★ ★ ★ ★ ★ ★ ★ ★
OPENS

The DEFEAT of the SPANISH ARMADA

It was clear to everyone in Europe that the Americas were extremely rich in resources and opportunity. The Spanish and the Portuguese dominated the Atlantic for the majority of the 16th century, but all that would change in 1588. The Dutch, the English, the French, and even the Swedish, ignoring the Catholic pope's division of the so-called New World, would soon explore and settle in the Americas as well as trade in Africa. The economic theory of MERCANTILISM said that a nation's power was in its wealth. European countries competed more than ever to establish colonies to get raw materials and gain new markets for exports.

Europeans were also fighting about religion. When ELIZABETH I, a Protestant, became queen of England in

1558, she ordered sailors to attack Spanish ships as they transported gold and silver back from America. She wanted to gain the wealth from the "New World" without incurring the expense of having colonies. One of the most successful and daring of these English sailors was SIR FRANCIS DRAKE.

TO THE ENGLISH HE WAS AN ADVENTURER, TO THE SPANISH HE WAS A PIRATE.

Motivated by these attacks and by his deep Catholic faith, in 1588, King Philip of Spain sent the mighty SPANISH ARMADA, a fleet of 130 ships, to conquer England and force them back to Catholicism. The two navies met in the English Channel, and England was the winner (with the help of a really massive storm). Spain never regained its previous power, and other nations saw they could challenge Spanish claims in the New World.

A FLURRY of EUROPEAN SETTLEMENT

Remember how the Spanish established Santa Fe in 1607? The same year, Englishmen settled Jamestown, Virginia. A year later, the French established Quebec, and seven years after that, the Dutch settled the Hudson River valley. All hoped to exploit the resources of the continent, though how they planned to do that depended on where they were able to establish colonies, the resources they found there, the labor available, and who had power over the colony. They all encountered Indigenous people but forged their own unique relationships with them. By 1650, European countries were in fierce competition. Remember that the lands they "claimed" and the lands they actually settled weren't always the same. (And remember that all of this claimed land was already inhabited by Indigenous people.)

TERRITORY CLAIMED BY EUROPE, 1650

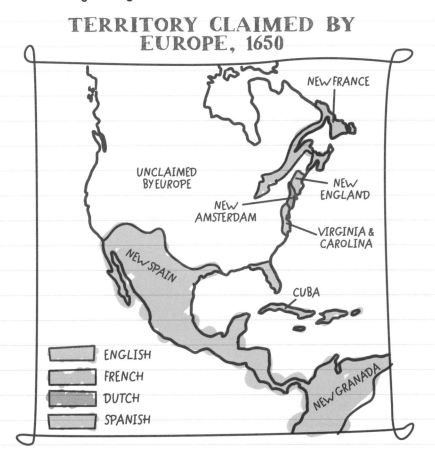

NEW FRANCE

UNCLAIMED BY EUROPE

NEW ENGLAND

NEW AMSTERDAM

VIRGINIA & CAROLINA

NEW SPAIN

CUBA

NEW GRANADA

- ENGLISH
- FRENCH
- DUTCH
- SPANISH

EARLY ENGLISH ENDEAVORS

In the late 1500s, explorer SIR WALTER RALEIGH received a **CHARTER**. He sent an expedition in 1584 to settle land they'd call Virginia. The next year, the expedition founded a colony on ROANOKE ISLAND in present-day North Carolina. Lack of food forced the settlers to sail back to England after a year.

CHARTER
permission from the monarch to start a colony

after Queen Elizabeth I, "The Virgin Queen"

In 1587, a group of about 150 English settlers tried again in the same place. One of the leaders, JOHN WHITE, returned to England for supplies but couldn't come back for three years because of the attack of the Spanish Armada. When he returned to Roanoke Island, the people had vanished.

The first person born in the Americas to British parents, **VIRGINIA DARE**, was John White's granddaughter. What happened to her and the other settlers is still a mystery. Her colony is now called the **LOST COLONY**.

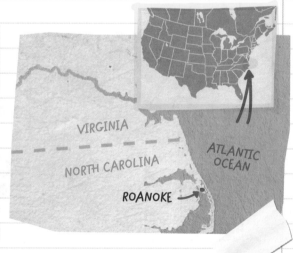

VIRGINIA

NORTH CAROLINA

ATLANTIC OCEAN

ROANOKE

Although the Roanoke Colony failed, the English were determined. A group of merchants formed the VIRGINIA COMPANY OF LONDON to make money from the colonies. On April 26, 1607, approximately 125 settlers (all male, mostly in their twenties) reached the Chesapeake Bay and founded the first permanent English settlement in North America, JAMESTOWN, on the banks of the JAMES RIVER. The company and the settlers who decided to go were hoping for an experience similar to that of the Spanish. (That lots of mineral wealth and forced Indigenous labor would make them all rich.) It was not to be.

WHAT'S WITH ALL THE JAMESES?

After Queen Elizabeth I died in 1603, James I became king of England. The settlers named Jamestown and the James River in his honor.

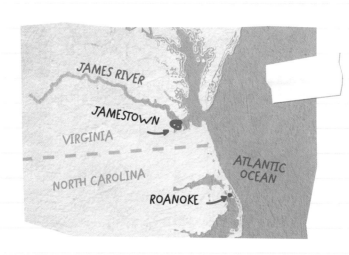

The JAMESTOWN SETTLERS

Although Jamestown eventually survived, most of its first settlers were unprepared for what was to come:

> They settled on an island near the river because it could be a defensive position should anyone approach by water, but the **WATER WAS DIRTY AND UNDRINKABLE** for most of the year.

> It was bitterly cold in winter, humid in summer, and full of **DISEASE-CARRYING MOSQUITOES** because of the marshy conditions.

> Most of the settlers were rich adventurers or explorers, not craftsmen or laborers, so they **FOCUSED ON SEARCHING FOR GOLD** (of which there was little) instead of building houses or planting food.

Fewer than half of the settlers survived the first winter. They owed their survival to the POWHATAN CONFEDERACY, a group of Indigenous communities led by CHIEF POWHATAN, who gave the settlers food and supplies, and later taught them how to grow maize.

CHIEF POWHATAN

The STARVING TIME

In 1608 CAPTAIN JOHN SMITH took charge of Jamestown, forcing settlers to plant and build ("work or starve"). Settlers spent more time searching for gold than farming, and they often raided Powhatan villages, stealing supplies and sometimes burning homes and villages. The Powhatans responded in kind and fighting escalated into the FIRST ANGLO-POWHATAN WAR.

In 1609 about 400 more settlers arrived, including women and children. That winter, disease and famine overtook the settlers. This period is called THE STARVING TIME. People were so hungry they ate anything within reach (maybe even each other). Only about 60 settlers survived to spring.

Jamestown was the first permanent **ENGLISH** settlement in North America. The Spanish town of St. Augustine, Florida (remember: explorer Ponce de Léon), was the first permanent **SPANISH** settlement in North America.

JOHN ROLFE

In 1610, more settlers arrived, including JOHN ROLFE, who was the first Jamestown settler to grow tobacco for export. A cash crop grown mainly in the West Indies, tobacco grew well in Virginia and made the settlement profitable for the first time.

Settlers started planting tobacco, taking more land from the Powhatans, and prolonging the war between them. In 1614, ~~POCHAHONTAS~~, who was

> **GET YOUR JOHNS STRAIGHT (DON'T LISTEN TO THE LEGENDS)**
> John ROLFE married Pocahontas. Although briefly captured by her father, John SMITH may or may not have been rescued by Pocahontas. Most historians believe John Smith exaggerated or completely made up the story about the princess.

the daughter of Chief Powhatan and had been held captive by the settlers for almost two years, married John Rolfe, beginning an era of relative peace between the Powhatans and the Virginia settlers.

TOBACCO and the FUTURE of VIRGINIA (and the U.S.)

Despite the success of tobacco, the Virgina Company's poor track record in Virginia still made it hard to attract settlers to the colony. The company decided to bribe Englishmen to move there. Under the HEADRIGHT SYSTEM (your RIGHT per HEAD, meaning per person), any man who paid his way across the ocean was granted 50 acres of land in Virginia. Labor for the tobacco plantations was needed, so a system of **INDENTURED SERVITUDE** was adopted. Indentured servants, often from Britain or Germany, signed a contract for four to seven years of service in exchange for passage

across the Atlantic. Landowners who could afford to pay the passage of an indentured servant got 50 additional acres of land for each person (head) the indentured servant brought with him, including women and servants of his own.

This labor system dominated the area for decades, and the first Africans, arriving in Jamestown in 1619, were actually treated like indentured servants. After the time of the contract was up, indentured servants were given land and were free to make a new life. There was, however, one catch. About 50 percent of these servants died before they fulfilled their contracts, because of abuse, poor nutrition, and hard labor.

The FRENCH STAKE CLAIMS

The French explored the St. Lawrence River as early as 1535, but the first settlements took some time to establish. In 1608, just a year after Santa Fe and Jamestown were founded, French explorer SAMUEL DE CHAMPLAIN founded a trading post in Quebec, where an active fur and metal trade developed. The settlers who moved to NEW FRANCE were few and far between, so many men married Indigenous women. That enabled them to build strong trading ties with the societies into which they had married. Although these settlers also brought European diseases, their small number and their need to get along with the many Indigenous societies they encountered meant they had better relations with the Indigenous population than either the Spanish or the English. They did not take over huge swaths of land for farming (the climate was not suited to it) but developed trading relationships with many groups. A number of Catholic priests also lived in New France, on a mission to convert the locals. As the French explored the inland waterways, they claimed large areas of territory but never really settled it.

In 1682, RENÉ-ROBERT CAVELIER, SIEUR DE LA SALLE sailed the length of the Mississippi River and claimed the area including what is now Louisiana for the French when he reached the southern end. The French later founded a trading post there in what is now New Orleans. In the 1700s, the French established trading posts in present-day Detroit, Michigan, and St. Louis, Missouri.

> Because of these French explorers, French culture in North America is still concentrated in the province of Quebec and the state of Louisiana.

And the DUTCH STAKE CLAIMS, TOO

The Dutch staked their claim in the Hudson River valley. In 1609, Henry Hudson, an Englishman hired by the Dutch, had fully explored what is now known as the Hudson River. In 1614, they set up Fort Nassau (near modern-day Albany) at the location where the river becomes too small for larger ships. THE DUTCH WEST INDIA COMPANY established the colony of New Netherland in 1621 along the river. In 1626, Peter Minuit "purchased" the island of Manhattan from the Indigenous MANHATES, who occupied the island, for what

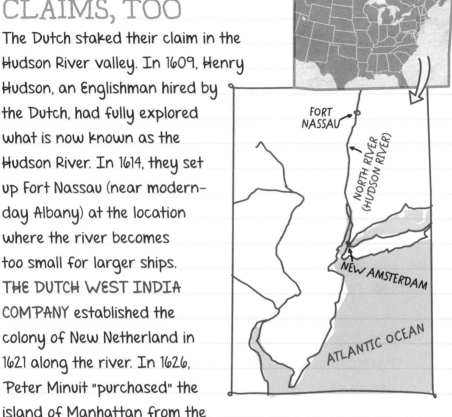

has been described as $24 worth of goods. It is likely that the Manhates did not consider this a sale of land. They probably considered the goods a gesture of goodwill, or an offering to ensure hunting rights. Historians are uncertain if this was a misunderstanding due to language and cultural barriers or deliberate theft. The city of New Amsterdam (today's New York City) became a prosperous center of the fur trade and eventually the slave trade as well.

The Dutch West India Company was a **CHARTERED COMPANY**. In that kind of business, investors joined to explore and trade together, with the support of the government of their home country. The government also gave permission to negotiate with foreign leaders and own colonial land. **THE DUTCH EAST INDIA COMPANY** (which did business in India and Asia) was another chartered company.

Ultimately, the Dutch, like the English, bribed settlers to come with the promise of land. Dutch families established farms the full length of the Hudson River. Taking land that was farmed and inhabited by the Esopus people caused conflict. The Dutch used diplomacy, violence, and trickery to get what they wanted from the local people.

The French and the Dutch shared a common interest in furs, which created conflict between these traders and their Indigenous allies. The French primarily traded with the St. Lawrence Iroquoians, the Wyandot (Huron), the Erie, and the Susquehannock. These groups were historic enemies with the Haudenosaunee Confederacy, who conducted their trade with the Dutch. The competition for European trade resulted in a series of wars that lasted from 1609 to 1701 and was known as the BEAVER WARS.

The ELUSIVE NORTHWEST PASSAGE

Europeans had not given up the idea of sailing west to get to Asia, and they were constantly exploring northern Canada, looking for a NORTHWEST PASSAGE. Remember John Cabot ("Giovanni Caboto"), who found all the fish in 1497? In 1498, this Italian, sailing on behalf of England, landed in Newfoundland, Canada. Cabot thought he was in Asia, so he set sail for Japan, but he was never heard from again.

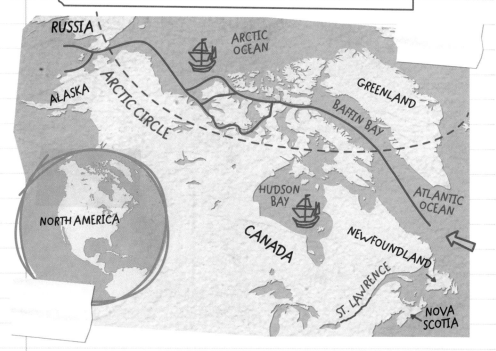

A northwestern route to Asia is what Samuel de Champlain was seeking when he explored the St. Lawrence Seaway and founded Quebec. And Henry Hudson was hired by the Dutch to find a way through North America to the Pacific Ocean when he reached the Hudson River in 1609. The next year, he returned on behalf of the British and "discovered" a bay (Hudson Bay). He planned to go on, but his crew **MUTINIED**, and he was either lost at sea or, more likely, killed. A northwest passage wasn't navigated until 1903.

MUTINY
to revolt or rebel against authority, especially by sailors against their officers

CHECK YOUR KNOWLEDGE

1. What impact did mercantilism have on the establishment of the colonies?

2. What were the repercussions of the Spanish Armada losing to England?

3. What challenges did the first settlers in Jamestown face?

4. Explain the system of indentured servitude.

5. Compare the ways French settlers of Quebec and Dutch settlers of the Hudson River region interacted with Indigenous people.

6. Although the Northwest Passage wasn't found by early explorers, what were two resulting explorations?

ANSWERS

CHECK YOUR ANSWERS

1. Mercantilism stated that a nation's power was in its wealth, so European countries wanted to gain wealth to prove their strength. This resulted in the rapid establishment of colonies.

2. After the defeat of the Spanish Armada, Spain lost power because other nations realized they could challenge Spain's claims in the "New World."

3. The first settlers in Jamestown faced undrinkable water, extreme weather, disease-carrying mosquitoes, and a lack of skilled laborers.

4. Indentured servitude was when a person signed a contract for several years of service to a landowner in exchange for paid travel to the "New World." Landowners who paid the way of an indentured servant were given additional land.

5. The French settlers built strong trading ties with Indigenous people and married into their societies.
The Dutch did not have a friendly relationship with the Indigenous people. They took over land that was settled by others, causing conflict.

6. John Cabot landed in Newfoundland, Canada, and Henry Hudson explored the Hudson River.

Unit 2

Colonial America 1607-1780s

The Americas were dominated by the Spanish and Portuguese in the 1500s, but the 1600s and 1700s saw new players on the east coast of North America. These colonists identified as British and also as Virginians, or Pennsylvanians, or Rhode Islanders. They did not identify as American. But after the French and Indian War, the colonists began to merge, based on the idea of independence from Britain. In the end, these colonies become independent states, which then joined to become "these United States."

☆ Chapter 5 ☆

VIRGINIA:

A CORNERSTONE COLONY

JAMESTOWN PROSPERS and VIRGINIA GROWS

The discovery, in 1614, that tobacco grew well in the area around Jamestown led to a transformation and expansion of the colony. Early settlers began to build plantations. Those planters who did well could increase their wealth by paying for the passage of their wives and children or indentured servants to the colony.

The HOUSE of BURGESSES

These increasingly wealthy men wanted to participate in making the rules that governed them, like Englishmen in England were able to do. In 1619, the **HOUSE OF BURGESSES**, a **LEGISLATIVE** body, held

> **BURGESS**
> a citizen representative in local government

> **LEGISLATIVE**
> having the function of making laws and, in reference to the House of Burgesses, imposing taxes

its first annual assembly. Under the overall governance of the Virginia Company, the people had their own **REPRESENTATIVE GOVERNMENT**.

The SECOND ANGLO-POWHATAN WAR

The powerful Indigenous societies of the Powhatan Confederacy already lived and farmed on the land the Virginia Company was giving away to Virginian settlers. There had been a period of peace between the settlers and the Powhatan, but as tobacco farms took up more and more land on the James River, the Powhatans, now led by CHIEF OPECHANCANOUGH, grew concerned. When a royal Powhatan adviser was murdered by the English, the Powhatans knew that peace could not last and staged a coordinated attack, killing 25 percent of the 1,200 settlers. The Powhatans retreated, expecting the settlers to pack up and leave. Instead, the settlers retaliated, and the second Anglo-Powhatan War broke out. Vicious fighting continued for the next 10 years.

Since the Virginia Company could neither protect the settlers nor make enough money to justify the cost of defending the colony, King James revoked their charter in 1624. Jamestown became a ROYAL COLONY, meaning the king was in charge. He chose a governor to rule the colony in his place and abolished the House of Burgesses. (After King James I's death, KING CHARLES I reinstated the House of Burgesses in 1629.)

HELP WANTED

In addition to resistance from Indigenous peoples, the colonies faced increasing labor shortages. Due to insufficient food provisions, awful working conditions, and the resulting 50 percent mortality rate, the flow of indentured servants coming from England slowed. Settlers began using enslaved African labor in larger numbers, starting in 1619, when the first enslaved African captives were brought to Jamestown. This meant that enslaved people of African descent and indentured servants worked shoulder to shoulder on the same plantations, under the same terrible working conditions. As a result, some developed alliances (like helping each other escape or start rebellions), and formed relationships and families.

These alliances made landowners nervous.

BLURRY LABOR LINES

At the same time, enslaved people were discovering loopholes in laws and using the legal system to fight for their freedom.

In 1656, an enslaved woman named ELIZABETH KEY, the daughter of an enslaved African woman and her white enslaver, sued for her freedom and the freedom of her children. Her attorney was William Grinstead: He was also her husband and a former indentured servant. They sued on the basis that under English law, a child inherited the free or enslaved status of their father. (In this case, the father was a free man.) English law also forbade the enslavement of a Christian person, and Elizabeth was a Christian. Elizabeth and William won the case, and both Elizabeth and her children were freed.

Landowners followed Elizabeth's case closely, knowing that the outcome would set a legal precedent that could empower more enslaved people to free themselves.

In the late 1600s, former indentured servants were forced to the frontier to claim their 50 acres of land. The Indigenous people who lived on the frontier retaliated, and the settlers demanded that the government protect them. In 1676, after Governor William Berkeley refused to send aid in, a group of frontiersmen led by **NATHANIEL BACON** attacked the Pamunkey people and the governor. **BACON'S REBELLION** quickly ended (when Bacon died from dysentery), but it was one of the first acts of rebellion by colonists.

RACE-BASED SLAVERY

Between the alliances formed by indentured servants and enslaved African people, and the loopholes that enslaved people found in English law, landowners and enslavers sitting on the Virginia General Assembly (of which the House of Burgesses was one chamber) began to revise and CODIFY the laws concerning the enslaved people in Virginia.

These SLAVE CODES included the following:

1640—Runaway indentured servants of African descent become enslaved for life.

1660—English servants who run away from their contract face harsher penalties if they run away with enslaved people.

1662—A child will inherit, at birth, the status of their mother.

1667—Conversion to Christianity does not alter the status of an enslaved person.

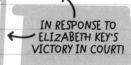

IN RESPONSE TO ELIZABETH KEY'S VICTORY IN COURT!

1669—It does not count as murder if an owner kills an enslaved person while punishing them.

These codes, over time, refined the meaning of what it was to be an enslaved person in the southern English colonies of North America. Virginians broke from English law to develop a homegrown definition of slavery: a race-based system of perpetual, inheritable property. The codes also worked to keep poor white people from allying with their enslaved peers. In later years, wealthy plantation owners used these codes to reassure poor white laborers that even though they had it bad, at least they were not enslaved.

> Interracial marriage was illegal in Virginia until the Supreme Court ruled such bans as unconstitutional in 1967!

The BEGINNINGS of BLACK AMERICAN CULTURE

Enslaved people were brought from all over Western Africa and were spread out once they arrived in the Americas. Because of this **DIASPORA**, enslaved Africans in the Americas formed new cultures built from their differing backgrounds and their common experiences. Enslavers knew that the people they purchased came from diverse societies in Africa. They intentionally tried to erase African culture by separating people with the same background or language. Enslavers sent some people to work in houses and others to work in fields, and they mixed people from different societies together.

Enslaved people in the Southern colonies often lived to old age (unlike

> **DIASPORA**
> the scattering of people from their homelands to a variety of diverse places, usually not voluntarily but through force or as refugees

enslaved people in the sugar islands). Despite the enslavers' attempts to erase their culture and identities, enslaved people formed families and communities and developed a distinct African American culture that blended Christianity with diverse African traditions and languages.

RELIGION: Many enslaved people adopted elements of Christianity. The enslaved Africans used their Christian faith to sustain themselves and to negotiate for work-free Sundays. And **SPIRITUALS** became a major element of their worship and resistance.

SPIRITUAL
a religious folk song created by enslaved African people in the Americas

SONG, DANCE, AND STORYTELLING: Influenced by African traditions, song, dance, and storytelling were essential for building community. Songs boosted morale during work and communicated secret messages. Stories taught traditional African morals and cleverly poked fun at their white enslavers. Dance preserved African culture and provided joy.

FAMILY: Though enslaved people were not legally allowed to marry, families were the central unit of society. However, the domestic slave trade meant it was difficult for families to stay together. Enslavers would often split up families by selling members to different plantations. Once forced apart, many enslaved families were never reunited.

OLAUDAH EQUIANO was an enslaved person brought to Virginia from Africa in the 1700s as a child. After buying his freedom, he wrote an autobiography depicting the horrors of slavery, which helped influence British lawmakers to abolish the slave trade in 1807. But slavery continued despite the end of legal trading.

VIRGINIA SETS the STAGE

By the late 1600s, Jamestown and the colony of Virginia had become:

→ THE FIRST PERMANENT ENGLISH SETTLEMENT IN NORTH AMERICA

→ THE FIRST ENGLISH ROYAL COLONY IN NORTH AMERICA

→ THE BIRTHPLACE OF REPRESENTATIVE GOVERNMENT IN THE UNITED-STATES-TO-BE

→ AND THE FIRST SLAVE SOCIETY (SOCIETY BASED ON SLAVERY) TO TAKE ROOT IN ENGLISH NORTH AMERICA

Virginia developed two foundational American institutions: representative government and **CHATTEL SLAVERY**—setting the stage for the United States to become what it is today.

CHATTEL SLAVERY
the practice of one person legally owning another; involuntary servitude for life passed down to future generations

Protecting the right to a democratically elected representative government united the thirteen colonies and pushed them to fight for independence from Britain.

Defending the other institution, chattel slavery, divided the country. The creation of a society that required brutal enforcement of oppressive slave codes challenged Christian morality and established systemic racism in government institutions and culture.

CHECK YOUR KNOWLEDGE

1. What was the first permanent English settlement in the Americas?

2. What were the powers of the Virginia House of Burgesses?

3. What happened when the Virginia Company lost its charter? Why did that happen?

4. What was Nathaniel Bacon angry about?

5. What were the slave codes?

6. How were enslaved Africans able to sustain themselves and build a community?

7. Which two foundational U.S. institutions did Virginia help to establish?

ANSWERS 69

CHECK YOUR ANSWERS

1. Jamestown was the first permanent English settlement in North America.

2. Taxation and creating local law

3. Virginia became a royal colony. The charter couldn't protect the settlers and wasn't making much money.

4. He was angry that the government was giving settlers land on the frontier and not protecting them against retaliation from the Indigenous people who lived there.

5. The slave codes were laws that restricted the freedom of African people in Virginia and led to the development of a race-based system of slavery in the United States.

6. Enslaved Africans turned to religion; used song, dance, and storytelling; and built close families to sustain themselves.

7. Virgina helped to establish a representative government (through the House of Burgesses) and a slave society (through slave codes).

☆ Chapter 6 ☆

The THIRTEEN COLONIES

As the colony of Virgina grew, more colonies developed on the eastern coast. There were three types of colonies:

1) CHARTERED COLONIES

under the control of a joint-stock company with a <u>charter</u>

 Examples: Connecticut, Rhode Island

2) PROPRIETARY COLONIES

under the control of the person whose <u>property</u> the land was

 Examples: Delaware, Maryland, Pennsylvania

3) ROYAL COLONIES

under the control, via an appointed governor, of English <u>royalty</u>

Examples: North Carolina, South Carolina, and Georgia, which started as proprietary colonies and later became royal colonies

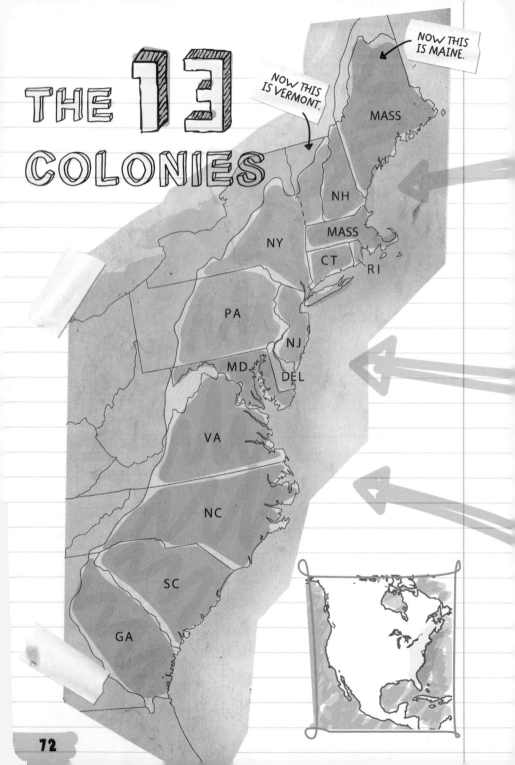

THE 13 COLONIES

NOW THIS IS VERMONT.

NOW THIS IS MAINE.

MASS

NH

NY

MASS

CT

RI

PA

NJ

MD

DEL

VA

NC

SC

GA

NEW ENGLAND COLONIES

Plymouth/Massachusetts Bay (1620)
New Hampshire (1629)
Rhode Island (1636)
Connecticut (1662)

MIDDLE COLONIES

New York (1624)
New Jersey (1664)
Pennsylvania (1681)
Delaware (1634)

SOUTHERN COLONIES

Maryland (1633)
Virginia (1607)
North Carolina (1663)
South Carolina (1663)
Georgia (1733)

PURITANS and PILGRIMS

Some people settled in North America for religious freedom. Catholics in England had been persecuted since the establishment of the CHURCH OF ENGLAND (Anglicans), and there was constant fighting between Catholic and Protestant nations.

Catholics weren't the only persecuted Christians.

PURITANS
wanted to <u>reform</u> the Church of England so that it would be more pure (or closer, they believed, to the text of the Bible)

SEPARATISTS
wanted to start <u>their own</u> church from scratch

In 1608, many Separatists fled England for the Netherlands. Later, they formed a joint-stock company and were given permission from the Virginia Company to settle in North America. They thought of themselves as **PILGRIMS**.

> **PILGRIM**
> one who travels to a sacred place as an act of religious devotion

The MAYFLOWER and the MAYFLOWER COMPACT

On September 16, 1620, a ship called the MAYFLOWER left England. Not everyone on board was a Pilgrim. They were bound for Virginia, but after two months of sailing, they spotted land farther north, in NEW ENGLAND. They decided to settle there instead, where they could make their own rules.

On November 21, 1620, before they went ashore, the men, led by WILLIAM BRADFORD, signed the MAYFLOWER COMPACT, a **COVENANT** agreeing to obey "just and equal laws" created for the "general good of the colony" in order to benefit "the glory of God" and the "honor of our king" (of England). The Pilgrims landed at Cape Cod and later chose to settle at PLYMOUTH ROCK in Massachusetts.

LAND HO!

PULL OVER!!!

> **COVENANT**
> an agreement or promise, with religious overtones

THANKSGIVING in PLYMOUTH

That first winter in Plymouth, about half the Pilgrims died from cold and starvation. The rest were saved when two Indigenous people, SAMOSET and SQUANTO, helped them make peace with the local WAMPANOAG tribe, whose leader was MASSASOIT, and taught them to grow maize and other crops. That's where we get the myth about the first Thanksgiving.

MASSACHUSETTS, CONNECTICUT, RHODE ISLAND, NEW HAMPSHIRE

MASSACHUSETTS

In 1630, led by JOHN WINTHROP, about 900 people settled in BOSTON. Their goal was to start a perfect Christian society, a concept known as a "city on a hill." A GENERAL COURT was established to create local laws. It was made up of representatives—but only male members of the church (those who were **ELECT**, or thought to be chosen by God) could vote. Meanwhile, the Puritans in England were feeling more and more threatened by religious persecution. Tens of thousands left between 1629 and 1640 in what is known as the GREAT MIGRATION. King Charles I granted the MASSACHUSETTS BAY COMPANY, a Puritan joint-stock company, a charter to establish a colony near Plymouth, creating Massachusetts.

ELECT
not "elected," but thought to be chosen by God

THE SALEM WITCH TRIALS
In 1692, in Salem, Massachusetts, some young girls accused people of casting spells on them. A special court was formed to judge witchcraft cases. The court often forced confessions from the accused. People eventually admitted that they had made false accusations, but by the time the witch scare had ended, 19 people had been executed for witchcraft.

CONNECTICUT

THOMAS HOOKER, a minister, disagreed with John Winthrop's leadership. He led his **CONGREGATION** to found Hartford, Connecticut, in 1636. Hartford and two other towns joined together to become their own colony, and Hooker drafted the FUNDAMENTAL ORDERS OF CONNECTICUT, the first written constitution in North America. Under the orders, male citizens who were not thought to be elect could still vote.

> **CONGREGATION**
> a group of people brought together for religious worship

RHODE ISLAND

ROGER WILLIAMS, another Massachusetts minister, believed that people shouldn't be forced to go to church, that settlers should pay Indigenous people for land, and that church and state should be separate. His beliefs were so controversial that he was **BANISHED** from Massachusetts in 1636. His congregation followed him and founded PROVIDENCE.

> **BANISHED**
> forced to leave or no longer welcome

In 1638, ANNE HUTCHINSON, a religious reformer, was banished from Massachusetts because she believed that ministers didn't need to be members of the elect. (Another reason for her banishment was probably that she was a woman who spoke out.) Hutchinson and her sympathizers founded Portsmouth, near Providence. In 1644, the area became the colony of RHODE ISLAND AND PROVIDENCE PLANTATIONS.

NEW HAMPSHIRE

In 1638, Anne Hutchinson's brother-in-law, JOHN WHEELWRIGHT, fled Massachusetts for similar reasons. He led people who agreed with him north and founded the town of Exeter. The area became the independent colony of NEW HAMPSHIRE in 1679.

KING PHILIP'S WAR

In 1675, three members of the Wampanoag tribe were tried and executed by the English for the murder of another Wampanoag. The Wampanoag chief, Metacomet (known as King Philip to the settlers), son of Massasoit, believed that the British had no right to execute his people. Also, the British continued to take the Wampanoag's land despite Metacomet's efforts to compromise with the British.

War broke out. Hundreds of settlers and most of the Wampanoag, including Metacomet, were killed. The English claimed victory, with help from their trading partners, the Pequot and Mohegan tribes. Afterward, the English expanded into Indigenous peoples' lands faster than ever.

THE MIDDLE COLONIES:
NEW YORK, NEW JERSEY, PENNSYLVANIA, DELAWARE

NEW YORK

New Netherland was a thriving Dutch colony. Seeing the large number of prosperous Dutch people between New England and Virginia, England wanted this land for itself. In 1664, England sent a fleet of warships to conquer the Dutch. Unprepared for a battle, the Dutch surrendered. The colony was renamed NEW YORK, after the Duke of York, who got it as a proprietary colony.

NEW JERSEY

The Duke of York gave some of his land to LORD JOHN BERKELEY and SIR GEORGE CARTERET, who named it NEW JERSEY. They attracted settlers by starting a representative assembly and offering large amounts of land. But because New Jersey had no harbor, it was hard to make a profit. They sold their shares of ownership in the colony, and the colony reverted to the king's control in 1702.

PENNSYLVANIA

New Jersey had a large population of QUAKERS, a religious group later called the RELIGIOUS SOCIETY OF FRIENDS who were said to tremble (or quake) before God and had been banished from New England. The Quaker beliefs in equality of the sexes, nonviolence, and tolerance felt like a threat to Puritans.

King Charles II handed over land to Quaker WILLIAM PENN in 1681 to pay off a debt Charles owed Penn's family. Penn established PENNSYLVANIA, where Quakers would have religious freedom, and founded PHILADELPHIA. It attracted thousands of people and became one of the largest cities in North America.

The MASON-DIXON LINE was originally a line of rocks laid down by two people named Mason and Dixon to mark the border between Pennsylvania and Maryland.

UGH, CAN'T WE JUST DRAW THIS ON A MAP?

DELAWARE

Penn also got land from the Duke of York. DELAWARE was south of his other holdings and was occupied by a large Swedish population. It was still officially part of Pennsylvania, but Penn let them govern themselves.

THE SOUTHERN COLONIES:
MARYLAND, THE CAROLINAS, GEORGIA

ESTABLISHED AFTER VIRGINIA...

MARYLAND

George Calvert, Lord Baltimore, wanted to set up a place for fellow Catholics. He requested a charter from King Charles I in 1632. His son Cecilius inherited the PROPRIETARY COLONY and named it MARYLAND. Although it was meant to be a safe place for Catholics, Protestants moved in too, causing conflicts. In 1649, Lord Baltimore issued the ACT OF TOLERATION, which made it illegal to **PERSECUTE** any Christian for his religion. However, in 1654, the Protestants gained control of the local government and revoked the act.

> **PERSECUTION**
> punishment/harrassment, usually because of one's identity

The CAROLINAS

> "Carolina" comes from "Carolus," the Latin form of "Charles."

After a civil war in England, CHARLES II became king in 1660. To reward the aristocrats who had supported him, he gave them a proprietary colony south of Virginia, which they named CAROLINA. Most people in the northern half were originally Virginians. Most in the southern half came directly from England, with enslaved people, attracted by farmland, religious tolerance, and self-government. It became difficult to rule both sides as one unit. The people of the more prosperous South Carolina split from the colony's rule. In 1729, North and South Carolina became royal colonies.

GEORGIA

Georgia was the last British colony founded in North America. In 1732, JAMES OGLETHORPE received a charter from King George II to establish a colony for **DEBTORS** (people who were unable to pay back money could be sent to jail at the time) and poor people to make a new start. The king saw Georgia as a buffer

> **DEBTOR**
> someone in debt

between the colonies and SPANISH FLORIDA. Oglethorpe had strict rules: no large plantations, no rum, few enslaved people, and no Catholics. Few settlers were actually debtors, however. Oglethorpe gave up on his plan, and in 1752, Georgia also became a royal colony.

England expected to profit from its colonies. So England passed the **NAVIGATION ACT OF 1651**, making it illegal for the colonies to sell to countries other than England, to use ships other than English ships, or go through ports other than English ports. The colonists soon saw that Navigation Acts limited their wealth by cutting back free trade. Many resorted to **SMUGGLING** (conducting illegal/secret trade).

1. What were the three types of British colonies in North America?

2. Why did Carolina split into North and South?

3. What is the difference between a Puritan and a Separatist?

4. What did the Mayflower Compact promise?

5. Why did Roger Williams leave Massachusetts to found Rhode Island?

6. What did Metacomet's loss in King Philip's War mean for the Wamapanog and other Indigenous people in the area?

7. How did the Quakers get their name?

CHECK YOUR ANSWERS

1. Royal, proprietary, and chartered
2. The Southern part of Carolina was wealthier, and the population was largely from England. The Northern part was poorer, and the population was largely from Virginia. The regions were so different and it was difficult to govern, and the Southern half split from the colony's rule.
3. Puritans wanted to reform the existing Church of England; Separatists wanted to start their own church.
4. The Mayflower Compact was a promise to obey "just and equal laws" created for the "general good of the colony" in order to benefit "the glory of God" and the "honor of our King" (of England).
5. He was banished from Massachusetts because he disagreed with the church that governed the colony. He believed in the separation of church and state, that settlers should pay Indigenous peoples for land, and people shouldn't be obligated to go to church.
6. Expansion of English settlers into their lands accelerated.
7. They were said to tremble before God.

Chapter 7

REGIONAL DIFFERENCES

As the populations of the thirteen colonies increased from immigration and high birth rates, the differences between them became more prominent. Vast distances and poor communication also led to differences. They developed individual cultures as well as a shared American culture.

The main differences between the colonies hung on **PEGS**:

POPULATION
ECONOMY
GOVERNMENT
SLAVERY

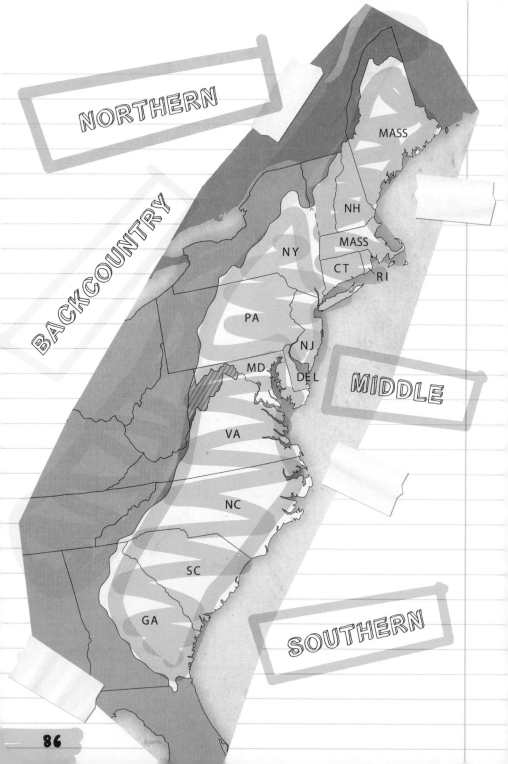

NORTHERN

BACKCOUNTRY

MASS

NH

MASS

NY

CT

RI

PA

NJ

MD

DEL

MIDDLE

VA

NC

SC

GA

SOUTHERN

86

SOUTHERN IDENTITY

Plantations: The South had a lot of plantations that grew cash crops, including tobacco, indigo, and rice. Each plantation was run individually, and people lived far apart. There was almost no manufacturing or other business.

Tidewater Aristocracy: Because plantations were large and few, a small number of wealthy people lived in the South. A tiny percentage of the population controlled almost all the money and power. The wealthiest planters lived along the Tidewater section of Virginia, which had good soil and navigable rivers and shipped tobacco and other crops to England.

Dependence on Slavery: Even though only a small percentage of the citizens were enslavers, the agricultural economy depended on slavery.

Population Imbalance: There were many more enslaved people and poor people than enslavers. Anticipation of rebellions caused local governments to make slave codes even stricter.

Elected Representative Assemblies: Starting with the House of Burgesses, most local government was in the form of assemblies. Often these assemblies were **BICAMERAL**, with one house elected by the people and the other appointed by the royal governor.

> **BICAMERAL**
> a legislature having two houses

NORTHERN IDENTITY

Town Life: Life for New Englanders revolved around the MEETINGHOUSE and church, which were usually the same building. The meetinghouse (where churchgoing men worked together to make laws) usually faced a town GREEN, which was shared land that belonged to the town. New Englanders owned small farms (for **SUBSISTENCE FARMING**) and lived close to their neighbors.

> **SUBSISTENCE FARMING**
> producing crops to live off of, not for profit

Trade and Industry: Unable to raise cash crops (because of long winters and poor soil), New England depended on trade, mills, lumber, shipbuilding, fishing, fur trading, whaling, and craftsmanship. New Englanders were, on average, better off than Southerners.

Use of Slavery: With no large plantations, there was a smaller enslaved population. Enslaved people were forced to work in households and businesses. Northern merchants participated in the slave trade and profited from it. However, the Northern economy did not depend on slavery.

Puritan Values: New Englanders adopted the Puritan values of hard work, modesty, and education. Massachusetts **MANDATED** schools in any town of more than 50 households. Puritan values did not include tolerance of religious differences.

> **MANDATE**
> to require, usually by law

MIDDLE-COLONY IDENTITY

The Middle Colonies linked the **NORTHERN** and **SOUTHERN** cultures:

Mixed Agriculture and Industry: The Middle Colonies grew some cash crops, especially grain, as well as fruits and vegetables. They developed industries such as ironworking and forestry. Trade was made easier by access to Philadelphia and New York City, the largest ports in the colonies and the centers of shipping.

Use of Slavery: Enslaved people were forced to work both in cities and on farms. Some were able to make money when their enslavers allowed them to work as longshoremen or shipbuilders in exchange for a portion of the enslaved people's wages. A rare few enslaved people were able to save enough to buy their freedom.

Mixed Populations: With large immigrant populations and a tradition of tolerance, the Middle Colonies were home to the most diverse populations.

Mixed Government: The Middle Colonies used a combination of assemblies, town meetings, and royal government.

BACKCOUNTRY IDENTITY

The BACKCOUNTRY, or the Western frontier, stretched along the APPALACHIAN MOUNTAINS, from the far north to the far south, and was populated by recent immigrants, former indentured servants, and Indigenous societies that had lived there for centuries. Although it wasn't very far west, it had a Wild West atmosphere. Few people had large farms or enslaved people.

NEW and UNIQUE AMERICAN IDENTITY

Even though regional identities became stronger, a culture was evolving, with:

COMMON HISTORY, from a shared English background

DISREGARD OF INDIGENOUS RIGHTS, which led to the belief that land was cheap and available

NOT THE CASE IN EUROPE!

SOCIAL MOBILITY (among white males) from lack of hereditary titles or classes

AN EMERGING MIDDLE CLASS, from wealth and social mobility because of the lack of aristocrats and use of enslaved people instead of poor workers

POWER FOR LANDOWNERS, because of the connection between landownership and the right to vote

TOLERANCE (mostly) **OF RELIGIOUS DIFFERENCES**, because of religious diversity

SHARED ENEMIES, from wars with Indigenous peoples and French and Spanish settlers

Women worked in the home (cooking, cleaning, raising children, gardening, making soap and candles, etc.) or running stores or inns in cities. Farming was mainly the job of men. Boys were often sent to **APPRENTICE** with a master craftsman, while girls learned their crafts at home.

APPRENTICE
to work for another in order to learn a trade

The ENGLISH BILL of RIGHTS

Changes in England meant changes in the colonies. In 1685, JAMES II became king. He wanted more control. He made the northern colonies the DOMINION OF NEW ENGLAND, a royal colony with very limited self-government. People on both sides of the Atlantic were unhappy with him. After three years, **PARLIAMENT** ousted him. His daughter and son-in-law, MARY AND WILLIAM OF ORANGE, invaded and took over in the GLORIOUS REVOLUTION (called that because it took place without bloodshed).

> **PARLIAMENT**
> the legislative body of Great Britain

In 1689, William and Mary approved an ENGLISH BILL OF RIGHTS, which limited the powers of the monarchy and asserted parliamentary power. The British government continued to make laws governing trade with the colonies, but there was little enforcement in the colonies—a hands-off approach called **SALUTARY NEGLECT**. Still, colonists believed they were full citizens of England and entitled to all of the same rights as someone living in England.

> **SALUTARY**
> good; healthy

> Considered one of the most important legal documents in history, the **MAGNA CARTA** of 1215 forced the king (at the time, King John) to obey the laws of the land. Ever since, British citizens have been determined to limit royal power and protect their rights.

The GREAT AWAKENING and the ENLIGHTENMENT

The GREAT AWAKENING was a religious movement led by traveling ministers in the 1730s and 1740s. Through fiery sermons at outdoor REVIVAL meetings, Americans were encouraged to seek a personal relationship with God.

MOST FAMOUS MINISTERS:
Jonathan Edwards of Massachusetts
George Whitefield of England

The ENLIGHTENMENT was a philosophical movement that emphasized human reason, scientific analysis, and individualism, and applied the laws of nature to politics and society. Led in England by such philosophers as JOHN LOCKE, it held that a SOCIAL CONTRACT ensured citizens' rights, in exchange for obedience to the government. The Enlightenment influenced BENJAMIN FRANKLIN, THOMAS JEFFERSON, and most of the Founding Fathers.

The Great Awakening and the Enlightenment prompted Americans to debate political, societal, and religious questions. Both put forth the idea that there was equality—whether in the eyes of God or the eyes of justice—among all individuals.

THE

New-York Weekly JOURNAL

Containing the freſheſt Advices, Foreign, and Domeſtick.

FREEDOM of the PRESS

JOHN PETER ZENGER, publisher of the NEW-YORK WEEKLY JOURNAL, was charged with **LIBEL** in 1735 and put on trial after printing negative statements about the governor of New York.

> **LIBEL**
> a printed statement that defames or misrepresents

(The governor was an appointee of the king and it was illegal to speak negatively about the king.) Zenger's lawyers, Andrew Hamilton and William Smith, urged the jury to determine whether or not Zenger spoke the truth and convinced them that people had the right to do so. It was the beginning of FREEDOM OF THE PRESS.

CHECK YOUR KNOWLEDGE

1. Were most people in the southern colonies enslavers?

2. Where was the center of town life in New England?

3. What values are emblematic of the Puritans and what region was known for them?

4. Why did the colonies have a successful middle class?

5. Who populated the Backcountry?

6. What is salutary neglect?

7. What did the Great Awakening and the Enlightenment have in common?

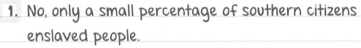

CHECK YOUR ANSWERS

1. No, only a small percentage of southern citizens enslaved people.

2. The meetinghouse and church, near the green

3. Puritan values of hard work, modesty, and education were adopted in New England.

4. There were no aristocrats, wealth was easier to acquire, and enslaved people did the work of poor workers.

5. Recent immigrants, former indentured servants, and the Indigenous people who had lived there for centuries

6. A hands-off approach to government that benefits the people

7. They both encouraged debate and individualism, and advocated that all people were equal.

Chapter 8

RISING

* * * * * * * * * * * * *

TENSIONS

TESTING the BOUNDARIES

As British colonists expanded westward, frontiersmen stole property and killed Indigenous people who lived there. They also challenged French claims to the land.

This map represents European claims to land (that was already settled by Indigenous people) by the mid 1700s:

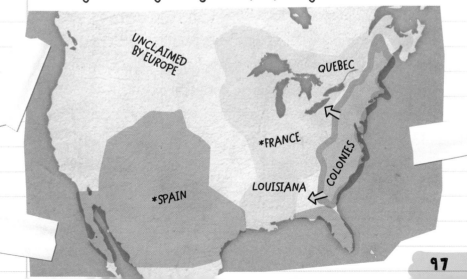

UNCLAIMED BY EUROPE

QUEBEC

*FRANCE

*SPAIN

LOUISIANA

COLONIES

FUR, PORTS, and FIGHTING

Some French colonists were JESUITS (priests), who aimed to convert Indigenous people to Catholicism, but most were in the fur trade. They depended on the rivers that provided access to the sea and French markets and built forts along the rivers to guard against English attack.

British traders had the same idea, and they built the settlement of PICKAWILLANY in present-day Ohio in 1748. The French responded by attacking Pickawillany. The British captured the French settlement of Louisbourg in Canada. France built more forts, such as FORT DUQUESNE in Pennsylvania.

ALLIANCES

Seeing that full-on fighting was coming, the British and French searched for Indigenous allies. Perhaps because the French were fewer in number, traded European goods, and didn't steal Indigenous peoples' land, the French had a better relationship with the local Indigenous peoples. They had allies in the Algonquin and Huron tribes, as well as others. The British got help from the Haudenosaunee Confederacy. Indigenous societies' main objective was to protect trade and their own land, so they joined whichever side seemed least harmful.

A POLITICAL CARTOON
BY BENJAMIN FRANKLIN

ALBANY PLAN

The British colonies sent representatives to Albany, New York, to discuss defense. In June 1754, Benjamin Franklin presented the ALBANY PLAN OF UNION (the ALBANY PLAN), the first formal attempt to unite the colonies. The plan was to join to raise money, train a **MILITIA**, and organize the government—but not a single local legislature was willing to give up its own power. So the colonies were left on their own to defend against attacks from Indigenous people that often resulted in their defeat.

GEORGE WASHINGTON

In 1753, a twenty-one-year-old surveyor named GEORGE WASHINGTON was sent by the Virginia governor to find French settlers in the Ohio River valley and persuade them to leave. The French refused, so in 1754 the governor made Washington an officer in the colonial militia and sent him back with troops. In what is now considered a military blunder (mistake), Washington attacked a French scouting party that was on a diplomatic mission. Among the 10 people killed was a French diplomat. Afterward, Washington built a smaller fort, FORT NECESSITY, near the French Fort Duquesne. Even though he had little experience and few men, Washington attacked Fort Duquesne. He was defeated, but the attack was the beginning of a war, the FRENCH AND INDIAN WAR, and Washington's actions made him a hero in Virginia.

The FRENCH and INDIAN WAR: 1754–1763 (PART of the SEVEN YEARS' WAR: 1756–1763)

The French and Indian War took place between the colonies of France and Britain, the parent countries, and Indigenous people who had allied themselves with either side or were forced to fight in the war. It became known as the SEVEN YEARS' WAR when Europe split into two factions—countries that sided with England and countries that sided with France—and war broke out across Europe.

> The **FRENCH AND INDIAN WAR** was the first war that started in the colonies and spread to Europe.

Meanwhile, the British didn't have a strong army in America. In 1755, King George II sent GENERAL EDWARD BRADDOCK to command the colonial forces. George Washington warned Braddock that the European style of combat—his army's bright red coats and method of lining up in columns—would not work in the American wilderness against people who knew the land well and had a greatly different fighting style. But Braddock ignored the advice. He was soon killed in a surprise attack. The **REDCOATS** took huge losses.

> **REDCOATS**
> British soldiers, so called because of their official uniform of a bright red jacket

The British secretary of state (later the prime minister) WILLIAM PITT was determined to drive the French out of British territory. The fighting was costly, and he had to send more troops to replace the many who were killed.

The TIDE TURNS

With additional troops, the British army and colonial militia began to capture French forts. Fort Duquesne became **FORT PITT**. Quebec, the capital of New France, seemed impossible to attack, but the British successfully ambushed the city under the cover of night. The BATTLE OF QUEBEC was a turning point in the war. When Montreal fell the next year, all of French Canada was in British hands.

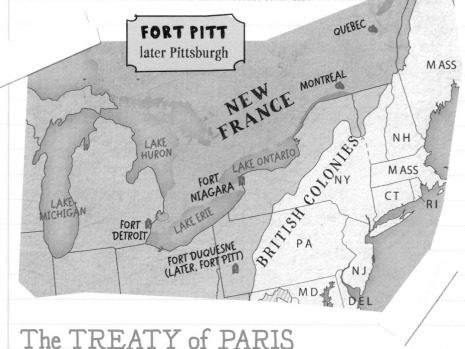

The TREATY of PARIS

The French and Indian War and Seven Years' War formally ended in 1763 when Britain and France signed the TREATY OF PARIS. The treaty gave England all the French territory east of the Mississippi as well as the Spanish territory of Florida (Spain had sided with France).

PONTIAC'S WAR

British expansion made life worse for Indigenous peoples. Trade with the British was less profitable, and more settlers were violently seizing land. An Ottawa chief named PONTIAC united many different Indigenous societies against the British. In early 1763, his forces took the fort at Detroit and attacked forts and settlements along the frontier. PONTIAC'S REBELLION, or PONTIAC'S WAR, continued until 1766. Over 400 British soldiers, more than 2,000 settlers, and more than 200 Indigenous people were killed. Pontiac signed a peace treaty with the British in 1766. He was killed in 1769.

The PROCLAMATION of 1763

To prevent more clashes between settlers and Indigenous peoples, KING GEORGE III issued the PROCLAMATION OF 1763, making it illegal for settlers to live west of the APPALACHIAN MOUNTAINS. This angered settlers, some of whom had already purchased land past this border. The local governments said the settlers were entitled to the land, and gave them permission to disobey the proclamation. The stage was set for more conflict.

The British perpetrated vicious warfare against Indigenous communities. They burned down food stockpiles and entire villages, and offered bounties for the heads and scalps of any Indigenous person. Settlers, not just soldiers, participated in this effort. There are also accounts of Indigenous leaders being presented with gifts of blankets that had been intentionally contaminated with smallpox, causing a deadly outbreak of the disease.

CHECK YOUR KNOWLEDGE

1. What did many French colonists do for a living?

2. Why did the French get along better with Indigenous peoples than the English did?

3. Who presented the Albany plan? What did the plan aim to do?

4. How did George Washington become a hero in Virginia?

5. What is the relationship between the French and Indian War and the Seven Years' War?

6. What were the elements of the traditional European style of combat? Were they successful in the French and Indian War?

7. What was the turning point in the Seven Years' War?

8. What were the terms of the Treaty of Paris?

9. How did Chief Pontiac respond to France's loss in the French and Indian War?

ANSWERS

CHECK YOUR ANSWERS

1. They were fur traders.
2. There were fewer French settlers, they traded with Indigenous people, and did not settle on their land.
3. Benjamin Franklin presented the Albany Plan. The plan was an attempt to unite the colonies, but it failed.
4. His attack on Fort Duquesne, which led to the start of the French and Indian War, made him famous.
5. The French and Indian War became known as the Seven Years' War when it grew into a larger European conflict.
6. Organized ranks, usually wearing bright uniforms. These elements were not successful in the French and Indian War because colonists and Indigenous people knew the land, and fought very differently. The bright uniforms made the Redcoats easy targets.
7. The Battle of Quebec
8. The treaty gave England all the French territory east of the Mississippi as well as the Spanish territory of Florida because Spain had sided with France.
9. He successfully united groups of Indigenous people and waged a three-year war against the British and invading settlers.

☆ Chapter 9 ☆

PARLIAMENT AND PROTESTS
★ ★ ★

The END of SALUTARY NEGLECT

The French and Indian War had been very expensive, so Great Britain had a large debt. In addition, the expanding British territory meant that Indigenous peoples were forced off their land by violence and deceptive treaties. England sent a **STANDING ARMY** to America to protect the colonists from Indigenous resistance, and those troops had to be paid, too. In order to pay off the war debt and maintain the standing army England had sent to America to protect the colonists, Parliament raised taxes.

MY FEET HURT!

> **STANDING ARMY**
> a professional army
> maintained even
> in peacetime

The SUGAR ACT ← SWEET! (NOT.)

The SUGAR ACT of 1764 actually lowered taxes on molasses that were brought into the colonies, in the hope that it would minimize SMUGGLING. Because customs officers were trying to stop smugglers, they searched ships, and any suspected contraband could be taken away, even before the smuggler was convicted. Colonists believed that the Sugar Act violated their legal rights as British citizens by denying the right to trial—and some went even further: JAMES OTIS, a lawyer in Boston, argued that Parliament didn't have a right to tax the colonists at all, since the colonists didn't have representatives there to debate the tax.

YE DREADED → STAMP!

The STAMP ACT

In 1765, the STAMP ACT was passed. Any printed paper goods, including legal documents, had to be taxed and have a stamp proving the tax was paid. The Stamp Act was the first direct tax on individual colonists. Protests broke out, including **BOYCOTTS** in which colonists refused to purchase British goods at all.

> **BOYCOTT**
> a protest in which people don't purchase controversial items

STAMP AGENTS WERE TARRED AND FEATHERED, AND MOBS PREVENTED STAMP DISTRIBUTIONS.

NOOOO!

That October, representatives from nine colonies met in New York for the STAMP ACT CONGRESS. They wrote a petition explaining how the Stamp Act was a violation of their natural and political rights. In March 1766, at the urging of British merchants who had been hurt by the boycotts, Parliament **REPEALED** the Stamp Act. But on the same day, they issued the DECLARATORY ACT, which basically reasserted Parliament's power to tax as it pleased.

> **REPEAL**
> to undo a law

NO TAXATION WITHOUT REPRESENTATION!

SAMUEL ADAMS and PATRICK HENRY

Boston businessman SAMUEL ADAMS agreed with Otis. He summed up Otis's position at a Boston town meeting in 1764 as "NO TAXATION WITHOUT REPRESENTATION." It became a rallying cry. Adams was a cofounder of a secret society called the SONS OF LIBERTY, which organized boycotts and protests, some of them violent. Women formed the DAUGHTERS OF LIBERTY, urging Americans to use homemade (rather than imported) clothes and household goods. This was some of the first political involvement by women in America.

PATRICK HENRY was a lawyer and member of the House of Burgesses. In 1765, he raised the cry of "No Taxation Without Representation" in Virginia and inspired the burgesses to protest the Stamp Act. Some people believed that these protests were headed toward **TREASON**. Henry said, "If this be treason, make the most of it," and implied overthrowing the king.

> **TREASON**
> a crime against a government to which one should be loyal

The TOWNSHEND ACTS

Parliament still wanted to raise more money to pay for British troops in America and the expenses of the French and Indian War. In 1767, it passed the TOWNSHEND ACTS, which taxed imports, including tea. Colonists were infuriated by another tax being passed without their permission. They were also angry about the WRITS OF ASSISTANCE, which gave customs officials permission to search for taxable goods without a search warrant. Soon tax collectors were among the most unpopular people in North America, and many went home to England to escape threats on their lives. The royal governor of Massachusetts asked England to send soldiers to maintain peace and enforce the law.

The BOSTON MASSACRE

In 1768, 1,000 Redcoats came to Boston. To the colonists, the Redcoats were not there to help, but were occupying troops. On March 5, 1770, a minor dispute broke out between a soldier and some Bostonians, who threw snowballs at him. More citizens and more soldiers came on the scene, and a mob formed. In front of the customhouse, where the taxes were collected, stones were thrown and some citizens dared the soldiers to fire. A few soldiers panicked and did, killing five Boston citizens. The event came to be known as the BOSTON MASSACRE. The five victims became heroes of the colonial cause—notably CRISPUS ATTUCKS, son of African and Wampanoag parents. Lawyer JOHN ADAMS, a cousin of Samuel Adams, argued that everyone, including the soldiers, was entitled to a fair trial. He and JOSIAH QUINCY defended the soldiers, who were freed on the grounds of self-defense. The trial demonstrated to the world that the colonists were committed to justice.

BOSTON TEA PARTY

Parliament repealed all of the Townshend Acts in 1770 except one: the tax on tea.

> **MONOPOLY**
> a situation in which one company has complete control of an entire market

People in Massachusetts were able to purchase smuggled tea. However, in 1773, when the British East India Company faced financial ruin, Parliament passed the new TEA ACT, giving the company a **MONOPOLY** on selling tea directly to the colonists and making taxed tea cheaper than smuggled tea. That reinforced taxes on the colonies and hurt local merchants who had made their living from tea.

> Many colonists began to drink coffee to replace tea.

At midnight on the night of December 16, 1773, while three East India Company ships were docked in Boston, the Sons of Liberty, disguised as Indigenous people, boarded the ships and dumped 342 chests of tea into Boston Harbor. This was dubbed the BOSTON TEA PARTY. Because they considered themselves loyal British citizens, the colonists attempted to pay England back for the tea in exchange for a repeal of the Tea Act. However, the king and Parliament had finally had enough and were determined to punish the colony of Massachusetts.

The INTOLERABLE ACTS

King George III acknowledged that England would either need to "master" the colonists or "leave them to themselves." He picked "master." In 1774, Parliament passed the COERCIVE ACTS, known in the colonies as the INTOLERABLE ACTS because...

Boston Harbor was closed until colonists compensated the East India Company for its lost tea.

INTOLERABLE!

Most town meetings were banned.

The charter of Massachusetts was revoked.

The Massachusetts legislature was put under the control of the new governor, General Thomas Gage. In effect, Boston was put under martial law.

INTOLERABLE!

Royal officials who committed crimes in the colonies couldn't be tried in colonial courts.

The Quartering Act forced colonists to let British soldiers stay in their homes.

VERY ANNOYING...
I MEAN,
INTOLERABLE!

Land the colonists thought belonged to them was given to Quebec (the Quebec Act).

The goal was to exert control in the colonies, but the Intolerable Acts had the OPPOSITE effect.

CHECK YOUR KNOWLEDGE

1. Why did England send a standing army to the colonies?

2. What rallying cry was developed by Bostonian James Otis and named by Samuel Adams?

3. How does a boycott work?

4. How were women involved in political protests in the 1760s?

5. What was the verdict in the case of the Boston Massacre deaths? What message did the trial send?

6. Who was responsible for the Boston Tea Party?

7. What was the reasoning behind the Coercive Acts?

ANSWERS

CHECK YOUR ANSWERS

1. To protect the colonists from Indigenous peoples who were protecting their land and their lives against settler attacks

2. "No taxation without representation."

3. Consumers stop buying or using a product in order to encourage those who sell it to make a change.

4. They encouraged Americans to use homemade (not imported) goods.

5. The soldiers were found not guilty. The trial demonstrated to the world that the colonists were committed to justice.

6. The Sons of Liberty

7. They were intended to help England maintain control over the colonies.

COERCIVE ACTS?
MORE LIKE...
INTOLERABLE!

☆ Chapter 10 ☆

THE BRITISH
★ ★ ★ ★ ★ ★ ★ ★ ★ ★ ★ ★ ★ ★ ★ ★
ARE COMING!

OOH, IS IT THE
BEATLES?

I BELIEVE THEY
MEAN US, SIR.

The FIRST CONTINENTAL CONGRESS

Seeing the Coercive Acts as truly intolerable, in September 1774 the colonies sent representatives to meet in Philadelphia and figure out how to respond. This was the FIRST CONTINENTAL CONGRESS.

Debate was about how to best oppose British policy or negotiate with Parliament.

The First Continental Congress was the first time delegates from all over the colonies got together. Georgia was the only colony that didn't send representatives, but later they agreed with its decisions.

"Congress" today is the legislative branch of the U.S. government. But back then, "congress" was just a fancy word for a meeting.

Patrick Henry—who told the Second Virginia Convention in 1775,

"GIVE ME LIBERTY OR GIVE ME DEATH" —argued on the side of war.

Congress decided to put on a different kind of pressure. They escalated the boycotts. They sent a petition, the VIRGINIA DECLARATION OF RIGHTS, to King George, informing him of the rights to "life, liberty, and property" they deserved as Englishmen. And they endorsed the SUFFOLK RESOLVES by the leaders of Suffolk County, Massachusetts, which called on colonists to form militias and declare the Intolerable Acts null and void. The delegates were hoping for the best and preparing for the worst.

The SONS of LIBERTY STRIKE AGAIN

Instead of repealing the Intolerable Acts, King George III sent more troops to Boston. So many people were spying for both sides that it wasn't long before General Gage, royal governor of Massachusetts, learned that the colonial militia was storing an arsenal of weapons in Concord, just outside Boston. In April 1775, he ordered his men to head there to destroy it and to arrest Samuel Adams and John Hancock (who also helped found the Sons of Liberty) in nearby Lexington.

On April 18, 1775, a Sons of Liberty spy came across a British regiment preparing to march. He ran to tell PAUL REVERE and

William Dawes, also members of the Sons of Liberty. Revere asked a man named Robert Newman to keep watch from the steeple in the Old North Church in Boston. Newman was told to light one lantern if the British troops were coming by land, and two if by sea.

THE REGULARS ARE COMING OUT!

When they saw two lanterns, Dawes took an overland route and Revere rowed across the harbor and took a MIDNIGHT RIDE through Charleston and on to Lexington and Concord. As he rode, he shouted, "The regulars are coming out," secret code words to warn the colonists that the British were coming.

LEXINGTON and CONCORD

The local militia, called MINUTEMEN (they could be READY IN A MINUTE), heard Revere and grabbed their weapons. When the 700 Redcoats reached Lexington around dawn, about 70 minutemen were waiting. Both sides were ordered not to fire unless fired upon, and to this day no one knows who shot first, but it was "THE SHOT HEARD ROUND THE WORLD," starting the BATTLE OF LEXINGTON AND CONCORD.

BANG!

BLIMEY, DID YOU HEAR THAT?

The British quickly defeated the outnumbered minutemen, killing eight of them, and marched on to Concord.

As the British were leaving Concord, they were surprised by more minutemen at the North Bridge. The colonists killed almost 200 Redcoats, using the bright red jackets as targets. The British retreated to Boston, and both sides pondered their next move.

Colonists who supported independence were called **Patriots**, and those who remained loyal to Britain were called **Loyalists**. Many Loyalists fled the colonies, often heading to Canada.

The SECOND CONTINENTAL CONGRESS

Initially most Indigenous peoples didn't take sides in the Revolutionary War, but the majority of those who fought supported the British. The British persuaded many tribes to fight against colonials settling in frontier regions.

Since King George III continued to ignore the Declaration of Rights, the colonial leaders from all thirteen colonies met on May 10, 1775, in a SECOND CONTINENTAL CONGRESS. They began to set up their own post office, make treaties with Indigenous peoples, and serve as an impromptu governing body. They formed the CONTINENTAL ARMY with the Virginian George Washington as its commander. The colonial leaders, who were mostly from Massachusetts, chose a Virginian as commander to make the resistance appealing to Southerners.

The BATTLE of BUNKER HILL

COLONEL WILLIAM PRESCOTT set up the Massachusetts militias on BUNKER HILL and BREED'S HILL, across the harbor from Boston. On June 17, 1775, more than 2,000 Redcoats

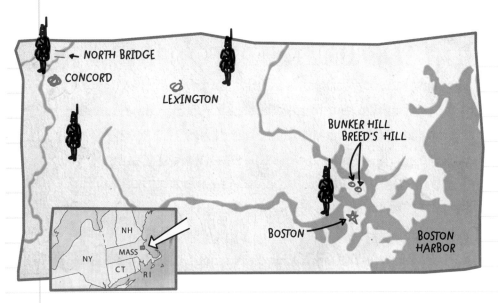

marched up the hill. According to legend, the militias were short on ammunition, so Prescott ordered them not to fire at the Redcoats until they could see "the whites of their eyes." Twice, the militias drove back the powerful British army. Although the British eventually forced them off Bunker Hill, the inexperienced colonial armies proved that they wouldn't be easily defeated.

The OLIVE BRANCH PETITION

On July 5, the Second Continental Congress sent King George III one last shot at peace, the OLIVE BRANCH PETITION. They still wanted to be part of England if the king would protect their rights. They urged the king to negotiate on disputed issues with recognition that the colonies should rule themselves on most matters. King George III rejected the petition and instead hired 30,000 German "Hessian" (or mercenary) troops to fight with the British.

TAKING BACK BOSTON

Washington took control of militias and began creating the Continental army to take back Boston. He came up with a plan to retrieve the weapons from FORT TICONDEROGA, which a militia known as the GREEN MOUNTAIN BOYS (led by ETHAN ALLEN) and a Connecticut militia (led by BENEDICT ARNOLD, most famous for turning traitor and selling information to the British army) had captured from the British earlier. Colonel HENRY KNOX and his troops hauled heavy cannons from the fort over 300 miles by foot in the middle of winter. The Redcoats, under the command of SIR WILLIAM HOWE, saw that defeat in Boston was inevitable. On March 17, 1776, the British retreated, fleeing north to Canada.

COMMON SENSE

In January 1776, a recent immigrant from England named THOMAS PAINE wrote an anonymous pamphlet arguing for democracy and independence titled COMMON SENSE. Paine blamed King George III personally—not just Parliament. Pretty radical for a time when most countries were ruled by kings (who claimed to have God on their side). Common Sense sold hundreds of thousands of copies throughout the colonies and persuaded many people to support independence.

COMMON
SENSE

ADDRESSED
TO THE
INHABITANTS
OF
AMERICA

The DECLARATION of INDEPENDENCE

JUNE 7, 1776:

RICHARD HENRY LEE of Virginia introduced a **RESOLUTION** in the Second Continental Congress calling the colonies free and independent states. Congress created a committee that included delegates Benjamin Franklin, John Adams, and Thomas Jefferson to draft a Declaration of Independence. Jefferson wrote it within two weeks, drawing on the ideas of **JOHN LOCKE**. It was meant to explain the LEE RESOLUTION.

> The Second Continental Congress came up with the national motto **E PLURIBUS UNUM**, meaning "out of many, one" in Latin.

> **RESOLUTION**
> a formal expression of an opinion

JULY 2, 1776:

Congress unanimously passed Lee's resolution. John Adams figured this date would become a national holiday.

> **JOHN LOCKE** wrote that all individuals have the right to "life, liberty, and property." "Property" became "the pursuit of happiness" in one of the most famous lines of the Declaration of Independence.

JULY 4, 1776:

The delegates adopted the Declaration of Independence. The United States of America was born ... provided the colonists won the war.

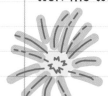

> ... and now we celebrate July 4 every year as Independence Day!

The DECLARATION

The Declaration of Independence has four parts:

1. **PREAMBLE** (introduction)
2. Declaration of Natural Rights
3. List of **GRIEVANCES** against the King
4. Resolution of Independence by the United States

PREAMBLE
introductory section

GRIEVANCES
complaints

From the Preamble:

"When in the Course of human events, it becomes necessary for one people to dissolve the political bands...they should declare the causes which impel them to the separation."

People must state their reasons for a revolution.

From the Declaration of Natural Rights:

"We hold these truths to be self-evident, that all men are created equal, that they are endowed by their Creator with certain unalienable Rights, that among these are Life, Liberty, and the pursuit of Happiness..."

Some rights come from the fact of just being human and can't be taken away by a king. When the Founding Fathers wrote "all men are created equal," they meant landowning white men. They did not include Indigenous people, enslaved people, free Black people, or women.

# of INDEPENDENCE

THE COLONIES'
JUSTIFICATION FOR
SEPARATION

From the List of Grievances:

"The history of the present King of Great Britain is a history of repeated injuries and usurpations, all having in direct object the establishment of an absolute **TYRANNY** over these States."

TYRANNY
rule by an often harsh absolute power

The grievances, or complaints, the colonists had against King George III, followed by a lot of examples.

RESTATES THE
LEE RESOLUTION

From the Resolution of Independence:

"We, therefore, the Representatives of the United States of America, in General Congress...do, in the Name, and by Authority of the good People of these Colonies, solemnly publish and declare, That these United Colonies are, and of Right ought to be Free and Independent States."

"We're independent!"

The DECLARATION of INDEPENDENCE in 40 WORDS

Government is a social contract. If the ruler doesn't protect the people and their natural rights, the contract is broken and the people can overthrow him. King George III broke the contract, so now the U.S. is its own nation.

PUT YOUR JOHN HANCOCK RIGHT HERE

John Hancock, president of the Congress, was the first to sign the Declaration of Independence. His signature was so large and stylish that people sometimes still call a signature a "John Hancock."

TOO MUCH?

actual size

CHECK YOUR KNOWLEDGE

1. What did the First Continental Congress debate about?

2. What was declared in the Virginia Declaration of Rights?

3. How did Paul Revere know which way the British were coming from?

4. What was the colonial militia nicknamed?

5. Who fired first at the Battle of Lexington?

6. What was the Olive Branch Petition?

7. What was the importance of the pamphlet *Common Sense*?

8. Who was considered "created equal" in the Declaration of Independence?

ANSWERS 123

CHECK YOUR ANSWERS

1. They debated about how to best oppose British policy or negotiate with Parliament.
2. That as Englishmen, colonists had rights to "life, liberty, and property"
3. Robert Newman lit two lanterns in the steeple of the Old North Church in Boston to indicate that the British were coming by sea.
4. The minutemen
5. Nobody knows!
6. It was the last attempt by the Continental Congress to make peace with King George III and remain part of England.
7. Thomas Paine's pamphlet persuaded many colonists that independence was a good idea.
8. The phrase "created equal" referred to landowning white men.

Unit 3

American Revolution and the Early Republic 1776-1791

Once the Declaration of Independence was signed, the United States was born, but Americans still had work ahead. First, they needed to win a war against one of the best armies and the most powerful navy in the world. Next, they had to invent a whole new form of government.

☆ Chapter 11 ☆

The AMERICAN REVOLUTION

TIMELINE to (REAL) INDEPENDENCE

Americans declared independence, but they weren't independent yet.

Washington was put in charge of the Continental army in 1775, but it was more like a collection of part-time volunteer militias contracted to fight for only one year. The Continental Congress suggested a **DRAFT**, but not everyone participated. The wealthy paid enslaved people, apprentices, or others to serve in their place.

> **DRAFT**
> a mandatory call of duty
> to serve in an army

The British—leaders of a well-trained, professional army and rulers of a great empire—were confident of victory.

The BATTLE of LONG ISLAND

Summer of 1776: Over 30,000 British soldiers under GENERAL WILLIAM HOWE arrived in New York City. Washington's troops were outnumbered.

August 1776: In the BATTLE OF LONG ISLAND, the Patriots were driven out of New York and then New Jersey, and forced to take refuge in Pennsylvania across the Delaware River.

The British were so sure the war would be over soon that they left the defense of New Jersey up to the HESSIANS, a group of German mercenaries, while the British army spent the winter in comfort in New York.

Thomas Paine, the author of *Common Sense*, also wrote a series of pamphlets called AMERICAN CRISIS. The first one, published in 1776, begins with the line, "These are the times that try men's souls."

WASHINGTON CROSSES the DELAWARE

Christmas Day 1776: During a terrible storm, Washington and thousands of his troops secretly rowed across the Delaware River while the Hessians were celebrating Christmas. The next morning, while the Hessians were camped out at Trenton and still sleeping, the Continental army attacked and won an important victory.

January 2, 1777: British general CHARLES CORNWALLIS, in charge of the British troops, tried to stop the Continental army, but Washington was a step ahead. His troops lit campfires near Princeton to make it look like they were resting. Instead, they followed the British troops and made another surprise attack.

The BATTLE of SARATOGA

Spring of 1777: The British plan was to capture the city of Albany and take control of the Hudson River to cut off New England from the other colonies. General William Howe would move north up the Hudson. GENERAL JOHN BURGOYNE would head south from Canada and recapture Fort Ticonderoga on the way. LIEUTENANT COLONEL BARRY ST. LEGER would travel down the Mohawk Valley. All three would meet in Albany. That was the theory, anyway.

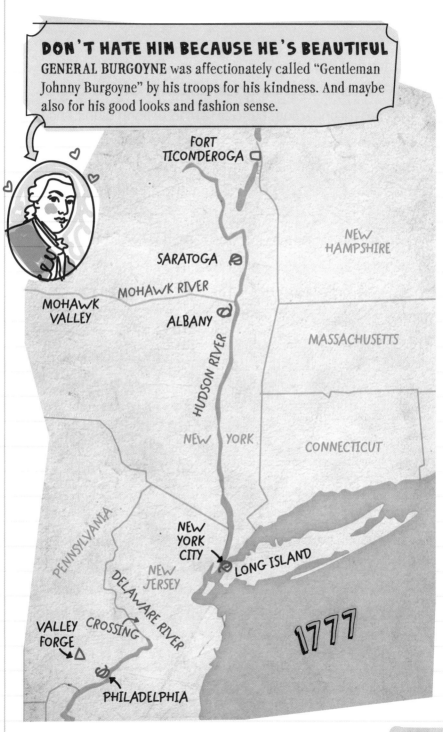

DON'T HATE HIM BECAUSE HE'S BEAUTIFUL
GENERAL BURGOYNE was affectionately called "Gentleman Johnny Burgoyne" by his troops for his kindness. And maybe also for his good looks and fashion sense.

FORT TICONDEROGA

SARATOGA

NEW HAMPSHIRE

MOHAWK RIVER

MOHAWK VALLEY

ALBANY

MASSACHUSETTS

HUDSON RIVER

NEW YORK

CONNECTICUT

NEW YORK CITY

LONG ISLAND

PENNSYLVANIA

NEW JERSEY

DELAWARE RIVER

VALLEY FORGE

CROSSING

PHILADELPHIA

1777

Howe decided it'd be better to capture Philadelphia. He forced the Continental Congress to flee the city. Burgoyne recaptured Ticonderoga, but Gentleman Johnny didn't know Howe wasn't on his way up the Hudson and was trapped in the woods by American militias. St. Leger was forced back en route to the Mohawk Valley by American general Benedict Arnold.

↖ TRAITOR! SPY! NOT-GOOD GUY!

Burgoyne eventually made it to Saratoga, New York, where he was met by the American forces of GENERAL HORATIO GATES. The British had no reinforcements and no escape route. On October 17, the British surrendered, and the BATTLE OF SARATOGA became the first major American victory of the Revolutionary War.

> The victory also led the French to get involved in the revolution. The French and British were bitter enemies, so the French began supporting the Patriots when they saw that the Americans could win and wouldn't be satisfied with anything less than independence.

WINTER at VALLEY FORGE

Winter of 1777: The Continental army suffered through one of the worst winters on record. While the British were comfy in Philadelphia, the Continental army was camped 20 miles west at VALLEY FORGE. The 12,000 troops had almost no food, clothing, or supplies. About a quarter of them died before spring. Those who survived had spent the winter training under Prussian officer Baron von Steuben. ←

They became a small but very skilled new Continental army.

HIRED BY CONGRESS FOR HIS MILITARY EXPERTISE

HELP from OVERSEAS

1778: The French had been secretly providing supplies and their navy to the Patriots. The victory at Saratoga, plus the charm of Benjamin Franklin as an American diplomat in France, persuaded the French to support the U.S. publicly. In 1778, King Louis XVI decided that France would officially become an ally and declare war on Great Britain.

PRIVATEER
a privately owned ship commissioned by the government to fight the enemy; in exchange, the ship could keep whatever they found on enemy ships

1779: Spain joined the war against England. Louisiana governor BERNARDO DE GÁLVEZ helped Spain take Natchez, Baton Rouge, and other cities from the British. Holland also helped the Patriots with loans and funding.

The **MARQUIS DE LAFAYETTE**, a young French nobleman, became a trusted aide to George Washington. Lafayette was such a strong believer in the Revolutionary War that he paid the troops under his command out of his own pocket!

WAR on the WESTERN FRONT

The British army had to spread out to cover a lot of land. West of the Appalachian Mountains, the British gained Indigenous allies like Mohawk chief JOSEPH BRANT. This area had been made more accessible thanks in part to DANIEL BOONE, who had **BLAZED** the WILDERNESS ROAD in 1775. GEORGE ROGERS CLARK, a lieutenant colonel in the Virginia militia, captured the British outposts and FORT SACKVILLE in modern-day Indiana.

> **BLAZED**
> cut a trail—as in, he was a trailblazer!

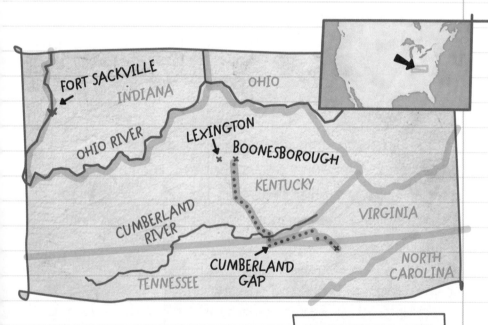

FORT SACKVILLE
INDIANA
OHIO
OHIO RIVER
LEXINGTON
BOONESBOROUGH
KENTUCKY
CUMBERLAND RIVER
VIRGINIA
CUMBERLAND GAP
TENNESSEE
NORTH CAROLINA

WILDERNESS ROAD

WAR in the SOUTH

1778-1780: The British offered freedom to people enslaved by Patriots if they would run away and join the British troops. In December 1778, British commander HENRY CLINTON captured Savannah, Georgia (and eventually the entire state of Georgia). In May 1780, Clinton also gained control of Charleston, South Carolina, in a battle that destroyed most of the American army in the South. GENERAL CORNWALLIS was put in charge of maintaining a British stronghold in the South.

Congress appointed GENERAL HORATIO GATES, who had led troops to victory in Saratoga, to create a new Southern army. Unfortunately, they were quickly defeated by Cornwallis.

1781: Congress replaced Gates with a new Southern general, NATHANAEL GREENE. Greene's army (under Patriot Daniel Morgan) defeated the British at the battle at Cowpens, South Carolina. It was the first time that militia units were deployed in battle.

GUERRILLAS and the SWAMP FOX

Instead of using the traditional European style of lining up for combat, Southern Patriots used their knowledge of the terrain by attacking supply and communication centers in small groups and escaping before they could be caught.

It was a style of warfare called **GUERRILLA WARFARE**. The most famous guerrilla of the South was FRANCIS MARION, leader of MARION'S BRIGADE. He was so difficult to catch that the British called him the "SWAMP FOX." Eventually, the British fled the Carolinas.

> **GUERRILLA WARFARE**
> system of warfare in which the soldiers fight using techniques such as surprise, ambush, and disruption

SWAMP FOX!

The BATTLE of YORKTOWN

Early 1781: Cornwallis moved his troops to YORKTOWN, Virginia, on the banks of the York River. Supplies and money were running low, and he needed a port to resupply his troops. Philadelphia and New York were controlled by the British. It was discovered that General Benedict Arnold was a spy and had been plotting to turn over the critical military fort, West Point, and conspiring to capture George Washington. Morale was low.

> Benedict Arnold wasn't the only spy around. **NATHAN HALE**, a young soldier for the Continental army, volunteered to go behind enemy lines and report on British troop activities during the Battle of Long Island. When he was caught and sentenced to hang in 1776, Hale's famous last words were this:
> **"I ONLY REGRET THAT I HAVE BUT ONE LIFE TO LOSE FOR MY COUNTRY."**

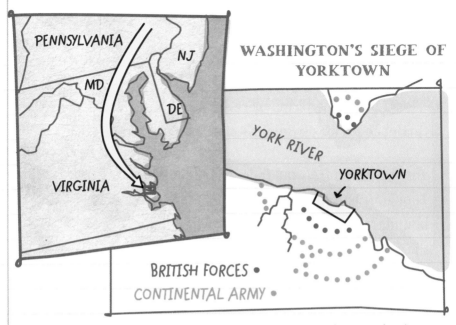

WASHINGTON'S SIEGE OF YORKTOWN

PENNSYLVANIA
NJ
MD
DE
VIRGINIA

YORK RIVER
YORKTOWN

BRITISH FORCES •
CONTINENTAL ARMY •

When Washington learned that Cornwallis had moved into Yorktown, he saw an opportunity. After a fast and top-secret march south, the Continental army (with the help of 7,000 French troops under Lieutenant General Rochambeau) surrounded the city of Yorktown. French ships had already blocked Chesapeake Bay, making it impossible for Cornwallis to escape or get reinforcements.

On October 19, 1781, after weeks of fighting, Cornwallis surrendered.

There were several small battles left to fight, but the war was over. Benjamin Franklin, John Jay, and John Adams began negotiations with the British in Paris to end the conflict. The last British troops left New York Harbor. Washington left for his home in Mount Vernon, Virginia.

The TREATY of PARIS (Again)

It took two years to finish negotiating the 1783 TREATY OF PARIS, but the terms were favorable for the U.S. On September 3, 1783, Britain officially agreed on the following:

> The U.S. was a free and independent nation. Though it had the potential to expand, its boundaries were now the Mississippi River, the southern border of Canada, and the northern border of Spanish Florida.

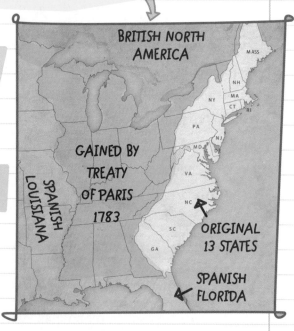

Americans could fish the waters of British North America.

Debts would be repaid.

Enslaved people would be returned.

The Congress agreed to RECOMMEND that property taken from Loyalists be returned. However, many Loyalists fled to New Brunswick and Nova Scotia. Also, Spain got Florida back.

The **1763 TREATY OF PARIS** ended the Seven Years' War. The **1783 TREATY OF PARIS** ended the Revolutionary War. In 1898, a completely different **TREATY OF PARIS** ended the Spanish-American War.

HOW the WAR WAS WON

So if the British army was better trained and better supplied, how did the Patriots win?

HOME-FIELD ADVANTAGE

KNOWLEDGE OF THE TERRAIN

MOTIVATION FOR THE CAUSE

CIVILIAN SUPPORT

GREAT LEADERSHIP

HELP FROM FRANCE AND SPAIN

WOMEN IN THE REVOLUTIONARY WAR

With the men away, women took more responsibility for the home front. They also supported the cause of independence: They sewed clothes and made supplies for the army, or became nurses. Many disguised themselves as men to fight or became spies. Some also followed their husbands to the battlefield and did a lot of domestic work at the camps. One famous example, **MARY LUDWIG HAYS McCAULEY**, actually fought in the war. She was probably the inspiration for mythical folk hero **MOLLY PITCHER**, who was famous for bringing pitchers of water to the soldiers. Molly Pitcher's name symbolizes the many women of the Revolutionary War.

BLACK PEOPLE IN THE REVOLUTIONARY WAR

At first, Black people weren't allowed to fight in the Continental army, mainly because the Southern states didn't want to give weapons to enslaved people. After the British recruited enslaved people, attitudes changed. A lot of free Black people served in the army; for example, the **FIRST RHODE ISLAND REGIMENT** consisted of 140 Black soldiers out of 225. By the end of the war, every state except South Carolina included Black people in their troops.

CHECK YOUR KNOWLEDGE

1. How did wealthy people get out of the draft for the Revolutionary War?

2. How long were most American troops contracted to fight at the time of the Revolutionary War?

3. What was the significance of the Battle of Saratoga?

4. What is a privateer?

5. Why was Francis Marion called the "Swamp Fox"?

6. What were the terms of the 1783 Treaty of Paris?

7. How did women participate in the American Revolution?

CHECK YOUR ANSWERS

1. They paid enslaved people or apprentices to go instead.
2. One year
3. It was the first major American victory and inspired the French to support the Patriots.
4. A privately owned ship asked by the government to attack the enemy in exchange for whatever they found on enemy ships.
5. He used guerrilla tactics and was hard to catch.
6. American independence was recognized and borders were determined. Debts were to be repaid and captive enslaved people returned to their enslavers. Americans could fish in British Canada, too.
7. Women made supplies for the army and became nurses. Many also fought, helped soldiers, or became spies.

Chapter 12 ☆

☆ A NEW ☆
GOVERNMENT

The ARTICLES of CONFEDERATION

Nobody wanted a new tyranny, but they needed a national government. Congress appointed a committee to draft a national **CONSTITUTION** called the ARTICLES OF CONFEDERATION. It established a CONFEDERATION CONGRESS, a national legislature responsible

> **CONSTITUTION**
> a set of laws that guides how a country, state, or organization operates

for borrowing and creating money, settling arguments between states, negotiating with Indigenous peoples, and making treaties. The Congress could ask the states to provide money and soldiers, but states could refuse, because they maintained their **SOVEREIGNTY**. Furthermore, each state had one vote in the Confederation Congress regardless of size or population, so they were all equal.

> **SOVEREIGNTY**
> authority or power

The Continental Congress (the governing body through which the colonial governments coordinated their resistance to British rule) approved the Articles of Confederation on November 15, 1777, but the articles still needed to be **RATIFIED**, or confirmed, by the states. Maryland was the last, and in March 1781, the Articles of Confederation became the constitution of a new nation.

> **RATIFY**
> to approve or confirm

The NORTHWEST TERRITORY

It was important for Congress to take control of the Western lands, because the U.S. was in debt. It hadn't paid its soldiers yet and needed to sell land to make money. The LAND ORDINANCE OF 1785 split land into TOWNSHIPS that could be sold off. This was land that had long been the home of many Indigenous societies, which led to conflicts and violence between the settlers and the Indigenous people of the land. The NORTHWEST ORDINANCE OF 1787 made these plots of land (parts of present-day Illinois, Indiana, Michigan, Ohio, Minnesota, and Wisconsin) the NORTHWEST **TERRITORY.**

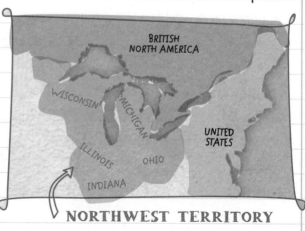

NORTHWEST TERRITORY

Territories within the Northwest Territory could apply to become states once they reached a population of 60,000 (non-Indigenous) people and

> **TERRITORY**
> in this context, a subdivision of land that is not a state but is governed by the U.S.

drafted a state constitution. Slavery was banned in them. Land there was cheap; the population quickly increased.

The TREATY OF GREENVILLE

Indigenous societies in the Northwest Territory united to fight American expansion into their land, with the support of the British. The Indigenous American forces were initially successful in defeating the expeditions that were sent to destroy them. However, they suffered a major defeat in 1794 at the BATTLE OF FALLEN TIMBERS. After that defeat, 12 Indigenous nations signed the 1795 TREATY OF GREENVILLE, **CEDING** most of their land in the Northwest Territory to the U.S.

> **CEDE**
> to yield or formally surrender

DIPLOMATIC and ECONOMIC PROBLEMS

The Articles of Confederation didn't give the federal government much power. It couldn't **LEVY** taxes to cover the war debt or build a unified army. Britain realized this. They refused to follow

> **LEVY**
> impose, raise

through on the terms of the Treaty
of Paris and wouldn't allow
American ships into British ports.
Spain closed the lower Mississippi

> **TARIFF**
> a charge or fee imposed
> by the government on
> imports or exports

to U.S. shipping and trade with foreign lands. Other European
countries placed high **TARIFFS** on American goods. The war
had seriously damaged harvests, particularly in the South, so
these states had few crops to trade.

Another problem was **INFLATION**.
The paper money printed by the
Continental Congress during the
Revolutionary War had little value,
because the states didn't have

> **INFLATION**
> an economic condition
> characterized by high
> prices and a decrease in
> the value of money

gold or silver to back it up. The states lowered the value of
paper currency by printing their own bills. The combination of
inflation and **TRADE DEFICITS** led to a **DEPRESSION**.

> **TRADE DEFICIT**
> when more goods are coming into
> the country than going out of it
>
> **DEPRESSION**
> an economic condition
> characterized by low employment
> and little economic activity

SHAYS' REBELLION

To pay its war debts, the state of Massachusetts decided to raise taxes on land. Farmers tended to own a lot of land but earn little money, and those who couldn't pay were forced to give up their land or go to jail.

In August 1786, a farmer and former captain of the Continental army named DANIEL SHAYS began SHAYS' REBELLION.

> **ARSENAL**
> a place where weapons are stored

He and a group of farmers closed down the state courts and marched on the federal **ARSENAL**. The Massachusetts militia finally stopped him and his men. Although Massachusetts had requested federal assistance, it did not receive any, because Congress didn't have the authority to help. If ordinary farmers could launch a revolt, it was clear that the national government needed more power.

The CONSTITUTIONAL CONVENTION

In May 1787, delegates met at a CONSTITUTIONAL CONVENTION in Philadelphia. After electing George Washington as the president of the convention, they discussed whether to **AMEND** or ditch the Articles of Confederation.

> **AMEND**
> to modify or change, usually by a formal procedure

DON'T MIX UP THESE MEETINGS:

THE CONTINENTAL CONGRESS
↳ signed the Declaration of Independence

THE CONFEDERATION CONGRESS
↳ created by the Articles of Confederation

THE CONSTITUTIONAL CONVENTION
↳ met to fix the Articles of Confederation and ended up creating a whole new Constitution

 THE FOUNDING FATHERS OF THE UNITED STATES

The men who attended the Constitutional Convention, signed the Declaration of Independence, framed the Constitution, and/or helped with the American Revolution are called the **FOUNDING FATHERS** of **THE UNITED STATES**. No women or nonwhite people were permitted to sign documents or attend conventions.

The GREAT COMPROMISE

Congress couldn't agree on how states should be represented: a bicameral legislature (two houses with votes per state based on the population—the VIRGINIA PLAN) or a **UNICAMERAL** legislature (one house with equal votes for each state—the NEW JERSEY PLAN). The Virginia plan appealed to large states that would have many representatives; smaller states like New Jersey wanted state size not to matter in terms of how much representation you got.

> **UNICAMERAL**
> consisting of a single chamber as a legislative body

Roger Sherman of Connecticut proposed the CONNECTICUT COMPROMISE (the GREAT COMPROMISE), which created the bicameral federal legislature we know today: a SENATE with two votes per state and a HOUSE OF REPRESENTATIVES with representation proportional to each state's population.

VIRGINIA PLAN
BICAMERAL: TWO HOUSES WITH VOTES PER STATE BASED ON POPULATION

NEW JERSEY PLAN
UNICAMERAL: ONE HOUSE WITH EQUAL VOTES PER STATE

CONNECTICUT COMPROMISE
SENATE: TWO VOTES PER STATE
+
HOUSE OF REPRESENTATIVES:
REPRESENTATION BASED ON STATE POPULATION

RECOGNIZING ENSLAVED PEOPLE... OR NOT

Southern states, which had large populations of enslaved people, preferred a system in which enslaved people counted for representation by size of population—but not taxation. Northern states, where there were fewer enslaved people, argued that if enslaved people were considered property, they should count for taxation but NOT representation. The delegates decided to count enslaved people as three-fifths of a person in a clause called the THREE-FIFTHS COMPROMISE.

Allowing slavery in a nation founded on the principles of liberty and equality didn't make sense to some delegates. All states except Georgia, North Carolina, and South Carolina had already banned the slave trade by this point. Southern states whose wealth depended on slavery disagreed. Georgia and South Carolina threatened to leave the Union if their right to enslave people was taken away. The delegates settled on the SLAVE TRADE COMPROMISE: The slave trade could not be restricted or abolished until 1808. The states pushed the decision to 1808 because the two sides could not agree on what to do. Many people were opposed to the importation of enslaved people and many people supported it, and the indecision was holding up the process of passing the Constitution and establishing a new government.

The CONSTITUTION

On September 17, 1787, 39 of the 42 delegates who assembled in Philadelphia signed the Constitution. However, it still needed to be ratified so it could take effect. Those who refused to sign, including George Mason of Virginia, thought that a formal summary of citizens' freedoms was necessary. The founders intended for the Constitution to be a living document, that could be changed with **AMENDMENTS**, and revised continually. They knew it wasn't perfect, but thought they needed to get the new government up and running as quickly as possible.

AMENDMENT
a change or addition made to improve a law; in this case, an article added to the U.S. Constitution

YOU MUST SIGN!

YOU CAN'T MAKE ME

The CONSTITUTION

The government that was established at that time still operates today. It is based on the principle of **FEDERALISM**: balancing power between the national government and the state governments in a **DIVISION OF POWER**, and balancing strong central authority with **POPULAR SOVEREIGNTY**.
These are the three branches of federal government:

THE LEGISLATIVE BRANCH	THE EXECUTIVE BRANCH	THE JUDICIAL BRANCH
the Senate and House of Representatives, where laws are made	the president and their office, where laws are applied	the courts, where laws are interpreted

A system of **SEPARATION OF POWERS** and **CHECKS AND BALANCES** keeps any one branch from getting too powerful.

The Constitution is the **SUPREME LAW OF THE LAND**, and no state can create a law that goes against it.

The Constitution **CAN BE AMENDED** so that it stays flexible and is a "living document."

FEDERALISM
system of government in which power is shared by the national government and the states

POPULAR SOVEREIGNTY
authority of the people

Just as the Declaration of Independence was inspired by John Locke, the Constitution was influenced and based on Enlightenment philosophy, the Magna Carta, the English Bill of Rights, and Thomas Jefferson's Virginia Statute for Religious Freedom.

FEDERALISTS and ANTIFEDERALISTS

Those who were in favor of ratifying the Constitution called themselves FEDERALISTS. The Federalists promoted their views in a series of essays called the FEDERALIST PAPERS. Written by Alexander Hamilton, James Madison, and John Jay, but published under a pseudonym of "Publius," the Federalist Papers argued that the Constitution would protect people from tyranny. The ANTIFEDERALISTS thought the Constitution gave too much power to the federal government.

In 1788, the Antifederalists published a pamphlet called *Observations on the New Constitution*. It was written by a woman, **MERCY OTIS WARREN**, the sister of James Otis. In the document she detailed her opposition to the Constitution because of its emphasis on a strong central government. Warren became a well-respected historian, playwright, and poet.

RATIFICATION of the CONSTITUTION

The Constitution required only nine states to ratify it for it to go into effect. The framers had already decided to move away from the Articles of Confederation and so did not need to honor its requirement of a unanimous vote for ratification. Delaware was the first state to ratify, in December 1787, and when New Hampshire became the ninth in June 1788, the new government had been approved. Virginia and New York, two of the largest and most influential states, had not yet agreed to it. James Madison argued that the Constitution had to be approved as written; no changes could be permitted because it would mean each state was signing a different document. Virginia ratified it, and New York soon followed. Two years later, in May 1790, Rhode Island became the last state to ratify. The BILL OF RIGHTS, the first 10 amendments to the Constitution, was ratified in December 1791.

FIRST!!!

DELAWARE

CHECK YOUR KNOWLEDGE

1. What were the powers of the Confederation Congress?

2. According to the Northwest Ordinance, how could a territory become a state?

3. What economic problems did the United States experience after the war?

4. Why did Daniel Shays lead a rebellion in Massachusetts?

5. What was the Three-Fifths Compromise?

6. What are the three branches of government?

7. What was the difference between the Federalists and the Antifederalists?

ANSWERS

CHECK YOUR ANSWERS

1. The Congress could borrow and create money, make treaties, settle disputes between states, and manage matters with Indigenous peoples.

2. Once it had 60,000 people and a draft of a constitution, it could apply for statehood.

3. Inflation and a trade deficit (due to damaged Southern harvests, and trade restrictions imposed by some European countries) that led to an economic depression

4. Because the state of Massachusetts was taking farmers' land or sending them to jail if they could not pay their taxes

5. A clause in the Constitution that said three-fifths of an enslaved population would count for both taxes and representation

6. Executive, legislative, and judicial

7. Federalists supported ratifying the Constitution. Antifederalists didn't, because they thought it would give too much power to the federal government.

The CONCISE CONSTITUTION

The Constitution is divided into seven ARTICLES, each of which includes SECTIONS. The Constitution also includes a BILL OF RIGHTS, as well as more AMENDMENTS added since it was originally framed.

> You should read the whole thing to get all the details. Considering how COMPLICATED government is, the Constitution is really SHORT.

The PREAMBLE

The Preamble sets out the reasons for a constitution. It says that the people are establishing the new government. The whole thing:

"**WE THE PEOPLE** of the United States, in Order to form a more perfect Union, establish Justice, insure domestic Tranquility, provide for the common defense, promote the general Welfare, and secure the Blessings of Liberty to ourselves and our **POSTERITY**, do ordain and establish this Constitution for the United States of America."

POSTERITY
future generations

The ARTICLES

QUORUM
the required number of people needed to legally do business

ARTICLE I describes the LEGISLATIVE BRANCH. The Legislature of the U.S. is bicameral: the House of Representatives and the Senate. The vice president of the U.S. is the president of the Senate but doesn't vote except in a tie. If a majority of the Congress is present, a **QUORUM** is reached, but if not, they can **ADJOURN**. Each **BILL** must be signed by the president before becoming law. If the president **VETOES** the bill, it could still become law if two-thirds of the Congress **OVERRIDES** the veto. Congress has the right to make any laws "necessary and proper" to carry out its duties.

VETO
to cancel the actions of another branch of government

ADJOURN
to end or postpone the rest of a meeting

BILL
a draft of a law

Article I, Section 8:18: The "**necessary and proper**" clause is also known as the "elastic clause" because it gives Congress the ability to stretch its powers.

OVERRIDE
to set aside or overturn

Before the Constitution, government positions were unpaid, and this favored wealthy people who could afford to work for nothing. The Constitution says that congressmen are paid a salary out of the treasury, which is important, because when that wasn't the case, government attracted only wealthy people.

SECTION 8: The powers of Congress are: levying taxes and tariffs as long as they are uniform throughout the states, paying debts, borrowing money, regulating commerce with other countries/between states/with Indigenous peoples, deciding how people become citizens, minting money and regulating it, punishing counterfeiters, making a post office, regulating copyrights, establishing federal courts inferior to the Supreme Court, punishing crimes against international law, declaring war, raising an army or navy and paying them, summoning militias, regulating law in the District of Columbia, and making any other laws "necessary and proper" to do all of that.

SECTION 9: But no discussing slavery until 1808, no overriding the WRIT OF HABEAS CORPUS (can arrest a person only for a specific cause) except in wartime suspension, no passing a BILL OF ATTAINDER (a law targeting one person or group without a trial), no passing an EX POST FACTO law (a law that applies to people who broke it before it was written), no levying export taxes, no favoring one state in any way, no levying direct taxes on people (aka CAPITATION, no set amount that everyone has to pay in taxes, only taxes determined by income or money spent), no taking money from the treasury without a specific budget being passed as law, and no creating a titled aristocracy.

ARTICLE II describes the EXECUTIVE BRANCH: the president's duties, the president's advisers, and the vice president. The president, like the vice president, serves a four-year term. The president receives a salary and takes an oath to protect the Constitution. The powers of the president include serving as COMMANDER IN CHIEF of the armed forces; **PARDONING** criminals; nominating ambassadors, judges, and officers; and making treaties, provided that two-thirds of the Senate approves. The president, vice president, and other civil officers may be **IMPEACHED** for treason, bribery, or other misdemeanors and "high crimes."

PARDON	**IMPEACH**
to release or excuse a person from being punished for an offense	to bring an accusation against a government official

ARTICLE III describes the JUDICIAL BRANCH, or the courts, and it establishes a Supreme Court. All judges appointed under Article III (such as judges on the Supreme Court, the federal courts of appeals, and district courts) can hold their jobs for life. In all cases involving ambassadors or entire states, the Supreme Court has **ORIGINAL JURISDICTION**, meaning it's the first court to hear the case.

JURISDICTION
the authority to administer justice

There is a reason judges hold their jobs for life—it's to prevent them from having to run for reelection or be influenced by politics.

ARTICLE IV defines the relationship between the states and says that the federal government guarantees each state a "REPUBLIC FORM OF GOVERNMENT."

In the *FEDERALIST PAPERS*, James Madison described a republican form of government as a representative democracy as opposed to a direct democracy. That is, people have control via representatives. Also, a monarch cannot rule the government. The Constitution created a republic—NOT a democracy.

ARTICLE V explains how AMENDMENTS to the Constitution can be proposed and passed.

An amendment requires two-thirds of both the House and Senate and three-fourths of the state legislatures for approval. However, legislators can bypass Congress completely and pass an amendment if two-thirds of the state legislatures approve a call for a convention, which would convene to draft the amendment. Then, the amendment would need three-fourths of the states' approval. This method, however, has never been used.

ARTICLE VI says that the Constitution is the SUPREME LAW OF THE LAND.

ARTICLE VII confirms that the Constitution is established once 9 of the 13 states ratify it.

The AMENDMENTS

The first ten amendments are known as the BILL OF RIGHTS. Ratified in 1791, they protect individual liberties and limit the powers of the federal government.

1. Individual rights: freedom of religion, freedom of speech, freedom of the press, the right to assemble, and the right to petition the goverment.

2. The right to bear arms (outlining the right to own and carry weapons).

3. The right not to have soldiers quartered in a person's house without consent of the owner.

> **WARRANT**
> the authorization of an officer to make an arrest, seize property, or make a search

4. The right not to have **WARRANTS** issued without probable cause.

5. The right to due process, meaning that nobody can serve as a witness against themself, and capital crimes cannot be charged without a grand jury (except in wartime).

6. The right of the accused to have a speedy and public trial by jury, to know what crime they are charged with, to confront witnesses against them, and to be represented by a lawyer.

7. The right not to have a case that was already decided by a jury reexamined in another court.

8. The right not to have to pay excessive bail or receive cruel or unusual punishments.

9. The right to other rights that may not be listed in the Bill of Rights.

10. The right of states to hold powers not specifically assigned to the federal government.

THE BILL OF RIGHTS CAN BE GROUPED LIKE THIS:

AMENDMENT 1 protects individual rights and minorities from majority rule.

AMENDMENTS 2–4 address mistakes made during the Revolutionary War.

AMENDMENTS 5–8 guarantee rights to people charged with crimes.

AMENDMENTS 9–10 maintain the rights of states and citizens.

Following the Bills of Rights, other amendments were made to the Constitution. There are 27 amendments in total.

Remember the **MAIN PRINCIPLES** of the Constitution:

Popular sovereignty
Limited government
Separation of powers
Checks and balances
Federalism
Republicanism
Individual rights

You can memorize these principles and the fact that Rhode Island was the last state to ratify with this mnemonic device:

Please,
Let's
Sign
Constitutions
Faster,
Rhode
Island.

☆ Chapter 13 ☆

PRESIDENT

* * * * * * * * * * * * * * *

PRECEDENTS

Since Washington
was the first president,
everything he (and FIRST LADY MARTHA WASHINGTON)
did became the start of a tradition, or a PRECEDENT.
For example, Washington chose to be called "Mr. President"
instead of "Your Highness," "Your Excellency," or "Your High
Mightiness" (someone seriously suggested that).

The FIRST PRESIDENT

In early 1789, the states that had
ratified the Constitution decided that an
ELECTORAL COLLEGE would meet and
elect a president. George Washington was
persuaded to come out of retirement, and he received ALL the

> **ELECTORAL COLLEGE**
> a group that represents the people's vote in electing a president

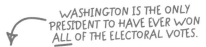WASHINGTON IS THE ONLY PRESIDENT TO HAVE EVER WON ALL OF THE ELECTORAL VOTES.

electoral votes. Nearly half of the voters cast their second vote for John Adams, who became the first vice president. They were inaugurated on April 30, 1789, in New York City, then the nation's temporary capital.

Each state legislature appointed a certain number of "electors" (based on its number of congressmen) to represent their state and elect a president. The electoral college system has changed a lot since then but is still in use today.

The CABINET

Congress created departments of the executive branch: the State Department (to deal with other countries), the War Department (to deal with defense issues), the Treasury (to deal with the economy), the Justice Department (to deal with administration of justice), and the Postal Service. Washington chose these people to head these departments:

Henry Knox (a general from the Revolutionary War): Secretary of War

Thomas Jefferson: Secretary of State

Alexander Hamilton: Secretary of the Treasury

Edmund Randolph: Attorney General

Samuel Osgood: Postmaster General

As a group, these heads of departments were THE CABINET. The cabinet members (except the postmaster) began to advise the president, as they do today.

The JUDICIARY ACT of 1789

ARTICLE III of the Constitution had few ⟵ ESTABLISHED THE JUDICIAL BRANCH

specifics about a federal court system, so Congress passed the FEDERAL JUDICIARY ACT OF 1789. This established federal courts consisting of 13 DISTRICT COURTS and three CIRCUIT COURTS OF APPEAL. The states still maintained their own courts, but a federal court could overturn their decisions. The Supreme Court, the final federal court of appeals, would consist of six JUSTICES who were nominated by the president. President Washington nominated John Jay as the first CHIEF JUSTICE of the Supreme Court.

ALEXANDER HAMILTON and the NATIONAL ECONOMY

The new nation faced a huge war debt, with debts to foreign nations, individual citizens, and soldiers who'd been paid with BONDS rather than cash. Alexander Hamilton proposed a three-prong solution in 1790:

> The U.S. would pay off all debts, including debts owed by states.

> Revenue would be generated by raising tariffs, which should also encourage people to buy American-made goods.

> A NATIONAL BANK would be established, owned jointly by the government and private investors, for the government to store money and make loans.
> A national mint would print paper money.

Hamilton ran into opposition:

The South had paid their few debts, so they saw Congress's decision as rewarding the North's failure to pay.

The South opposed tariffs, which don't benefit an economy that doesn't rely on manufactured goods.

People who lent money to the government in exchange for bonds often sold their bonds for cheap to **SPECULATORS**, who would now get a profit.

SPECULATORS
people who buy items at a low price with the hope that their value will later increase and they can be sold at a profit

Some people argued that Congress didn't have the right to found a bank.

Hamilton supported a LOOSE CONSTRUCTION VIEW OF THE CONSTITUTION, noting that the ELASTIC CLAUSE of Article I gives Congress the authority to do what is "necessary and proper" to carry out its powers.

Thomas Jefferson and James Madison favored a STRICT CONSTRUCTION VIEW OF THE CONSTITUTION, arguing that the "necessary and proper" clause put stronger limits on what was truly necessary.

Whereas Hamilton seemed to favor businessmen, Jefferson and Madison supported small farmers. Whereas Hamilton advocated having a strong central government, Jefferson and Madison favored local and state governments. The disagreement between "Hamiltonians" and "Jeffersonians" over the scope and extent of federal powers laid the foundation for the first political parties in the U.S. TWO AGAINST ONE, NO FAIR!

Partly by assuring Southern congressmen that the location of the nation's capital would move, Hamilton was able to persuade them to accept his plan. Congress assumed the state debts, enacted low tariffs, and established the Bank of the United States in 1791. The bank had a 20-year charter that would have to be renewed, and states had the right to start their own banks. Washington had tried to stay neutral, but he agreed with Hamilton.

☆ WASHINGTON, D.C. ☆

New York City was a large and bustling metropolis, but some worried that keeping the capital there favored Northern interests. A piece of land on the Potomac River, between Maryland and Virginia but part of neither state, was chosen as the site of a new capital. In 1790, the capital moved temporarily to Philadelphia, and in 1800, Washington, the District of Columbia, became the new capital.

WASHINGTON, D.C.

VA

MD

1801 BORDER, NOW PART OF VA

The WHISKEY REBELLION

Alexander Hamilton also encouraged Congress to pass a tax on whiskey. In western Pennsylvania, farmers who grew the corn used to make the whiskey saw the tax as an attack because it cut into the profits they lived off of.

In the summer of 1794, farmers attacked tax collectors in the WHISKEY REBELLION. That November, Washington personally led an army to stop the rebellion, and the farmers surrendered right away. Washington proved that the U.S. government was powerful and would use force if its people did not follow the law.

The **WHISKEY REBELLION** is the only time in U.S. history that a sitting president has personally commanded an army.

The NEUTRALITY PROCLAMATION

In 1789, when the French Revolution began, Americans were supportive of a revolution that seemed similar in spirit to their own. But the French Revolution turned bloody and violent—a period that came to be known as the "Reign of Terror"—and war broke out between the French and other European nations. Jefferson felt that the U.S. shouldn't abandon its ally France—its people were fighting for liberty.

Hamilton thought it was more important for the U.S. to protect relations with Britain, its biggest trading partner.

On April 22, 1793, Washington issued the NEUTRALITY PROCLAMATION. Americans wouldn't fight or help EITHER side, and foreign warships couldn't use American ports. Madison argued that only Congress had authority over foreign affairs. Jefferson resigned as secretary of state.

IMPRESSMENT and JAY'S TREATY

The British kidnapped American ships that traded in the French West Indies and forced the American sailors to fight for Britain. This practice, called IMPRESSMENT OF SEAMEN, pushed the U.S. closer to another war with England.

Washington sent Chief Justice John Jay to England to discuss the seized U.S. ships. In 1795, Jay was able to get the British to agree to pay for the losses. JAY'S TREATY prevented another war with Britain, and also . . .

improved trade between the countries

withdrew British troops from Western outposts in the U.S.

established commissions to settle border disputes

WASHINGTON'S FAREWELL

Concerned that he had too much power for one man, and overdue for retirement, George Washington announced in 1796 that he wouldn't be running for a third term (he could've run—there wasn't any precedent yet about how many terms a president got). In his FAREWELL ADDRESS, Washington warned against forming political parties, **FACTIONS**, or "permanent alliances" with foreign nations.

> **FACTION**
> a group that shares a common goal or belief

POLITICAL PARTIES FORM

Despite Washington's warnings, the disagreements with Jefferson and Madison on one side and Hamilton on the other grew into the first full-fledged political parties in American politics.

The DEMOCRATIC-REPUBLICAN PARTY (Jefferson and Madison) supported the ideas of REPUBLICANISM, including:

- **strict construction view of the Constitution**
- **reliance on agriculture**
- **the ideal of a nation of small farmers**
- **sympathy for the French**

The Democratic-Republican Party was favored in the South and on the Western frontier.

> The Democratic-Republican Party was also just called the Republican Party. It's not related to today's Republican Party. It actually evolved into today's Democratic Party.

The FEDERALIST PARTY (Hamilton) was named after those who had supported the Constitution from the beginning. This party supported:

- **strong, central representative government**
- **loose construction view of the Constitution**
- **reliance on trade (especially with England)**
- **the importance of urban merchants**

Most Federalists did business and lived in urban areas in New England.

The ELECTION of 1796

The Democratic-Republicans chose Thomas Jefferson to run for president and Aaron Burr to run for vice president at a **CAUCUS**. The Federalists chose John Adams and Charles Pinckney. Adams received the most electoral votes and became president. Jefferson, the runner-up, became vice president.

> **CAUCUS**
> a meeting of party leaders to select candidates

> ADAMS: 71
> JEFFERSON: 68
> CLOSE ELECTION!

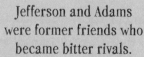

Jefferson and Adams were former friends who became bitter rivals.

The XYZ AFFAIR

France began attacking American ships because they were upset about a treaty the Americans had signed with the British. They considered it an anti-French treaty. In 1797, President

> This insult outraged Americans and led to the slogan "Millions for defense but not one CENT for tribute."

Adams sent Charles Pinckney, Elbridge Gerry, and John Marshall to Paris to negotiate. The French foreign minister, Charles Maurice de Talleyrand-Périgord, aka TALLEYRAND, refused to meet. Instead, Talleyrand sent three agents to discuss a treaty in exchange for a huge bribe. Adams was furious. Referring to the agents as Agent X, Agent Y, and Agent Z, he urged Congress to prepare for war.

Congress expanded the navy, but Adams ← CONSIDERED TO BE THE FATHER OF THE AMERICAN NAVY
didn't REALLY want war.

The ALIEN and SEDITION ACTS

> SEDITION
> rebellion against the government

American citizens were now unsure of the allegiances of new immigrants. Congress passed the ALIEN AND SEDITION ACTS in 1798. These controversial laws allowed the president to deport or imprison immigrants in wartime. They also made **SEDITION**, or opposing the government, illegal, taking away basic civil liberties such as freedom of speech and freedom of the press.

The KENTUCKY and VIRGINIA RESOLUTIONS

Democratic-Republicans thought the Alien and Sedition Acts were an abuse of power. Jefferson wrote a resolution for the Kentucky legislature in 1798, and Madison wrote one for Virginia in 1799 (although the authorship was kept secret). The KENTUCKY AND VIRGINIA RESOLUTIONS argued that the Acts were unconstitutional because they interfered with constitutional rights granted to states. The Kentucky Resolution insisted that states could **NULLIFY** laws they found unconstitutional. The resolutions didn't change the law—Congress just let the Acts expire after Adams left office—but they showed that states could challenge the federal government.

> **NULLIFY**
> to cancel or make void

The CONVENTION of 1800

In 1800, Adams sent another set of delegates to Paris. In the CONVENTION OF 1800, France agreed to stop naval attacks. Adams was pleased, but many Federalists from his own party had wanted a war. And ever since the Alien and Sedition Acts, the Democratic-Republicans saw Adams as an enemy to their cause. When election season rolled around, Adams was in a bad position for reelection.

CHECK YOUR KNOWLEDGE

1. What is the role of the president's cabinet?

2. Who nominates Supreme Court justices?

3. Why did Alexander Hamilton support raising tariffs?

4. Why is Washington, D.C., the capital of the U.S.?

5. What did Washington say in his Farewell Address?

6. What were the first two politcal parties to form in the U.S.? Name one Founding Father who was in each party.

7. What did the Kentucky Resolution argue?

FAREWELL AND DON'T FORGET MY WARNINGS!

ANSWERS 173

CHECK YOUR ANSWERS

1. To advise the president
2. The president
3. To raise revenue and encourage people to buy American goods
4. Washington, D.C., sits between the North and the South, and is not part of any state.
5. He advised the nation to avoid forming political parties, factions, and permanent alliances with foreign countries.
6. The Democratic-Republican Party (Thomas Jefferson, James Madison) and the Federalist Party (Alexander Hamilton)
7. That the states have the right to nullify, or cancel, laws that they find unconstitutional.

Unit 4

American Expansion
1801-1861

As settlers moved west into the newly claimed territory, Indigenous people were forced off their land. These changes created new tensions and increased settler violence between the groups. Against this backdrop, the continental U.S. grew to fill the borders it has today, and the number of settlers skyrocketed.

U.S.

☆ Chapter 14 ☆

PRESIDENT THOMAS
JEFFERSON

The ELECTION of 1800

Democratic-Republicans tried to paint Federalist candidate John Adams as a MONARCHIST. Adams tried to label Thomas Jefferson, the Democratic-Republican candidate, as a radical and an **ATHEIST**. Adams clearly lost, but Jefferson tied with Aaron Burr, at 73 votes in the Electoral College.

> **ATHEIST**
> a person who rejects belief in gods

The House of Representatives voted 35 TIMES, trying to break the tie. Finally, Alexander Hamilton persuaded a congressman not to vote for Burr. Jefferson became the third U.S. president and called his election the Revolution of 1800 because it was the first time a peaceful transfer of power occurred between opposing political parties.

The mess of trying to break the tie led to the **TWELFTH AMENDMENT** in 1803, which made the election of the president and vice president two separate ballots. It also led to a lifelong grudge between Hamilton and Burr that ended in a duel on July 11, 1804. Hamilton died the next day of a gunshot wound to the stomach.

Jefferson owned Monticello, a plantation where he enslaved more than 600 people. After he was elected, newspapers accused Jefferson of fathering multiple children with Sally Hemings, a woman he enslaved. DNA evidence has proved he fathered six children with Hemings. Enslaved women did not have the legal right to refuse unwanted sexual advances from their enslavers, and many women bore children fathered by men who enslaved them. Hemings's own father was Jefferson's father-in-law, the man who enslaved her mother, Elizabeth. Jefferson freed Hemings's children when they turned twenty-one. They were the only enslaved people he freed. Hemings was unofficially emancipated shortly after Jefferson's death.

JEFFERSON as PRESIDENT

Jefferson emphasized the central stances of the Democratic-Republican Party:

limited government with a
LAISSEZ-FAIRE approach

focus on agriculture

political unity through
individual independence

LAISSEZ-FAIRE
French for "leave it alone,"
a theory, particularly in
economics, that insists on
minimal government intervention

Taxes were repealed, the Alien and Sedition Acts expired, the military and military spending shrank, and the number of employees working for the federal government decreased.

The MIDNIGHT JUDGES

At the very end of Adams's presidency, Congress had passed the JUDICIARY ACT OF 1801, creating new federal judge positions. Once the judges were in office, they would keep their jobs for life, so Adams made sure to appoint them before he left. Because of the last-minute timing, they were called the "MIDNIGHT JUDGES."

When Jefferson became president, some of the judges hadn't yet gotten their COMMISSIONS, the documents that made it official. It was the job of the new secretary of state, JAMES MADISON, to deliver the commissions, but Jefferson told Madison, well, just not to deliver them. One of the judges left in limbo was WILLIAM MARBURY.

MARBURY v. MADISON (1803)

It gets complicated and there's *Latin*, but it's important. Marbury took his case straight to the Supreme Court, where he requested a WRIT OF MANDAMUS against James Madison, which basically asked the court to force Madison to give him his commission. The JUDICIARY ACT OF 1789 gave the Supreme Court the power to settle the case. Although CHIEF JUSTICE JOHN MARSHALL agreed that

Marbury deserved his commission, he ruled against Marbury, saying the Supreme Court didn't have the power to grant the writ and settle the case because . . .

Congress had no right to pass the Judiciary Act of 1789 in the first place.

The Constitution is the "supreme law," so when the Constitution and the law were in disagreement, the Supreme Court could cancel out the law.

The case of MARBURY v. MADISON is important because it established **JUDICIAL REVIEW:** the power of the Supreme Court to nullify a law by

JUDICIAL REVIEW
the power to declare an act of Congress unconstitutional

declaring it unconstitutional. It made the Supreme Court equal in power and status to the executive and legislative branches. MARBURY v. MADISON strengthened the idea of checks and balances in the federal government and made the Supreme Court the final word on the constitutionality of the law.

WESTERN EXPANSION

KENTUCKY was admitted to the Union in 1792, TENNESSEE joined soon after in 1796, and OHIO in 1803. The Mississippi River was officially the western border of the United States, based on the treaty signed at the close of the American Revolution. The lands provided a buffer zone between the expanding American settlements and the existing Spanish ones. But American settlers continued the pattern first established on the Eastern Seaboard: They pushed west, taking over land inhabited by Indigenous groups, who, in turn, had to move west themselves, accommodate their new neighbors, or take a stand, which might go badly for them. This push west was fueled by a desire to reach the Mississippi River, which merchants and farmers wanted to use to conduct trade.

TROUBLE with SPAIN

Spain controlled the river and its major port, New Orleans, but the river did not belong to them. Spain had secretly traded the Louisiana Territory (all of the land between the Mississippi River and the Rocky Mountains, including New Orleans) to France in 1800.

But the land didn't belong to France either. The land claims were just "claims." None of the Indigenous nations had given this land to any foreign power or taken part in any negotiations. Two powerful nations who had acquired and mastered horses dominated the Great Plains and are credited by historians as having built empires. The LAKOTA EMPIRE (sometimes referred to as the Sioux) dominated the northern plains, and the COMANCHE EMPIRE dominated the southern plains.

Although neither Spain nor France owned the land or the Mississippi River, they coordinated their efforts to control the river's mouth and its major trading center.

In 1802, Spain closed the port to American shipping. NAPOLEON BONAPARTE, the ruler of France, was planning to expand his empire in the Americas, using New Orleans as a critical point of entry for troops headed to the country. New Orleans also controlled the Mississippi River, which was a major port of exit for goods from the American West. France was essentially threatening the sovereignty and economic stability of the U.S.

The LOUISIANA PURCHASE

Jefferson sent ROBERT R. LIVINGSTON and JAMES MONROE to France to meet with Minister Talleyrand ← NAPOLEON'S FOREIGN MINISTER to discuss buying the territory of New Orleans, but they got a surprise. Haitian leader TOUSSAINT-LOUVERTURE led enslaved people in a revolt that forced the French out of Haiti. ← FRENCH TROOPS WERE ALSO DECIMATED BY YELLOW FEVER. France was losing interest in the Americas and needed to fund its war with England.

Talleyrand offered to sell the whole Louisiana Territory, which was larger than the entire U.S. at the time. The price of $15 million to transfer the paper ownership of this land was a bargain (roughly 3 cents an acre). In October 1803, the LOUISIANA PURCHASE extended the borders of the U.S.

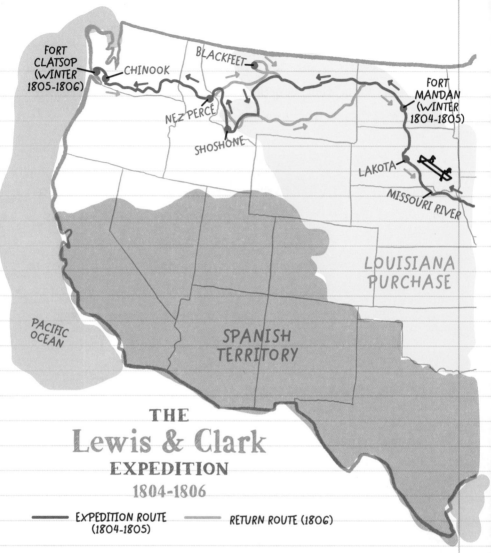

THE
Lewis & Clark
EXPEDITION
1804-1806

——— EXPEDITION ROUTE (1804-1805)   ——— RETURN ROUTE (1806)

to the Rocky Mountains. The actual cost was much higher:
Jefferson violated his own understanding of the role of
the federal government to make the purchase. In addition,
actually taking control of the territory would involve millions
of dollars in treaty negotiations with and warfare against
the Indigenous people living on this land.

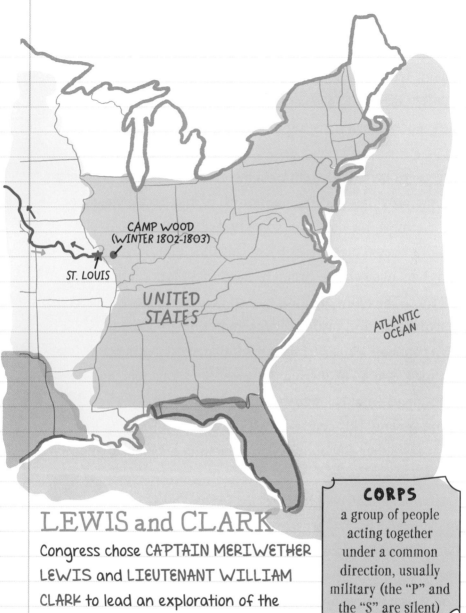

CAMP WOOD
(WINTER 1802-1803)

ST. LOUIS

UNITED
STATES

ATLANTIC
OCEAN

LEWIS and CLARK

Congress chose CAPTAIN MERIWETHER
LEWIS and LIEUTENANT WILLIAM
CLARK to lead an exploration of the
West. Their group of about 50 soldiers

> **CORPS**
> a group of people
> acting together
> under a common
> direction, usually
> military (the "P" and
> the "S" are silent)

and militia—the "**CORPS** OF DISCOVERY"—set out to map
the new land, gather information on the nations they

encountered, and document the plant and animal life they found. In May 1804, the LEWIS AND CLARK EXPEDITION left St. Louis and followed the Missouri River. By winter, they had reached modern-day North Dakota.

The corps benefited from both the information that Indigenous people provided and the generosity of the people they met. For example, the corps was warned about the powerful Lakota (Sioux) by several tribes, and the Mandans and Hidatsas allowed the group to build Fort Mandan near their villages. The Mandans also helped Lewis and Clark recruit a translator and guide, a Frenchman named Toussaint Charbonneau. He joined the expedition, along with his 16-year-old wife; SACAGAWEA was a Lemhi Shoshone who had been kidnapped from her people by the Hidatsa and then sold to Charbonneau. This couple joined the group at Fort Mandan, and six weeks later Sacagawea gave birth to a son, Jean-Baptiste.

Sacagawea was able to translate for and even guide the corps. The presence of a woman and a baby helped the corps gain the trust of many of the tribes they met. They didn't believe any war party would have a woman and baby with them!

SACAGAWEA

Upon arriving at the Pacific coast, the group faced another difficult winter and was helped by the Chinook people. They returned to St. Louis on September 23, 1806, 27 months after beginning their "voyage of discovery." In 1809, Charbonneau and Sacagawea and their son moved to St. Louis at the invitation of William Clark. Clark then took charge of Jean-Baptiste's education and ultimately adopted him.

A TALE OF TWO COINS

During the expedition, Lewis and Clark gave the tribal leaders they met "Jefferson Peace Medals" as gifts. President Jefferson was featured on the flip side of the coin.

In 2000, a dollar coin with an image of Sacagawea and Jean-Baptiste was forged for the first time. Originally the other side featured an eagle in flight, but in 2007, under the Native American $1 Coin Act, it was decided that each year the other side would feature a new image that celebrated the contributions of Indigenous peoples to the development of the United States.

TRADE TROUBLES

Even though the U.S. had remained neutral in the conflict between Britain and France, each of those countries tried to stop America from doing business with the other.

Jefferson, who had been reelected to a second presidential term, decided to punish England and France by cutting off their access to American trade altogether. In December 1807,

Congress passed the **EMBARGO ACT**, ending all international trade between the U.S. and the rest of the world. But Britain and France just traded with other countries instead. It was a disaster for American merchants and for Jefferson's image.

EMBARGO
a government order prohibiting commercial ships sailing into or out of its ports

CHECK YOUR KNOWLEDGE

1. How was the tie in the election of 1800 broken?

2. What were the central stances of the Democratic-Republican Party?

3. To whom does the term "midnight judges" refer?

4. What was the decision in the case *Marbury v. Madison*?

5. Why were the Mississippi River and the port of New Orleans important?

6. What did Napoleon Bonaparte intend to do with the Louisiana Territory?

7. Which two Indigenous Empires controlled the Great Plains in the early 1800s?

8. What were the goals of the Lewis and Clark Expedition?

ANSWERS

CHECK YOUR ANSWERS

1. Hamilton persuaded a congressman not to vote for Burr.

2. Limited government and laissez-faire economics, individual independence, and agriculture

3. The judges appointed by President Adams right before he left office

4. Marbury had a right to his commission, but Congress had no right to extend the jurisdiction of the Supreme Court to apply to the case.

5. Merchants and farmers needed the Mississippi River to conduct trade. New Orleans was a major trading center.

6. He wanted to expand France's empire into the Americas, using New Orleans as a point of entry.

7. The Lakota Empire and the Comanche Empire

8. To map the land aquired in the Louisiana Purchase, gather intel about Indigenous nations, and document plants and animals

☆ Chapter 15 ☆

The ★ WAR ★ of ★ 1812

JAMES MADISON, the primary author of the U.S. Constitution, was elected in 1808 to take the place vacated by his fellow Virginian Thomas Jefferson. Madison would soon face problems within the country because of expansion and encroachment on the frontier, and internationally with the British. The problems were connected: The British had promised in the Peace of Paris (1763) to leave the forts they held in the interior of the continent, but they kept them. From these forts, the British encouraged Indigenous peoples to resist American expansion. In addition, while at war with France, the British navy often stopped American commercial ships, took sailors they thought were British, and forced them into the service of the British navy. These acts—instigating rebellions and kidnapping sailors—led to Americans fighting a second war for independence, the War of 1812.

TECUMSEH and FRONTIER CONFLICTS

Indigenous peoples in the Northwest and Louisiana Territories were determined to hold on to their land. Led by Shawnee chief TECUMSEH, who was supported by Great Britain, several tribes united to fight settlers.

> Tecumseh attended a large intertribal gathering in 1783, held at the end of the American Revolution, where tribal leaders met to make a plan about how to deal with the Americans. Tecumseh understood the need to unite all tribes and to convince Indigenous leaders that the lands of the continent were the collective property of all the Indigenous peoples and no single tribe had the authority to negotiate land deals with the Americans.

By 1810, Tecumseh was working to unite as many Indigenous nations as possible. The American authorities on the frontier understood that he was a threat to continued expansion and settlement.

WILLIAM HENRY HARRISON, governor of Indiana Territory, sent a warning to Tecumseh, urging him to stick to the terms of earlier treaties and past agreements. Tecumseh responded that the few chiefs who signed the treaties didn't have the authority to represent other tribes and give away their land.

The BATTLE of TIPPECANOE

The first major battle of the War of 1812 took place on November 7, 1811. While Tecumseh was away, rallying Indigenous nations to unite, Harrison prepared to attack Prophetstown, a settlement near the Tippecanoe River that Tecumseh built to be the headquarters of the confederacy.

Harrison's soldiers defeated the Shawnee people at the BATTLE OF TIPPECANOE. They burned Prophetstown to the ground and Techumseh's confederacy never came to be.

DEMANDS for WAR

On June 18, 1812, under pressure from **WAR HAWKS**, Congress declared war (for the first time!). That summer, Tecumseh and his remaining allies crossed the border into Canada to join the British forces, and later that fall, James Madison was elected to his second term as president.

> The term "**WAR HAWK**" refers to anyone in government who supports war.
> The term "**PEACE DOVE**" refers to someone who advocates peace.

The WAR of 1812 BEGINS

The first American plan of attack was to invade Canada, but the British and their Indigenous allies seized Detroit before the Americans could head north. It was also difficult to invade Canada because the British controlled Lake Erie.

> Keep in mind that Canada was claimed by Britain. The reason only 13 colonies engaged in the American Revolution is that the Patriots couldn't persuade colonists in Canada to join the revolution.

By September 1813, the Americans had gained control of Lake Erie. Then, in October 1813, William Henry Harrison— commanding the troops in the area—defeated the British and their Indigenous allies near the U.S.-Canadian border in the BATTLE OF THE THAMES. Tecumseh was killed. Although the Americans had pushed the British out of the Northeast, battles with Indigenous peoples, including the CREEK WAR, continued. The Creek War took place in what is today Alabama, where the Red Stick Creeks, following Tecumseh's lead, had asked the British for support. In March 1814, ANDREW JACKSON, leader of the Tennessee militia, defeated the Creek Nation in the BATTLE OF HORSESHOE BEND, forcing them to sign the TREATY OF FORT JACKSON and cede Creek/Muscogee land to the U.S.

ATTACK on WASHINGTON, D.C.

By 1814, Napoleon had fallen from power and British forces could focus on enemies to the west. On August 24, 1814, the American troops were defeated in the BATTLE OF BLADENSBURG, Maryland, which allowed the British to sail into the Chesapeake Bay. They invaded Washington, D.C., setting fire to the Capitol and the White House and forcing President Madison to flee. (The first lady, Dolley Madison, stayed behind until the last moment to save a portrait of George Washington.)

The British continued up the Chesapeake to Baltimore, Maryland, intending to capture FORT McHENRY. On September 13, British warships began their attack. But because of the Americans' refusal to surrender, the British armada eventually withdrew.

"The Star-Spangled Banner"

Before the British attack on Baltimore, Americans raised a large flag over Fort McHenry. When FRANCIS SCOTT KEY, a lawyer who had witnessed the night-long bombardment, saw at dawn that the flag was still there, he was so moved that he wrote a poem to it. The poem was later set to music, and it eventually became the U.S. national anthem.

CAPITAL VS. CAPITOL

A **capital** (with an "a") is a city or place that is the official seat of government of a country or state. The **U.S. Capitol** (with an "o") is a building in Washington with a famous dome and is named after an ancient Roman hill called the Capitoline.

The BATTLE of LAKE CHAMPLAIN and the BATTLE of NEW ORLEANS

In September 1814, British forces trying to seize the city of Plattsburgh, New York, faced the U.S. Navy at Lake Champlain. The Americans refused to surrender in the BATTLE OF LAKE CHAMPLAIN, and the British retreated.

The British forces in the South decided to attack New Orleans. As they advanced on Louisiana on January 8, 1815, an army organized by Andrew Jackson waited. Marching in their typical style across an open field, the British were easy targets. Winning the BATTLE OF NEW ORLEANS boosted Jackson's popularity. It was the final battle of the War of 1812—and it occurred <u>after</u> the war had officially ended.

The END of WAR

The British decided war wasn't worth the time and money it cost and reached an agreement with the Americans. But the news took a while to reach Andrew Jackson and the Federalists. From December 15, 1814, to January 5, 1815, Federalists met at the HARTFORD CONVENTION to show opposition to the war. Little did they know that on December 24, 1814, the British and Americans had signed the TREATY OF GHENT in Belgium. The Hartford Convention embarrassed the Federalists for opposing a war that had already been won.

The Treaty of Ghent did not resolve border and trade disputes between the U.S. and Britain, but it increased patriotism and inspired a growing American identity. Although the treaty returned the countries to the way things were before the war, Americans were proud to have held their own. Because the War of 1812 cemented America's independence, it is also called "America's Second War for Independence." American manufacturers profited, since British goods weren't available. Americans decided that their destiny lay in the West, not in Canada, and the nation seemed destined for success.

The War of 1812 may have been the second war for independence, but it was also a war of dominance over resistant tribes. The boundaries between the United States and Canada remained unchanged, but the Indigenous people of the continent lost a powerful ally, because the British were no longer supporting their resistance to expansion.

CHECK YOUR KNOWLEDGE

1. How did Tecumseh try to protect Indigenous peoples' lands?

2. What was the first major battle of the War of 1812? What effect did this battle have on the frontier?

3. Who were the "war hawks" and what did they want?

4. What was the first time Congress ever declared war?

5. When did the U.S. push the British out of the Northeast?

6. What inspired "The Star-Spangled Banner"?

7. What was the last battle of the War of 1812?

8. What did the Treaty of Ghent accomplish?

9. What effect did the War of 1812 have on the national mood?

10. Why is the War of 1812 called America's Second War for Independence?

CHECK YOUR ANSWERS

1. He led several united societies to fight settlers. He also established an alliance of nations to form a federation, a unified government to protect Indigenous peoples' land.

2. The battle of Tippecanoe was the first major battle of the War of 1812. As a result of the battle, the violence on the frontier got worse.

3. They were people in government who wanted war with England.

4. The War of 1812, on June 18, 1812

5. After the Battle of the Thames, in October 1813

6. Francis Scott Key was inspired by a flag troops raised at Fort McHenry as they defended Baltimore from the British.

7. The Battle of New Orleans, which took place after the war ended

8. The Treaty of Ghent helped to increase patriotism and helped inspire America's identity.

9. Patriotism increased, as did confidence in the success of the nation.

10. The War of 1812 is called America's Second War for Independence because it solidified America's independence from Britain.

☆ Chapter 16 ☆

THE YOUNG NATION

★ ★ ★ ★ ★ ★ ★ ★ ★ ★ ★ ★

GROWS

After the War of 1812, feelings of **NATIONALISM** spread through the U.S.

> **NATIONALISM**
> patriotism; a sense of national identity

NATIONALISM and the ERA of GOOD FEELING

James Monroe was elected America's fifth president in 1816 with little opposition from the now fractured Federalist Party. Monroe toured the country and was widely supported and welcomed everywhere he went. This era was marked by so little disagreement about national politics that it was called the ERA OF GOOD FEELING.

> ERA OF GOOD FEELING? MAYBE FOR THOSE IN POWER....

In 1820, Monroe was reelected almost unanimously. Monroe was the third and final president who made up the "Virginia Dynasty."

> JEFFERSON, MADISON, AND MONROE

The AMERICAN SYSTEM

In order to strengthen the national economy and further promote national unity, HENRY CLAY, Speaker of the House (the congressperson who runs the House of Representatives), proposed a program called the AMERICAN SYSTEM. This system consisted of three parts: a national bank, tariffs, and infrastructure.

> A Bank of the United States would issue a single U.S. currency.

The bank, whose original charter expired in 1811, received a new charter in 1816 and was called the Second Bank of the United States, but it was still controversial. The South opposed tariffs because they hurt its economy. And some people argued that the Constitution did not say that Congress could spend money on public works within the individual states.

> Protective tariffs would be increased to encourage American manufacturing.

Britain had kept the colonies dependent on British-manufactured goods because that was good for British businesses. But men like Henry Clay understood how important manufacturing was to the new country. Tariffs would give young companies a fair shot at growing.

Money collected from taxes and tariffs would be spent building roads and canals (infrastructure).

Congress had already approved the construction of the CUMBERLAND ROAD from Cumberland, Maryland, to Vandalia, Illinois (later called the NATIONAL ROAD). Congress also invested in the ERIE CANAL, built almost entirely by hand between 1817 and 1825, to connect New York City with the Great Lakes region. The Erie Canal led to increased trade and a population surge in the Midwest. It inspired the building of many more canals in pre-railroad-era America.

The idea of investing federal dollars in transportation was controversial, so the Erie Canal was largely the work of Governor DeWitt Clinton of New York. It was so successful that New York became known as the Empire State.

The INDUSTRIAL REVOLUTION

> The **INDUSTRIAL REVOLUTION** was the first
> time many people in America needed a clock.
> On a farm, you can plan your day by the movement
> of the sun; in a factory, not so much.

The American Industrial Revolution is said to have begun in
Rhode Island in 1793, when SAMUEL SLATER built the first
American spinning mill, a factory that makes cloth. Rhode
Island's geography was perfect for water-powered mills,
and the War of 1812 made it tough to get imported goods,
inspiring Americans to find more efficient ways to produce
their own. The most famous factory was a textile mill started
by Francis Cabot Lowell in 1814 that mostly employed young
women. It was so successful that it led to the founding
of an entire town, called LOWELL, MASSACHUSETTS.
The "Lowell girls" were paid well, but they worked long
hours in grueling conditions.

The Industrial Revolution was a time of great innovation.

NEW TECHNOLOGY

OF THE ERA INCLUDED

INTERCHANGEABLE PARTS:
ELI WHITNEY (who invented the **COTTON GIN**) introduced premanufactured, identical musket parts for the army. This created the possibility of **MASS PRODUCTION**.

The **TELEGRAPH**, invented by **SAMUEL F. B. MORSE** in 1837, improved communication. Using **MORSE CODE**, telegraphs sent short pulses of energy along a wire that were translated into letters that spelled out messages.

STEAM POWER:
Once **STEAM ENGINES** were improved by **JAMES WATT** in 1780, factories no longer had to be located near rivers.

The **STEAMBOAT**, perfected by **ROBERT FULTON** in 1807, improved river transportation.

The **STEAM LOCOMOTIVE**, created by **PETER COOPER** in 1830, improved land transportation and led to the development of railroads.

NEW TECHNOLOGY AFFECTS REGIONS DIFFERENTLY

New technology helped people who were headed west. They could now use better agricultural tools, like the JOHN DEERE PLOW and the McCORMICK REAPER. Wheat became a cash crop, cities such as Chicago sprang up, farms in the Midwest began to supply the factory workers in the Northeast with food, and the Northeast began to supply the Midwest with manufactured goods. Long distances seemed to become shorter, thanks to American innovation.

In the South, the most significant invention was the COTTON GIN. Invented by Eli Whitney in 1793, it could clean seeds from cotton quickly. Taking seeds out by hand was so labor intensive that it was not worth growing cotton. Now, all that changed. The cotton gin also increased the use of enslaved people. When the Constitution was written, the South insisted that slavery be kept legal, but many Northerners believed that slavery would eventually die out, and even made a plan to phase out the international slave trade in 1808. The cotton gin ended the hope that slavery would quietly fade away.

Plantation owners, who made up only about 3 percent of the Southern population, generated huge profits. In the Deep South, cotton was "king," and little attention was paid to either manufacturing or infrastructure.

The North and South developed economic systems with very different needs.

> The development of the Erie Canal, roads, and, later, railroads actually meant that the Midwest was deeply connected to the eastern trading hubs. This made the Midwest the natural partner of the North rather than the South, adding a new layer to the regional divisions.

SLAVERY and RESISTANCE INTENSIFIES

Cotton farming is very hard on the soil, so the cotton gin also led to westward expansion in the South. By 1808, the international slave trade had been abolished, but a terrible domestic slave trade that separated family members from one another developed. Enslavers even came to use the fear of sale as a weapon. An enslaved person who was considered "uncooperative" might be told that they would be sold "downriver." That meant one thing: life on a cotton plantation where enslaved people were out in the field before the sun came up and not back in their quarters until the sun went down, and being watched all day by overseers with whips. By the early part of the century, almost every enslaved person in the U.S. had been born into slavery.

As Southern wealth became even more dependent on enslaved labor, resistance to slavery grew. Enslaved people were determined to win their freedom. NAT TURNER, one of the most famous enslaved rebels, led a violent uprising in 1831 in Virginia. Many Southern whites earned their living as YEOMEN, small-scale farmers who owned land but not enslaved people, or as TENANT FARMERS, who rented their land. These people tended to be poor and were left unharmed in the uprising.

Nat Turner's rebellion scared many Southerners and hardened their position. Nat Turner could read and write. He was deeply religious, read the Bible, and believed God had signaled him to rebel. Some states passed even harsher laws to control enslaved people, which included making it illegal to teach an enslaved person to read and forbidding gatherings of enslaved people. The rebellion also proved that enslaved people were not content to live enslaved (as Southerners often argued) and drew the attention, as Turner had hoped it would, of antislavery groups in the North. In the end, Turner was caught and hanged, as were approximately 150 other enslaved people.

SECTIONALISM

The Industrial Revolution swept the economy and social structure of each region as they became specialized and distinct. This led to a rise in SECTIONALISM, or loyalty to one's specific region. As always, the Northeast focused on factories and trade, and the South relied on plantations. Now the West was a place for people to exploit newly colonized land.

This created regional politics: The North advocated high tariffs so that people would buy American-made goods. The South supported slavery, and they also supported low tariffs, because they imported most of their goods. Northerners wanted the government to sell its land at a high price to discourage poor workers from leaving the cities, but Westerners wanted the government to sell them land at a low price and give them roads and other public improvements.

The MISSOURI COMPROMISE

A conflict rooted in sectionalism happened when Missouri applied for statehood in 1817. At the time, the U.S. consisted of 11 slave states and 11 free states. If Missouri entered the Union as a slave state, as it wanted, it would upset a balance of power in the Senate between slave and free states.

THE UNITED STATES 1820

In 1820, Henry Clay came up with a solution for the land from the Louisiana Purchase—the MISSOURI COMPROMISE. The Missouri Compromise divided the land from the Louisiana Purchase into separate regions defined by slavery. It stipulated that Missouri would enter the Union as a slave state, whereas Maine, which was still a part of Massachusetts, would enter at the same time as a free state. In all future applications for statehood, slavery would be illegal north of the southern border of Missouri, at latitude 36°30'. Slavery was increasingly becoming an issue that divided the North and South.

So, the increased unity that emerged from the War of 1812, and the Era of Good Feeling that followed, did not last.

RELATIONS with ENGLAND and SPAIN

> **PARALLEL**
> another word for a
> line of latitude

The U.S. and Britain agreed that neither nation would maintain a navy in the Great Lakes region or along the U.S.-Canada border. A demilitarized border between the U.S. and Canada was created at the **49TH PARALLEL**, stretching as far west as the Rocky Mountains.

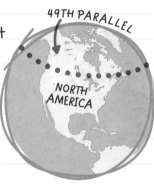

Relations between the U.S. and Britain improved, but tensions with Spain were high. The U.S. claimed western Florida belonged to the U.S. because it was part of the Louisiana Purchase. Spain disagreed. As American settlers moved into the Florida territory, the Seminole people, who were indigenous to the area, raided the settlements and helped enslaved people escape.

In April 1818, without government permission, Andrew Jackson, already famous for his victory over the Creek warriors at the Battle of Horseshoe Bend during the War of 1812, invaded Spanish territory and captured two Spanish forts, starting the FIRST SEMINOLE WAR. Instead of punishing Jackson, and knowing that Spain could not fight back, Secretary of State JOHN QUINCY ADAMS (former President Adams's son) gave Spain two choices: They could control the Seminole living in Spanish Florida or sell the territory to the U.S. in the ADAMS-ONIS TREATY of 1819. Spain sold Florida and their claims to part of the Pacific Northwest to the U.S. for $5 million.

The MONROE DOCTRINE

Spain was losing territories not only in the U.S. but also throughout Latin America. (The people living in the 13 British colonies that

> **DOCTRINE**
> a theory or position on an issue

staged the American Revolution weren't the only ones in the Americas unhappy about being ruled by Europeans living across the Atlantic.) SÍMON BOLÍVAR led revolutions that freed people from Spanish rule in modern-day Bolivia, Colombia, Panama, Venezuela, Ecuador, and Peru. MIGUEL HIDALGO Y COSTILLA won independence for Mexico in 1821. When France, Russia, Prussia, and Austria discussed helping Spain regain its land, President Monroe feared that European countries would also attempt to recolonize other territories claimed by the U.S.

On December 2, 1823, Monroe issued the MONROE DOCTRINE. It established American foreign policy for years to come and set the stage for America to become a world power.

Its three major points were:

1. European interference in U.S. affairs would not be tolerated and the U.S. would stay **NEUTRAL** in European colonies or conflicts.

2. The U.S. wouldn't tolerate **NEW COLONIZATION** in either North or South America.

3. Any attempt by Europe to further colonize the Americas would be considered an act of **AGGRESSION**.

The ELECTION of 1824

All of the candidates of the 1824 presidential election belonged to the Democratic-Republican Party. The North was in favor of John Quincy Adams, the South supported Andrew Jackson or William Crawford, and the West wanted Henry Clay or Andrew Jackson. Andrew Jackson won the **POPULAR VOTE** but didn't receive a majority of electoral votes.

> **POPULAR VOTE**
> method of electing a candidate based on a majority of votes

Jackson got the most votes—about 40%—but **NOT** a majority.

ELECTORAL VOTES:	POPULAR VOTE:
JACKSON: 99	151,271
J.Q. ADAMS: 84	113,122
CRAWFORD: 41	40,856
CLAY: 37	47,531

NO CANDIDATE WON A MAJORITY OF THE ELECTORAL COLLEGE VOTE—THERE WERE TOO MANY CANDIDATES.

According to the Constitution, the House of Representatives would decide the winner in that situation. Henry Clay, the Speaker of the House, who finished in last place, persuaded his colleagues to vote for John Quincy Adams. When Adams became the country's sixth president and appointed Clay as his secretary of state, his opponents argued that a backroom deal had been made.

The ELECTION of 1828 and JACKSONIAN DEMOCRACY

The bitterness and anger over the 1824 election led to the development of two new political parties and a rematch of the previous election: The Democrats supported Jackson; the National Republicans supported Adams. Jackson was seen by many as a hardworking national war hero and had earned the nickname "OLD HICKORY" for his toughness. He won an overwhelming victory, and JOHN C. CALHOUN, who had been John Quincy Adams's vice president, became his vice president.

"OLD HICKORY"

One reason for Jackson's victory was that he promoted expanding democratic privileges to a wider population. Called JACKSONIAN DEMOCRACY, this movement included the extension of **SUFFRAGE**. Before, only white men who owned

> **SUFFRAGE**
> the right to vote

property or paid taxes could vote, but Jackson loosened these restrictions to include all white men over the age of 21. Jackson's win was considered a triumph for the common man. Well over half the population still had no right to vote. His vision for democracy did not extend the right to vote to either free or enslaved Black Americans, Indigenous peoples, or women of any class or race.

Jackson began to replace government bureaucrats with his friends and supporters. Called the SPOILS SYSTEM, this was criticized as favoritism and political payback, but Jackson argued that it was good to clean house. Jackson appointed MARTIN VAN BUREN as secretary of state and depended on his advice. He also relied on his "KITCHEN CABINET," friends who gave him advice, often in the White House kitchen.

TARIFFS and the NULLIFICATION CRISIS

In 1828, before Jackson took office, Congress passed a tariff that taxed raw materials and manufactured goods so much that the South called it the TARIFF OF ABOMINATIONS. The South argued that the tariff was unconstitutional because it favored one region over another. Also, the states could nullify laws that were unconstitutional because of the THEORY OF STATE SOVEREIGNTY, which says that the power of the federal government comes from the states and that the states are more powerful.

In the NULLIFICATION ACT OF 1832, South Carolina declared a federal tariff null and void, and threatened to secede from the Union. Jackson had shown support for states' rights by vetoing a renewal of the charter for the Second Bank of the United States, so it surprised many people when he pushed for Congress to pass the FORCE BILL, which would allow him to use the army to enforce the tariff. In 1833, Henry Clay came up with a plan that would gradually reduce the tariff. South Carolina agreed to the compromise.

None of this resolved the debate about states' rights vs. federal power. But historians argue that South Carolina's nullification of the tariff was a dress rehearsal for the fight the state thought was sure to come over the issue of slavery. In a twist of history, Abraham Lincoln later used Jackson's assertion of federal power over state power to justify the Civil War.

The WHIG PARTY and the PANIC of 1837

MORE WIGS, FEWER CROWNS!

Partly in opposition to Jackson's destruction of the Second Bank of the United States, a new political party formed. The WHIG PARTY was formed in opposition to what its members saw as a danger of majority parties. Led by Henry Clay, the Whig Party nominated three candidates for president in 1836 in hopes of throwing the election. They took their name from the

English anti-monarchy party because they were opposed to choosing electors by popular vote. They thought it led to the tyranny of "King Andrew" Jackson. However, Van Buren, the presidential nominee for Jackson's supporters, now called the DEMOCRATS, still won and took office in 1837 as the eighth president.

By then the economic boom of the 1830s was over, partly as a result of Jackson's closure of the national bank. During the PANIC OF 1837, the values of land, cotton, and paper money decreased, leading to terrible inflation. Van Buren, not Jackson, was blamed for the depression that followed, particularly because he believed in laissez-faire economic policies.

"TIPPECANOE and TYLER TOO"

In 1840, the Whig Party nominated William Henry Harrison for president and JOHN TYLER for vice president. Using a log cabin as their symbol, the Whig Party tried to show that Harrison was a common man from the Ohio frontier, whereas Van Buren was a man of privilege. (But Harrison also came from a rich family, so...) These personal attacks on Van Buren are called the LOG CABIN CAMPAIGN.

The Whigs also used the catchy slogan "TIPPECANOE AND TYLER TOO" to remind people that like Jackson,

TIPPECANOE...

...AND TYLER TOO!

Harrison was a decorated military campaigner, and of his connection to the Battle of Tippecanoe. The Whigs' plan worked, and William Henry Harrison was elected the ninth president.

On Inauguration Day, which was bitterly cold, Harrison (who was 68 years old) didn't wear

LONGEST INAUGURAL ADDRESS IN HISTORY! BRRR!

a coat while he delivered his speech. He caught pneumonia and died about a month later. Tyler became president and went back to the beliefs of his former party, the Democratic Party. Like the other parties, the Whig Party was destined to fall victim to sectional differences.

???

BAH!

FIRST TIME A PRESIDENT DIED IN OFFICE AND WAS SUCCEEDED BY HIS VICE PRESIDENT. ALSO SHORTEST PRESIDENCY!

CHECK YOUR KNOWLEDGE

1. Why was the period after the War of 1812 known as the Era of Good Feeling?

2. What are the three major points of the Monroe Doctrine?

3. Name a factor behind increased sectionalism at the end of the Era of Good Feeling.

4. What were the terms of the Missouri Compromise?

5. What is the theory of state sovereignty?

6. Andrew Jackson expanded suffrage in the United States. To whom did he give the right to vote?

7. What were the values of the Whig Party?

ANSWERS ➤

CHECK YOUR ANSWERS

1. Nationalism increased and there was little disagreement about national politics.

2. American neutrality, no more European colonies in the Americas, and that European intervention in the Americas would be considered an act of aggression

3. Each region's economy became even more specialized and different from the others'.

4. Missouri would be a slave state, Maine would be free, and all future states north of 36°30' would be free.

5. That federal power comes from the states, so states are the most powerful body in U.S. government

6. All white men over the age of 21. (Before, only white men who owned land had the right to vote.)

7. They were against majority parties having too much power and potential presidential "tyranny."

☆ Chapter 17 ☆

WESTWARD MIGRATION:
AGAIN

As canals, railroads, and roads were built westward, travel became easier, and Americans moved west looking for new opportunities. But the land that migrants were after was already occupied by peoples who had lived there for centuries! A pattern was created: White settlers entered an area, pushing the local population west. If the Indigenous population chose to stay put, settlers used forced **ASSIMILATION**, violated treaties, or engaged in warfare and outright military removal. If one strategy failed, the settlers simply tried another one.

> **ASSIMILATION**
> to take on the cultural habits of a larger group

The INDIAN REMOVAL ACT

Thomas Jefferson hoped that Indigenous peoples would accept white ways and become his version of "American." In the Southeast the Cherokee Nation thought this sort of assimilation was the best chance to live side by side with white Americans. The Cherokee Nation had developed a written language and had a constitution of their own, as well as newspapers. They had been farmers for centuries but adopted the use of white American tools and techniques and in some cases kept enslaved people. Intermarriage was not uncommon.

The Cherokees of Georgia were the most assimilated of the southeast tribes, but the state of Georgia had motivation to **DISPLACE** them: In 1828, gold had been found on their land. Georgia began to pass laws that helped the settlers take over Cherokee lands.

> **DISPLACE**
> to force people to leave their home or country

The Cherokees were part of a separate nation recognized in an 18th-century treaty, and they had a deep understanding of American law. They took their case to the Supreme Court. In 1832, in the case of *WORCESTER V. GEORGIA*, the Supreme Court ruled that the Cherokees were a **SOVEREIGN** nation and that only the federal government (not Georgia) had the power to form a treaty with another sovereign nation. Both the state of Georgia and President Jackson decided to ignore the ruling. The Supreme Court had no power to enforce it.

> **SOVEREIGN**
> independent

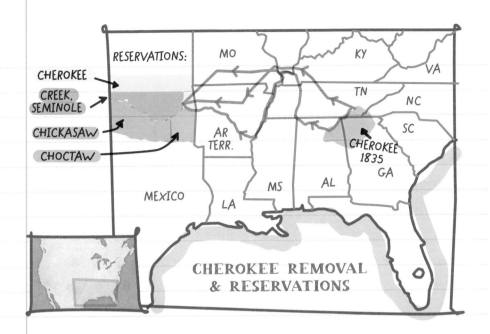

CHEROKEE REMOVAL
& RESERVATIONS

Meanwhile, at the urging of President Jackson, Congress had passed the INDIAN REMOVAL ACT of 1830, which authorized the federal government to force the Cherokee, Chickasaw, Choctaw, Muscogee (Creek), and Seminole, who lived on valuable farmland, off their land. These nations had assimilated into American culture to varying degrees with the hopes that doing so might protect their sovereignty over their land. The plan was to send them to the Great Plains, which Congress mistakenly believed was barren, worthless desert. Congress selected an area of modern-day Oklahoma to be INDIAN TERRITORY (also known as a RESERVATION). Within the next few years, Congress also established the BUREAU OF INDIAN AFFAIRS to manage the removal and transport of Indigenous peoples.

The TRAIL OF TEARS

The policy of removing Indigenous people to what is now Oklahoma lasted from 1830 to 1850 and involved the forced displacement of 60,000 people. The Muscogee (Creek) had never recovered from their defeats in the War of 1812, and internal conflict made it easy to force them out of Georgia. The Choctaw Nation split, with half the nation moving to Oklahoma, while the other half remained in the South and faced hostile laws and constant harassment. The Chickasaws sold their lands to the federal government. Once in Oklahoma, they merged with the Choctaw.

The Cherokee continued to resist. Ignoring the Supreme Court, the federal government had one more trick to try. In 1835, Congress was able to persuade a very small number of Cherokees to sign a treaty ceding their land. The government disregarded the law and decided to view the treaty as an agreement with the entire tribe. President Van Buren sent GENERAL WINFIELD SCOTT and thousands of U.S. Army troops to invade the Cherokee Nation in 1838. Sixteen thousand Cherokees were moved into holding camps and then forced to go to their new land. During their 800-mile trek to Indian Territory, a quarter of the population died from disease, starvation, poor weather conditions, and harsh treatment. Their painful march became known as the TRAIL OF TEARS.

SEMINOLE RESISTANCE to the INDIAN REMOVAL ACT

In Florida, the Seminoles also resisted being displaced. Although they were forced to sign removal treaties too, their chief, OSCEOLA, urged his people to go to war against the Americans, starting the SECOND SEMINOLE WAR. Even after

OSCEOLA

Osceola was captured in 1837, his people hid in the Everglades, continued to aid runaway enslaved people, made surprise attacks, and used guerrilla tactics against the Americans. In 1842, the U.S. Army gave up after spending half a billion dollars (in today's money) on the war.

OREGON COUNTRY

Back in Europe, hats made from beaver fur became a popular fashion accessory, prompting an explosion of the American beaver fur trade. It became so large that it nearly wiped out the Eastern beaver population.

People who made their living from beavers traveled to the Northwest to find more. A lot of these MOUNTAIN MEN immersed themselves in Indigenous culture and married into Indigenous families, choosing to live in the Northwest.

As the beaver population in the Northwest also died out, and as beaver hats grew less fashionable, some mountain men started farming in Oregon, but many went back east and became guides to help other people make the journey west.

The land the mountain men settled in was called OREGON COUNTRY (modern-day Oregon, Washington, and Idaho, along with parts of Montana and Wyoming). The land had been claimed by the U.S., Britain, Spain, and Russia, but the 1819 ADAMS-ONÍS TREATY ← and another treaty between Russia and the U.S. in 1824 kept Spain and Russia out. The U.S. and Britain still both wanted the territory, but they decided not to go to war over it, instead choosing to control it jointly.

> ADDED FLORIDA TO THE U.S. AND DEFINED SPANISH-AMERICAN BORDERS. IT ALSO RECOGNIZED THE 42ND PARALLEL AS THE SOUTHERN BOUNDARY OF THE OREGON TERRITORY.

The OREGON TRAIL

SCHOONER
a kind of sailboat

After the Panic of 1837 and at the height of the economic depression, many Americans chose to make the 2,000-mile trip from Independence, Missouri, to Oregon on the OREGON TRAIL. The difficult journey generally took six months in a wagon train of "prairie **SCHOONERS**" (wagons that looked like ships from a distance).

MISSIONARIES were among the first to travel the Oregon Trail. Their reports of the beautiful land of the West encouraged others to

follow. It was widely believed that American expansion to the Pacific coast was part of MANIFEST DESTINY: the idea that the U.S. was chosen by God to spread across the continent and that the expansion of the United States was the people's "manifest," or obvious, destiny.

The SANTA FE TRAIL

The SANTA FE TRAIL also began in Independence, Missouri, and led to Santa Fe. After Mexico gained its independence and took control of New Mexico Province, which stretched from California to Texas, this area became an ideal place for trade. Although the 800-mile trip was long and often dangerous, the prospect of large profits inspired many traders.

The MORMON TRAIL

The Church of Jesus Christ of Latter-day Saints had been founded by JOSEPH SMITH in 1830 in New York. The church's members, called Mormons, were persecuted because they practiced **POLYGAMY** and communal ownership of property, among other reasons. The Mormons moved to the Midwest (to Nauvoo, Illinois), but

225

conditions there were equally difficult and dangerous. Smith was murdered by an anti-Mormon mob in 1844. The new Mormon leader, BRIGHAM YOUNG, led his people in 1846 to an area they called DESERET. When Deseret became the UTAH TERRITORY in 1850, Brigham Young was appointed governor. Utah didn't become a state until 1896, nearly 50 years later.

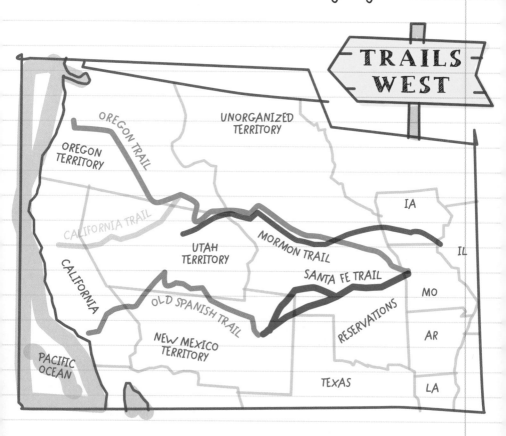

TRAILS WEST

OREGON TRAIL

OREGON TERRITORY

UNORGANIZED TERRITORY

CALIFORNIA TRAIL

UTAH TERRITORY

MORMON TRAIL

SANTA FE TRAIL

IA

IL

MO

CALIFORNIA

OLD SPANISH TRAIL

NEW MEXICO TERRITORY

RESERVATIONS

AR

PACIFIC OCEAN

TEXAS

LA

CHECK YOUR KNOWLEDGE

1. What tactics did white settlers use to take land from the Indigenous people?

2. Why did Georgia want to force the Cherokee off Cherokee land?

3. How did the Cherokee resist being displaced?

4. Why were sovereign Indigenous nations in the east forcibly relocated to Oklahoma?

5. What happened to the beaver population in the Northeast?

6. Why were wagons known as prairie schooners?

7. What is the idea behind Manifest Destiny?

8. Why did the Mormons go to Utah in 1846?

ANSWERS 227

CHECK YOUR ANSWERS

1. They tried to force the Indigenous people to assimilate, they went to war against them, forced them to move, and violated treaties.
2. Gold was discovered on Cherokee land, and Georgia wanted to profit from it.
3. They brought a case against Georgia to the Supreme Court (*Worcester v. Georgia*) and won (at least in court).
4. Their land was valuable, and the government took it from them and moved them to land in the west that was not considered valuable.
5. They were killed off to make hats.
6. Because they looked like ships (called schooners) sailing across the prairie
7. That God created the U.S. to spread across the continent, so American expansion was destiny
8. They were persecuted in the East for practicing polygamy and owning property as a group, and were in search of a safe place to settle.

☆ Chapter 18 ☆

The LONE STAR
★ ★ ★ ★ ★ ★ ★ ★ ★ ★ ★ ★
NON-STATE

After Mexico gained its independence from Spain in 1821, it became a **REPUBLIC** with a government based in Mexico City. Its territory included present-day Texas, which the Spanish called Tejas (pronounced "Tay-hoss"). Spain had tried to attract families to the land but settled for building about two dozen missions. Their goal? To convert Indigenous peoples to Christianity and cultivate their loyalty to Spain that way. The local population of Coahuiltecans and Jumanos were unenthusiastic but did accept help defending themselves against the Apaches and Comanches who had only recently moved into the region.

> **REPUBLIC**
> a form of government in which a state is ruled by representatives of its citizens

SETTLERS in TEXAS

At the beginning of the 19th century, very few people lived in Texas, aside from a few thousand TEJANOS, or Spanish Texans. While Tejanos were leaving, the Indian population was growing because of displacement: Caddos, Cherokees, Alabamas, and Coushattas moved west into the area. To promote growth, the newly independent Mexican nation offered large, inexpensive land grants to EMPRESARIOS, people who agreed to find settlers to purchase these grants. One of those settlers, STEPHEN F. AUSTIN, also received permission to start a new colony, on the condition that the new settlers follow Mexican law. Austin agreed, and after arriving in Texas in 1821, he recruited 300 new families, who became known as the "OLD THREE HUNDRED," to settle in the area. These families encouraged many more Americans to move to Texas in the upcoming years.

Migration to Texas led to the first text messaging. "GTT" carved into a cabin door meant "Gone to Texas."

The new American settlers broke three Mexican laws immediately: They did not speak Spanish or practice Catholicism, and they brought enslaved people into the territory. Within a decade, there were 20,000 Americans in Texas, 5,000 enslaved people, and only 600 Tejanos, and the U.S. decided to pressure the Mexican government to sell its land. In 1830, fearful of the growing, dissatisfied American population in Texas, the Mexican government outlawed immigration from the U.S. to Texas and began to enforce their antislavery laws.

The TEXAS WAR for INDEPENDENCE

American Texans grew increasingly unhappy about following Mexican law and drafted a constitution for Texas as an independent state of Mexico. In 1833, Stephen Austin met with Mexico's vice president to urge Mexico to lift the ban on immigration and to discuss the independent state idea. Instead, Mexico's new president, ANTONIO LÓPEZ DE SANTA ANNA, took this as proof of Austin's support for rebellion. He arrested Austin in Satillo and jailed him in Mexico City. Santa Anna, who had angered Mexicans as well by seizing power, also declared himself a dictator, thereby violating and subsequently abolishing Mexico's constitution, which protected the Tejanos' rights. By the time Austin was released eight months later, even he, typically so diplomatic, agreed it was time for independence.

In 1831, the Mexican government had lent a cannon to the small Texas settlement of GONZALES to help its inhabitants protect themselves from Comanche raids. In 1835, Santa Anna gathered troops and sent them to Gonzales with orders to seize this cannon. The Mexicans failed to retrieve the weapon, but the attempt set off the first battle in the TEXAS WAR FOR INDEPENDENCE.

The ALAMO

THE ALAMO

Having no army of their own, the Texans put out a call for volunteers. The 180-person volunteer militia (including free Black people, rebel Tejanos, local residents, and adventure-seeking Americans like DAVY CROCKETT and JAMES BOWIE) occupied an abandoned mission called the ALAMO from February 23 to March 6, 1836. The volunteers were no match for Santa Anna, who had the entire Mexican military at his disposal. Mexican cannons broke down the walls of the Alamo, but the Texans did not surrender. After killing every soldier at the Alamo, the Mexicans captured and executed the remaining militia, who were stationed at a fort called Goliad, in the GOLIAD MASSACRE. But rather than become discouraged by these events, more Texans were inspired to join the militia.

The BATTLE of SAN JACINTO

> **AMBUSH**
> to attack unexpectedly

As Santa Anna remained on the attack, the Texas militia, now more than double in size and led by SAM HOUSTON, headed eastward. On April 21, 1836, Houston's troops **AMBUSHED** Santa Anna's army at their camp near the San Jacinto River. Shouting "REMEMBER THE ALAMO!" the Texans quickly defeated the Mexicans, taking Santa Anna captive and forcing him to sign a treaty recognizing Texan independence.

The LONE STAR REPUBLIC

During the siege of the Alamo, Texan leaders met to draft their own constitution, which they modeled on the U.S. Constitution. On March 2, 1836, they declared their independence and established the REPUBLIC OF TEXAS, or the "Lone Star Republic." After Santa Anna signed the treaty, elections were held and Sam Houston became president. Stephen Austin, whom the capital of Texas was later named for, became secretary of state.

> **ANNEX**
> to attach or add on

Because the Republic of Texas was in debt and still in conflict with the Mexicans, Houston requested that the U.S. **ANNEX** Texas in 1836 so it could apply for statehood. At the time, Jackson was president of the U.S., and he feared admitting another slave state to the Union, as well as provoking Mexico, so he denied the request. Instead, he offered Texas diplomatic recognition as its own nation. The next president, Martin Van Buren, inherited the Texas issue from Jackson. Annexation debates took place under the Van Buren administration. Mexico never recognized the new nation, forcing Texas to create the TEXAS RANGERS, a militia devoted to guarding the border. Texas would not be admitted to the Union until 1845.

CHECK YOUR KNOWLEDGE

1. What was the form of government in Mexico following the 1821 revolution?

2. How did the Mexican government try to attract settlers to Texas?

3. How did General Santa Anna get control of the Mexican government?

4. Why was Stephen F. Austin jailed in 1833?

5. Why is Gonzales, Texas, famous?

6. What was the Alamo? Why should we remember it?

7. What was the Goliad Massacre?

8. What forced Santa Anna to recognize Texan independence?

9. Why was Texas's request to be annexed by the U.S. denied?

ANSWERS

CHECK YOUR ANSWERS

1. A Republic; a form of government in which a state is ruled by representatives of its citizens

2. It offered land grants and hired empresarios to sell the land to people.

3. He overthrew the government and declared himself dictator.

4. Santa Anna jailed Austin because he thought Austin was planning a rebellion.

5. The people of Gonzales did not allow Mexico to take their cannon, which began the Texas War for Independence.

6. It was an abandoned mission where a volunteer militia fought against the Mexican military for Texan independence. Mexican soldiers killed all Texan militia members who fought, inspiring more Texans to join the fight.

7. It was when the remaining Texan militia were executed by the Mexican army, shortly after the fall of the Alamo.

8. He was taken captive by Sam Houston's troops.

9. Because it would have been a slave state, and annexation might have made Mexico angry.

☆ Chapter 19 ☆

THE MEXICAN-AMERICAN

Even after Congress approved the U.S. annexation of the Lone Star Republic in 1845, Texas remained a disputed territory. A new Mexican government declared that the treaty Santa Anna had signed was not valid, and Texas still belonged to Mexico. Oregon Country and California also remained in question.

FIFTY-FOUR FORTY or FIGHT!

When John Tyler fell out of favor with the Whig Party, the Whigs nominated Henry Clay as their candidate in the 1844 presidential election. The Democrats nominated JAMES K. POLK, whose main campaign promise was in the slogan of "FIFTY-FOUR FORTY OR FIGHT!" That is, he supported moving the northern border of Oregon Country, which the U.S. jointly occupied with Great Britain, at latitude 54°40' north, giving the U.S. more land.

On this promise, and the popularity of Manifest Destiny, Polk was elected president. Because he was more interested in territory than war, Polk eventually compromised with Britain to extend the border to the 49th parallel, which previous U.S. administrations

MOVEMENT OF OREGON BORDER

54°40' LINE

BRITISH NORTH AMERICA

OREGON

1846 TREATY BOUNDARY

49TH PARALLEL

COUNTRY

UNITED STATES

OREGON TRAIL

MEXICO

↑42ND PARALLEL

had already proposed. THE OREGON TREATY of 1846 reset the borders between the U.S. and British-controlled Canada, creating the OREGON TERRITORY.

U.S.-MEXICO TENSIONS

Mexico eventually acknowledged that Texas was an American territory, but the border between the two nations

MEXICAN BORDER DISPUTE

MEXICAN TERRITORIES

DISPUTED TERRITORY

U.S.

NUECES RIVER

MEXICO

RIO GRANDE

was not yet settled. The U.S. government considered the Mexican border to be along the RIO GRANDE RIVER; the Mexican government believed the border was much farther north, along the NUECES RIVER.

The MEXICAN-AMERICAN WAR BEGINS

In 1845, President Polk sent Ambassador John Slidell to offer Mexico $30 million for the disputed areas of Texas, California, and New Mexico, but Mexico refused to negotiate. In a controversial move, Polk also sent GENERAL ZACHARY TAYLOR and his troops to Texas, with instructions to make camp in the disputed region between the Rio Grande and the Nueces.

Polk's stance was that this land was American land, so the U.S. was not invading Mexico. Mexico argued that the U.S. Army was making hostile moves. When Mexican troops engaged Taylor's men on April 25, 1846, Polk informed Congress that Mexico had attacked U.S. troops on U.S. soil without being provoked. In early May, Congress declared the MEXICAN-AMERICAN WAR. Public support for war with Mexico was mixed: Gaining another Southern territory would create more slave states in the Union. Still, the vote in Congress was a landslide since it would gain a lot of land at a very low cost.

THE SECOND DECLARED WAR UNDER THE CONSTITUTION

Abraham Lincoln, a first-term representative from Illinois, thought Polk had deliberately provoked Mexico. In the first speech he ever made in Congress, Lincoln demanded that Polk identify the exact "spot" on which Polk claimed that American blood had been spilled on American soil. Many Americans called the war "Polk's War."

SUPPORT for the WAR

Mexico had taken control of California
from Spain after Mexico's war
for independence. The Mexican
government replaced the Spanish
mission system with *RANCHOS* (ranches), large parcels
of land owned by wealthy rancheros and managed
by *VAQUEROS*, or cowboys. Given the distance between
California and Mexico, the Mexican Californians, called
CALIFORNIOS, felt a stronger sense of local identity than of
national identity. Like Tejanos before them, Californians felt
little loyalty to Mexico, and there was a growing American
population in the region. The white settlers in California, or
ANGLOS, took this to an extreme: They didn't think California
should be part of Mexico at all. In June 1846, a small group
of Anglos in California decided to declare independence
and proclaimed themselves the REPUBLIC OF CALIFORNIA.
Because of the bear motif on the flag they flew, California
briefly became known as the BEAR FLAG REPUBLIC.

Immigrants also signed up to fight for the United States. By this time, immigration from Europe was rising. However, many Catholic immigrants (from Germany, Canada, France, and Ireland), disgusted by the treatment of Catholic churches at the hands of the American military, deserted the U.S. Army and joined the Mexican army. Because of the large number of Irish in this group, they became known as the SAINT PATRICK'S BATTALION. These men faced severe punishment if caught deserting: More than 50 members of the battalion were executed by the U.S. military.

MEXICO DEFEATED

Despite political and physical resistance the war went well for Polk. President Polk's plan for the Mexican–American War was to push the Mexican army out of Texas, take New Mexico and California, and then march on Mexico City. By the beginning of 1847, Zachary Taylor had invaded Mexico by crossing the Rio Grande and capturing the city of Monterrey. Meanwhile, GENERAL STEPHEN KEARNY had taken control of New Mexico without firing a single shot and continued on to California, where there was also little resistence. By September 1847, GENERAL WINFIELD SCOTT and his troops captured Mexico City. Mexico surrendered and the war was won.

The TREATY of GUADALUPE HIDALGO

The Mexican–American War ended in 1848, when Mexico and the U.S. signed the TREATY OF GUADALUPE HIDALGO.

> **CESSION**
> something that is ceded, or given up

Mexico gave up present-day California, Nevada, and Utah, along with parts of Arizona, New Mexico, Colorado, and Wyoming (a region referred to as the MEXICAN **CESSION**). Mexico also recognized the U.S. annexation of Texas and agreed to set the border between Texas and Mexico at the Rio Grande. In exchange, America gave Mexico $15 million and granted land rights and protection to Mexicans and Indigenous people who would now be living in the U.S.

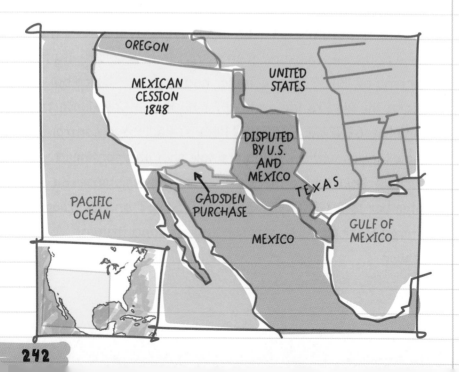

In 1853, Mexico also sold the U.S. a strip of land in present-day Arizona and New Mexico for $10 million. Negotiated by AMBASSADOR JAMES GADSDEN, the GADSDEN PURCHASE set the border between the two nations.

SETTLING the SOUTHWEST

After the U.S. took control of the Southwest, more Americans flocked there. Many followed the CALIFORNIA TRAIL, an offshoot of the Oregon Trail that ran through the Sierra Nevada Mountains. Although the Treaty of Guadalupe Hidalgo granted land rights to the Mexicans and Indigenous peoples who already inhabited land in the Southwest, these grants were generally not enforced by the U.S. government. Over time, Mexican, Indigenous, and Anglo cultures mixed, forming the distinct heritage of the American Southwest.

Maybe the most famous travelers on the California Trail were the **DONNER PARTY**, a group that set out for California, tried to find a shortcut, and then became stranded in the Sierra Nevada Mountains during the winter of 1846–1847. Why are they famous? When they ran out of food, some of them resorted to the only nourishment they could find: They ate each other.

Gold Rush

One of the first American men to settle in California was John Sutter, who founded SUTTER'S FORT in 1839. His homestead became a popular stop for people traveling or trading in the area near the Sacramento River, so he hired James Marshall, a carpenter, to build a sawmill. While he was working in January 1848, Marshall discovered gold. It wasn't long before the entire country learned that there was **GOLD** in the rivers and mountains of California.

In 1849, tens of thousands of people from the U.S. and all over the world flooded into California to try to strike it rich. Because most of the miners arrived that year, they became known as FORTY-NINERS. The miners usually agreed that the first person to begin looking for gold in a certain area could stake a claim to it, but conflicts often arose over mining rights. And although some people did get very wealthy, most miners ended up finding little or nothing of value.

BOOMTOWN LIFE

The sudden influx of people in California led to the creation of mining camps. These camps quickly became BOOMTOWNS, cities that came to life almost overnight. Few women lived in the towns, but those who did could earn money running businesses. For example, some women ran restaurants or boardinghouses. Merchants also prospered in the mining towns, where there was little competition for their goods and services.

One of the most famous and successful boomtown merchants was Levi Strauss, a Jewish German immigrant who sold miners sturdy work pants called "Levi's."

As gold supplies began to decline, the (incorrect) perception developed that Chinese miners were taking American gold. In 1852, the FOREIGN MINERS TAX made mining too expensive for many Chinese immigrants. Instead of paying the tax, many Chinese miners decided to find other work. Some founded successful businesses, and these became the foundations of thriving Chinese communities throughout California.

CALIFORNIA STATEHOOD

Even after the gold rush died down, many miners remained to farm or ranch. After just two years as a territory, California had a large enough population to apply for statehood. California wasn't granted statehood immediately; because it would be a free state, California would upset the Union's 30-year-long balance. It would also mean that the South would lose some of its power in Congress. In 1850, in another compromise between Northern and Southern interests, California became the 31st state to be admitted to the Union, but tensions between the North and South mounted.

CHECK YOUR KNOWLEDGE

1. What is the meaning of the phrase "Fifty-four Forty or Fight"?

2. Before the Mexican-American War, the Texas-Mexico border was disputed. Where did the U.S. consider the border? Where did Mexico?

3. How did President Polk get Congress to declare war on Mexico?

4. Why did some people support the Mexican-American War while others did not?

5. What was the nickname of the Republic of California? Why?

6. What was the Mexican Cession?

7. What happened to the land granted to Indigenous people in the Southwest in the Treaty of Guadalupe Hidalgo?

8. Who were the forty-niners?

9. Why did California institute the Foreign Miners Tax?

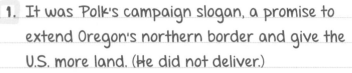

CHECK YOUR ANSWERS

1. It was Polk's campaign slogan, a promise to extend Oregon's northern border and give the U.S. more land. (He did not deliver.)

2. The U.S. thought it was the Rio Grande and Mexico thought it was the Nueces River.

3. He sent Zachary Taylor to camp in the zone between the disputed borders so it would be seen as an attack on American soil when the Mexicans defended what they thought was their territory.

4. Some supported the war because the U.S. would gain land. Others did not support the war because another Southern territory would create more slave states.

5. The Bear Flag Republic, after the image on its flag

6. A region of land that Mexico ceded to the U.S. in the Treaty of Guadalupe Hidalgo. It included present-day California, Nevada, Utah, and parts of Arizona, New Mexico, Colorado, and Wyoming.

7. The land was flooded with white American settlers and the U.S. government did not enforce the land rights of Indigenous people.

8. They were the miners who went to California during the gold rush of 1849.

9. In response to the perception that Chinese miners were taking American gold. It was designed to make mining too expensive for Chinese immigrants.

☆ Chapter 20 ☆

THE AGE OF

★ ★ ★ ★ ★ ★ ★ ★ ★ ★ ★

REFORM

As the physical shape of the U.S. changed, so did its people and culture. Influenced in part by the Industrial Revolution, more immigrants poured into the country; those already here began movements to secure more rights.

IMMIGRATION

Millions of people immigrated to America in the mid-1800s. They often traveled in **STEERAGE**, but they made the journey in spite of

> **STEERAGE**
> the lowest class on a ship, which usually had bad conditions

the rough conditions. Many Irish people crossed the Atlantic because of the IRISH POTATO FAMINE and to escape anti-Catholic persecution from the Protestants in Great Britain, who colonized the small country. Mostly poor and uneducated, they settled in northeastern cities to work as industrial and domestic laborers.

Driven out by an 1848 revolution in their homeland and general poverty, Germans made up another significant percentage of U.S. immigrants in the mid-19th century. Germans tended to settle in the Midwest, where they found inexpensive land and the opportunity to farm. Most large groups of immigrants settled in clusters: Scandinavians tended to head for the northern Midwest, and Chinese people, who immigrated across the Pacific, went to California.

NATIVISM

Many Americans were afraid the new arrivals would take their jobs for lower pay. Those who opposed immigration became known as NATIVISTS, and nativist politics soared in popularity.

In 1849, a secret society of nativists founded the American Party, though they were often called the KNOW-NOTHING Party because they refused to speak about the details of their organization. The Know-Nothings were anti-Catholic and supported longer waiting periods for **NATURALIZATION** and a ban on foreign-born people holding public office. Within a few years, however, the party fell apart over disagreements about slavery.

NATURALIZATION
when a foreigner
becomes a citizen

CITY LIFE

City life proved challenging for many immigrants. Most cities lacked adequate sewer systems, police and fire departments,

and enough housing
for a population boom.
Immigrants tended to live
in crowded **TENEMENT**

TENEMENT
a low-rent,
low-quality
apartment

apartment buildings, where disease spread easily. Others,
however, prospered as middle-class business owners.

The SECOND GREAT AWAKENING

The SECOND GREAT AWAKENING was a new religious
revival movement in the early 19th century, with millions
of supporters (like the Great Awakening). Preachers in the
movement

> challenged traditional Protestant views

> encouraged an emotional attachment to religion

> emphasized the power of each person (rather than churches,
> priests, and rules) to control their own soul and salvation

> taught personal responsibility

> wanted to improve the world

REFORM MOVEMENTS

The Second Great Awakening's principles quickly spread
outside religion. Many Americans, particularly middle-class
women who had time and money to spare, developed a spirit

of reform. The popularity of reform movements was so great that the 1820s to 1860s became known as the AGE OF REFORM. Major reform movements of this time were

THE TEMPERANCE MOVEMENT: This blamed society's problems on liquor and wanted a ban on alcohol.

THE PRISON-REFORM MOVEMENT: This was led by Dorothea Dix, who encouraged the creation of mental institutions so that the ill wouldn't be imprisoned with criminals anymore. The juvenile justice system also began in the same time period.

EDUCATION REFORM: This included the creation of the first teachers' training schools; ← CALLED "NORMAL SCHOOLS"
Catherine Beecher's first all-girls school; Samuel Gridley Howe's school for the blind; ← HELEN KELLER WENT THERE.
Thomas Gallaudet's school for the deaf; the expansion of public education; and the founding of liberal arts colleges, including Oberlin, the first college to admit women and Black people.

UTOPIAN SOCIETIES: These were attempts to create perfect communities based on religious or philosophical ideals. The Shakers, whose faith-based society prohibited marriage and having children, lasted longer than you'd expect, through converts and the adoption of orphans.

UTOPIA
a perfect place

ABOLITIONISM

One of the most significant reform movements of the 1830s was the antislavery movement. They called themselves **ABOLITIONISTS** because their goal was to "abolish" slavery. They were a small but growing group of Black and white people taking on the pro-slavery South. They considered many ways to end the institution of slavery.

ABOLISH
to do away with

One short-lived idea was to send people back to Africa. In 1821, the AMERICAN COLONIZATION SOCIETY founded the African nation of LIBERIA as a free home for Black people. As it turned out, it wasn't feasible to send large numbers of people to Liberia. Though some Black people thought their rights in the U.S. would never be upheld, and chose to return to Africa, most had lived their whole lives in the U.S. and wanted to stay.

In 1831, WILLIAM LLOYD GARRISON of Massachusetts began to publish *THE LIBERATOR*, an abolitionist newspaper.

253

He also founded the AMERICAN ANTI-SLAVERY SOCIETY. He advocated for an immediate freeing of all enslaved men and women, with no payment to enslavers. This contradicted the British abolitionist plan that was put into place in 1833, which was gradual and paid compensation to enslavers. Abolitionists also included writer HENRY DAVID THOREAU, who refused to pay taxes for six years because those taxes would be used to support the Mexican-American War, which to him was all about spreading slavery. People who preferred novels to newspapers could read HARRIET BEECHER STOWE's novel *UNCLE TOM'S CABIN*, which detailed the horrors of enslavement.

In addition to written materials, abolitionists traveled the North giving lectures. The Southern-born sisters ANGELINA AND SARAH GRIMKÉ shared their personal accounts of growing up in the South and stirred their audiences to action. Former enslaved people such as FREDERICK DOUGLASS and SOJOURNER TRUTH drew the most attention as they traveled the nation and the world, educating people about their enslaved lives.

Frederick Douglass wrote *Narrative of the Life of Frederick Douglass, an American Slave* and delivered one of the most important antislavery orations on July 5, 1852, which became known as "What to the Slave Is the 4th of July?"

The UNDERGROUND RAILROAD

In the mid-1800s, a network of abolitionists, free Black people, and formerly enslaved people organized to help thousands of enslaved people escape to the North or to Canada. The UNDERGROUND RAILROAD (not an actual railroad) organized transportation and hiding places for **FUGITIVES** from slavery. Its most famous guide, or "conductor," was ~~HARRIET TUBMAN~~, a formerly enslaved person who made more than a dozen trips to guide enslaved people to freedom.

> **FUGITIVE**
> a person fleeing from intolerable circumstances; a runaway

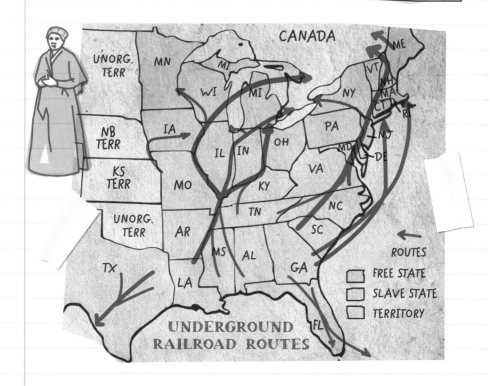

UNDERGROUND RAILROAD ROUTES

ROUTES

☐ FREE STATE
☐ SLAVE STATE
☐ TERRITORY

OPPOSITION to ABOLITIONISM

The South was one of the five richest economies in the world by this time, and abolitionism was a threat to Southerners' way of life. Even in the North, some people worried that free Black people would take jobs from white people. In addition, most Northerners didn't know enough about slavery to care about ending it. That is why abolitionists worked so hard to educate Americans about it and why Southerners worked so hard to shut them up.

Abolitionists faced physical violence and political persecution. Abolitionism was illegal in the South, and while President Jackson was in office, he banned the U.S. Postal Service from delivering abolitionist materials. In 1833, a white man was whipped in Nashville for having abolitionist literature with him. In 1836, the House of Representatives passed a resolution that postponed any discussion of slavery in the House. This became known as the "gag rule." Publishers of abolitionist newspapers faced particular violence. Their presses were smashed, and several, like ELIJAH LOVEJOY, were murdered.

WOMEN'S RIGHTS MOVEMENT

The women's rights movement grew hand in hand with the abolitionist movement. Women couldn't vote; most weren't educated; they didn't receive equal pay for equal work; and if they did earn money, it belonged to their husbands or fathers. Many supporters of abolition, such as the Grimké sisters, Sojourner Truth, and Frederick Douglass, also wanted gender equality.

In 1840, ELIZABETH CADY STANTON tried to attend an abolitionist convention in London, but women weren't allowed to sit with men in the main hall. Instead, they were hidden behind a curtain where they could hear but not see. She and her friend LUCRETIA MOTT decided to organize a women's rights convention. The SENECA FALLS CONVENTION, in July 1848 in Seneca Falls, New York, was the first meeting of its kind. Activists drafted a DECLARATION OF SENTIMENTS AND RESOLUTIONS, based on the Declaration of Independence, to lay out the injustices in gender relations. For example, it stated that "all men AND WOMEN are created equal." (Women didn't get the right to vote for another 70 years.)

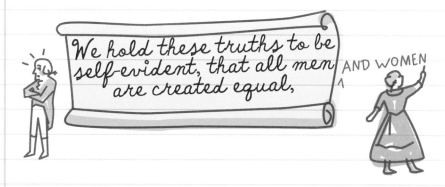

We hold these truths to be self-evident, that all men AND WOMEN are created equal, ^

The two pillars of the women's rights movement were abolition and temperance. Women saw that alcohol abuse led to domestic problems and felt that they could relate to the status of enslaved people.

Women working to end slavery began to see the parallels between their lives and the lives of enslaved people.

The arguments against abolitionism and women's rights followed the same pattern:

> Some people argued incorrectly that people of African descent were incapable of taking care of themselves and were better off enslaved.

> Some people argued incorrectly that women were incapable of taking care ofthemselves and were better off being protected from the world.

LUCY STONE, originally a women's rights advocate, became a spokesperson for the American Anti-Slavery Society. SUSAN B. ANTHONY, like Cady Stanton, originally an abolitionist, encouraged New York State to pass laws allowing women to own property. Frederick Douglass attended the Seneca Falls Convention and endorsed the Declaration of Sentiments. The abolitionist movement and the women's rights movement had common roots, but to some extent they disagreed over which had greater priority.

CHECK YOUR KNOWLEDGE

1. What drove Europeans to immigrate to the U.S. in the mid-1800s?

2. What were the main values preached during the Second Great Awakening?

3. Who were most active in the reform movements of the mid-1800s?

4. What were the major reform movements during the Age of Reform?

5. What was the Underground Railroad?

6. What were some of the ways that women were oppressed in society?

ANSWERS

CHECK YOUR ANSWERS

1. Famine, poverty, and religious persecution in Europe

2. The Second Great Awakening challenged traditional Protestant views and taught personal responsibility. It also emphasized individual power of destiny and salvation, as well as an emotional attachment to religion. The preachers wanted to improve the world.

3. Middle-class women

4. The Abolition Movement, the Women's Rights Movement, the Worker's Rights movement, the Temperance Movement, Education Reform, and Prison Reform

5. It was a network that organized transportation and hiding places for fugitives from slavery.

6. Most women were not educated, could not vote, and did not receive equal pay for equal work. If they did work, the money they earned belonged to their husbands or fathers.

Unit 5

Civil War and Reconstruction
1850s–1870s

As the U.S. approached its 70th year of independence, the relationship between the states and the federal government still wasn't resolved. Slavery remained a contentious issue. How would the North and South reconcile their differences? They couldn't, and the result was the Civil War.

☆ Chapter 21 ☆

The SECTIONAL CRISIS

By the mid-19th century, the U.S. stretched from the East Coast to the West Coast. As states continued to apply for statehood, the debate over abolition went on.

The WILMOT PROVISO

Representative David Wilmot of Pennsylvania had proposed the **WILMOT PROVISO**, suggesting that slavery be banned in any territory acquired through the Mexican Cession. It passed in the House, but Southerners prevented its passage in the Senate.

> **PROVISO**
> a part of a law that restricts something

The ELECTION of 1848

When the Wilmot Proviso failed, a new political party formed: the FREE-SOIL PARTY. They wanted to keep new territories and states free of slavery. They nominated former president Martin Van Buren against the Whig candidate

ZACHARY TAYLOR and Democrat Lewis Cass (a senator from Michigan). Taylor won the presidential election. The Free-Soil candidates won some seats in Congress.

COMPROMISE of 1850

HE PROPOSED THE MISSOURI COMPROMISE, TOO

When California applied to the Union as a free state, some Southern states threatened to secede. Henry Clay had a compromise:

California would be admitted as a free state.

Texas would give up some of its land, and the government would help pay off its war debts.

Popular sovereignty would decide positions on slavery in territories and new states, which meant that settlers would decide the issue.

DON'T FORGET—THIS MEANS AUTHORITY OF THE PEOPLE

The slave trade (but not slavery itself) would be banned in Washington, D.C.

Congress would pass stronger laws requiring the capture and return of runaway enslaved people.

After President Taylor died suddenly and his vice president, MILLARD FILLMORE, took his place, the Compromise of 1850 was passed into law.

The FUGITIVE SLAVE ACT

A controversial part of the Compromise of 1850 was the
FUGITIVE SLAVE ACT, which required Northern citizens
to cooperate with and assist slave-catchers, and denied
fugitives a fair trial (they were tried in a separate court).
It divided the nation even further. The South supported it,
and felt vindicated. The North hated it. Many free Black
people fled to Canada, and some Northern whites practiced
CIVIL DISOBEDIENCE, refusing
to follow the new law. The North
also passed PERSONAL LIBERTY
LAWS, which basically negated
the Fugitive Slave Act and proved
to the South that the North was
not uniformly enforcing the law.

> **"CIVIL DISOBEDIENCE"**
> was an essay written by
> Henry David Thoreau on
> the idea that people should
> refuse to follow the laws or
> commands of a government
> when they seem unjust.

In Massachusetts, abolitionist Harriet Beecher Stowe was
inspired to write *Uncle Tom's Cabin* (1852), a novel about the
harsh realities of slavery. It turned abolition into a topic of
household discussion and became one of the most influential
books of the 19th century.

The KANSAS-NEBRASKA ACT

In the presidential election of 1852, little-known Democratic
candidate FRANKLIN PIERCE of New Hampshire defeated
the Whig nominee, war hero Winfield Scott. At this time,
some Western land, including Kansas and Nebraska,
was not yet organized into states, and Illinois senator

STEPHEN A. DOUGLAS wanted to build a railroad that ran through it from Chicago to the Pacific. He initially proposed making KANSAS and NEBRASKA U.S. territories that, under the terms of the Missouri Compromise, would be free. However, Douglas also knew that Southerners would object to this idea. Backed by President Pierce, he proposed the KANSAS-NEBRASKA ACT, which would invoke the **DOCTRINE** of popular sovereignty and allow the people living in the new states to determine the slavery issue. The act passed, and the Missouri Compromise was made obsolete.

> **DOCTRINE**
> a theory or position on an issue

BLEEDING KANSAS

KANSAS

During the March 1855 territorial elections in Kansas, thousands of so-called **BORDER RUFFIANS** from the slave state of Missouri crossed the border to vote illegally. In fact, about four times more people voted in Kansas than lived there. A pro-slavery local government took control. Antislavery settlers started their own government, creating two governments for one state.

> **RUFFIAN**
> a tough, lawless person; a bully

In May 1856, the pro-slavery government sent a group to Lawrence, Kansas, to arrest the antislavery government, but they had fled. The pro-slavery group ransacked the city in the **SACK OF LAWRENCE**. In response, the passionate abolitionist JOHN BROWN led his group in the POTTAWATOMIE CREEK MASSACRE of pro-slavery Kansans. Over the summer, hundreds of people were killed in "BLEEDING KANSAS" before federal troops restored order.

> **SACK**
> to pillage and plunder

BLEEDING SUMNER

Violence also broke out in Congress after Senator CHARLES SUMNER of Massachusetts criticized people who were pro-slavery, specifically Andrew Butler of South Carolina. Butler's cousin, Representative PRESTON BROOKS, beat Sumner over the head with a cane in the Senate chambers. Sumner was badly injured.

The REPUBLICAN PARTY and the ELECTION of 1856

Both the Democratic and Whig parties were splitting along sectional lines. The antislavery Whigs decided to join the Northern Democrats and Free-Soilers to create the REPUBLICAN PARTY.

> Though some names have stayed the same, modern political parties are not the same as their roots.

The Republican Party nominated John C. Frémont of California for president, and the Democratic Party nominated JAMES BUCHANAN, a Pennsylvanian who

> Frémont's campaign slogan was "Free Soil, Free Men and Frémont."

favored compromise. The Know-Nothing Party nominated former president Millard Fillmore. Buchanan won the South and won the election.

The DRED SCOTT DECISION

In 1857, a Supreme Court case about an enslaved man named DRED SCOTT fueled the abolitionist cause. Scott was enslaved by an army doctor in Missouri, John Emerson, who brought him along on travels to Illinois, where slavery was illegal. After Emerson passed away in 1843, Scott petitioned Emerson's widow for his and his family's freedom, but she refused. Scott, his wife, Harriet, and his two daughters continued living in slavery. A few years later, with the help of lawyers from the North, Scott sued for his family's freedom, making the argument that they were free after having lived in a free place.

After a decade of appeals, the Supreme Court took on the issue in the case of *DRED SCOTT v. SANFORD* (also called the DRED SCOTT DECISION). They voted 7-2, against Scott. Chief Justice Roger Taney wrote the decision that ruled:

1. Scott didn't have the right to sue because he was legally considered a piece of property, not a citizen.

2. The government can't seize private property (Scott and his family) from a citizen (Emerson) without due process of law.

3. Congress can't ban slavery in the territories, because that would violate the property rights of people bringing enslaved people there.

4. Therefore, the Missouri Compromise and other popular sovereignty decisions were unconstitutional.

The nation's highest court had ruled that Black people, whether they were free or enslaved, were not citizens of the United States and did not have a right to protection from the federal government or the court system. Ultimately, the Scott family were freed when Emerson's widow moved to Massachusetts and married an abolitionist, but the damage of the decision had been done.

Abolitionists like Frederick Douglass had spoken for years about the **SLAVOCRACY**, and this decision seemed to confirm that the federal

SLAVOCRACY
the power of enslavers inside the federal government

government, including President Buchanan (who had pressured several justices in this case) and the Supreme Court were being influenced by Southern plantation owners. The chief justice believed that his ruling was a "compromise" that would settle the issue of slavery and its expansion, when in fact, it proved to be a turning point in the abolitionist cause in addition to dividing the Democratic Party.

The LINCOLN-DOUGLAS DEBATES

In the senatorial election of 1858, prominent Democratic senator Stephen A. Douglas of Illinois faced a new, young challenger, ABRAHAM LINCOLN, a Republican lawyer who had served one term in the House of Representatives and eight years in the state legislature.

Since Lincoln was not very well known, he challenged Douglas to a series of debates, the LINCOLN-DOUGLAS DEBATES. They met seven times in cities and towns throughout Illinois to debate what to do about slavery.

Douglas was a strong proponent of **POPULAR SOVEREIGNTY**, believing the voting population of each state should decide whether to allow slavery. Lincoln argued against the expansion of slavery. He centered his campaign on the immorality of slavery and the need to resolve the issue as a nation once and for all. Before the debates he summarized the problem in his famous House Divided ⟵ speech. He believed that the nation ultimately would have to decide if slavery was to be allowed everywhere or nowhere.

POPULAR SOVEREIGNTY
the political position that people living in the state should vote to decide about slavery

THIS WAS KNOWN AS THE IRREPRESSIBLE CONFLICT DOCTRINE.

When Douglas accused Lincoln of supporting equality of the races, Lincoln acknowledged that he didn't believe that the races were equal. He said, though, that people of African descent deserved all the rights spelled out in the Declaration of Independence.

Douglas rejected the idea that all states had to hold the same policy. He argued that the FREEPORT DOCTRINE proved that territories could exclude slavery despite the Dred Scott decision by refusing to protect the rights of enslavers. He argued that the nation should be a loose collection of states with equal and independent powers, whereas Lincoln wanted a unified nation.

The debates attracted local and national attention, deepening the rift in the Democratic Party and boosting Lincoln's reputation.

The RAID on HARPERS FERRY

In 1859, John Brown led another raid, this time in HARPERS FERRY, VIRGINIA. The plan was to seize weapons from an armory and use them to arm a group of both white and Black abolitionists. That group, who had already been in contact with enslaved people on nearby plantations, would then begin regular nighttime missions to help them escape. Brown believed that such a constant threat would convince enslavers that slavery could never be protected and give it up.

The raid began on October 16, 1859. Two tactical errors led to the failure of the mission: Brown's men stopped a passenger train passing through Harpers Ferry. Brown lectured the passengers for more than an hour, then let the train continue on its journey. Once the train arrived in Baltimore, Maryland, passengers alerted the authorities. In the meantime, Brown waited too long for members of his party to bring reinforcements. Brown and his men were captured on Tuesday, October 18.

John Brown wrote about the need to end slavery every day of his trial until he was executed for treason and murder in early December. Rumors spread about Brown and his intentions. Though he was remembered as a mentally ill man intent on creating a slave uprising and making himself a **MARTYR**, his stated goal was to free as many enslaved people as he could, and he was willing to put his freedom at stake to do so. Although the raid failed, it inspired Northern abolitionists and frightened the people who profited from enslaving others.

> **MARTYR**
> someone who dies for their beliefs

The ELECTION of 1860

Northern Democrats nominated Stephen Douglas, who supported popular sovereignty; Southern Democrats chose JOHN BRECKINRIDGE from Kentucky, who supported slavery. A new party, the CONSTITUTIONAL UNION PARTY (compromise and union at any cost), nominated JOHN BELL of Tennessee. Abraham Lincoln, who believed slavery should be banned in the territories, received the nomination from the Republican Party. Lincoln received only 40 percent of the popular vote and did not carry a single Southern state. However, he swept the North, along with California and Oregon, and became the 16th president of the U.S.

SECESSION

Although at the time Lincoln did not favor abolishing slavery in states where it already existed, he believed that restricting the expansion of slavery would, sooner or later, cause the institution of slavery to fall apart. That idea made the South very worried about having him in the White House. Within days of Lincoln's victory, the South Carolina legislature met for a special session, arguing that if a state could choose to enter a union it could also choose to leave. On December 20, 1860, South Carolina **SECEDED** from the U.S. by repealing its ratification of the Constitution. Some people believed that secession was a state's legal right, and

> **SECEDE**
> to formally withdraw from membership in an organization

others believed that South Carolina's decision was a revolt. However, Southern lawmakers claimed that the government had violated its rights by not protecting slavery.

The CONFEDERATE STATES of AMERICA

CONFEDERATE
part of an alliance or confederacy

Following in South Carolina's footsteps, Texas, Louisiana, Mississippi, Alabama, Florida, and Georgia also seceded. On February 4, 1861, representatives from these states met to establish their own government as the **CONFEDERATE STATES OF AMERICA** (the CSA). They elected JEFFERSON DAVIS as president.

LINCOLN'S FIRST INAUGURAL ADDRESS

INAUGURAL
having to do with an inauguration, the ceremony at which someone is sworn into office

Abraham Lincoln was inaugurated on March 4, 1861. The main points of his first **INAUGURAL ADDRESS** were:

Legal **REDRESS** and revolutionary actions are different; secession is not an acceptable choice.

REDRESS
relief from an injury or wrongdoing

The Union is perpetual; therefore the CSA doesn't actually exist and is a band of rebels living in the U.S.

Federal property in the South will remain federal property.

Slavery shouldn't be completely abolished, but it shouldn't spread.

War is not a reasonable option.

The people of the United States should all be friends, not enemies, because the United States is one country.

The address was meant to reassure Southerners that Lincoln would not interfere with slavery in the states where it already existed.

Lincoln's inaugural address is well known for its eloquence: "In your hands, my dissatisfied fellow-countrymen, and not in mine, is the momentous issue of civil war. The Government will not assail you. You can have no conflict without being yourselves the aggressors. You have no oath registered in heaven to destroy the Government, while I shall have the most solemn one to preserve, protect, and defend it....I am loath to close. We are not enemies, but friends. We must not be enemies. Though passion may have strained it must not break our bonds of affection. The mystic chords of memory, stretching from every battlefield and patriot grave to every living heart and hearthstone all over this broad land, will yet swell the chorus of the Union, when again touched, as surely they will be, by the better angels of our nature."

CHECK YOUR KNOWLEDGE

1. What was the platform of the Free-Soil Party?

2. What did the Fugitive Slave Act require of Northern citizens?

3. What is popular sovereignty? How was it used in the Compromise of 1850?

4. How was the Republican Party founded?

5. What was one ruling by the Supreme Court in the Dred Scott decision?

6. What were Lincoln's prewar opinions about racial equality?

7. What were the secessionists' arguments for the legality of their actions?

8. What did Lincoln think about the legality of secession?

ANSWERS 275

1. They believed that new states and territories ought to be free of slavery.

2. Northern citizens had to cooperate with and assist slave-catchers and Northern courts had to try fugitives in separate courts.

3. Popular sovereignty means authority of the people. The Compromise of 1850 ruled that popular sovereignty, the settlers, would determine if slavery was allowed in a new state.

4. Antislavery Whigs joined forces with the Northern Democrats and the Free-Soilers.

5. Dred Scott did not have the right to sue because he was not a citizen.

6. He did not believe in racial equality, but he thought slavery was wrong and that Black people should be citizens.

7. They believed that the federal government had violated their rights by not protecting slavery.

8. Lincoln believed that secession was not legally possible and that the Confederacy was in rebellion.

#5 has more than one correct answer.

☆ Chapter 22 ☆

✯ ✯ ✯ ✯ ✯ The ✯ ✯ ✯ ✯ ✯
CIVIL WAR

FORT SUMTER

> **CIVIL WAR**
> a war within one country, rather than between two different nations

Soon after his inauguration, President Lincoln learned that supplies for federal troops at FORT SUMTER, which was in the harbor of Charleston, South Carolina, were running out. Sending more supplies could provoke war. After alerting the CSA, Lincoln sent unarmed supply ships. In response, on April 12, 1861, the Confederacy attacked Fort Sumter. The fort surrendered two days later. The **CIVIL WAR** had begun.

BORDER STATES

Lincoln called on state militias to supply troops for what he estimated would be three months of fighting. In response, border states North Carolina, Tennessee, Virginia, and Arkansas seceded—they refused to bear arms against their fellow Southerners and saw Lincoln's actions as unjust. Border states where slavery was legal but not such a big part of the economy—Delaware, Kentucky, Maryland, and Missouri—stayed in the Union. In 1863, the part of Virginia loyal to the Union—WEST VIRGINIA—became the USA's 35th state.

NORTH VERSUS SOUTH

The North (the **YANKEES**, or the **UNION**, who wore blue uniforms) had a bigger population, more transport options (especially railroads), more factories and production capacity, and more money.

The South (the **REBELS**, or the **CONFEDERATES**, who wore gray uniforms) had influence on the world's cotton market.

The South needed to fight a defensive war. They hoped for foreign intervention and planned to hold out until the North got weary of the war.

The North needed to fight a more active war and subdue the Rebels.

Both armies consisted mostly of inexperienced volunteers who signed up for only 90 days of fighting.

Together, North and South faced the scary reality of a war that pitted countrymen against one another.

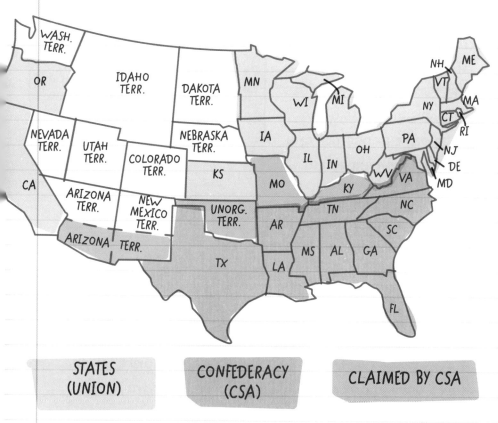

| STATES (UNION) | CONFEDERACY (CSA) | CLAIMED BY CSA |

The FIRST BATTLE of BULL RUN

In July 1861, the Union army tried to take Richmond, Virginia, which had become the CSA capital. The Confederate troops met the Union army at MANASSAS, Virginia, which was a key railroad junction near BULL RUN CREEK. Neither side was ready. On July 21, the Union forces crossed the creek and pushed back all of the Rebels, except for the unit led by General Thomas Jackson, who received the nickname "Stonewall" for refusing to move. Under STONEWALL JACKSON, the Confederate army pushed the Union troops back to Washington, D.C. The First Battle of Bull Run showed both sides that this war was going to be more dangerous and difficult than expected.

GEORGE McCLELLAN and ULYSSES S. GRANT

Lincoln brought in GENERAL GEORGE McCLELLAN to lead the Union ARMY OF THE POTOMAC. McClellan trained his troops for almost a year but, convinced that the Confederate troops were too powerful, hesitated to attack. Meanwhile, Union forces in the West, led by ULYSSES S. GRANT, were taking forts, gaining ground, and seizing control over trade and supply routes. ADMIRAL DAVID FARRAGUT led navy troops to take New Orleans, wrapping his wooden ships in heavy chains to protect them like IRONCLADS.

NEW MILITARY TECHNOLOGY

One of the most significant new inventions of the Civil War was the **IRONCLAD** warship, a ship that was armored with iron. Other major innovations were the **REPEATING RIFLE** (which could fire more than one bullet before it had to be reloaded) and the **MINIÉ BALL BULLET**; soldiers could shoot farther and more accurately. War became a whole lot deadlier.

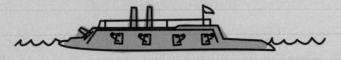

THE BIG BATTLES

The BATTLE of SHILOH

The Confederacy's western troops retreated to Corinth, Mississippi. Grant's army followed closely behind, stopping near SHILOH CHURCH, in Tennessee, to wait for reinforcements. On April 6, 1862, Albert Sidney Johnston, leader of the Confederacy's western troops, and his soldiers ambushed Grant's camp. Over two days, the Union forces were able to push the Confederates back into Mississippi, but both sides lost huge numbers of soldiers in the BATTLE OF SHILOH.

The PENINSULA CAMPAIGN

Because Lincoln was frustrated with McClellan's hesitations, McClellan finally announced a plan to move the entire army by boat from Alexandria, Virginia, to Virginia's Lower Peninsula—a huge and slow operation. But Confederate troops were able to retreat to Richmond faster than the Union army could cut them off at either Yorktown

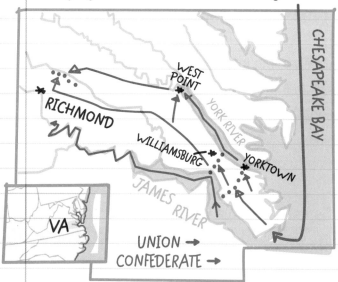

WEST POINT

RICHMOND

YORK RIVER

WILLIAMSBURG

YORKTOWN

JAMES RIVER

CHESAPEAKE BAY

VA

UNION →
CONFEDERATE →

or West Point. The city had time to prepare. Three months into the campaign, when Union forces reached Richmond, the Confederates, under the command of a new leader, ROBERT E. LEE, pushed them back in a major defeat ending July 1, 1862.

The SECOND BATTLE of BULL RUN

In August 1862, in the SECOND BATTLE OF BULL RUN, the Rebels gained another victory.

ANTIETAM

Lee decided to attack the North. A victory there would take the war to Northern soil. (It was also designed to help Virginia

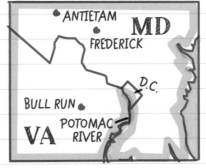

farmers harvest their crops by moving the battle north.) In September 1862, the Confederate army crossed the Potomac into Frederick, Maryland (a Union state).

Lee planned to divide his army into three units, which made him vulnerable to attack. A Union soldier found a copy of Lee's marching orders in an abandoned Rebel camp. When McClellan learned of the plan, he was slow to act when he could have used this secret information to get an advantage.

COMBINED CASUALTIES WERE 23,000 KILLED, WOUNDED, OR MISSING.

Two days later, on September 17, the two armies met near Sharpsburg, Maryland, at the BATTLE OF ANTIETAM, which became the deadliest one-day battle in all of U.S. history.

After Lee retreated, McClellan didn't follow with an attack. Lincoln fired McClellan.

The EMANCIPATION PROCLAMATION

EMANCIPATION
setting free

Lincoln said that the Civil War wasn't being fought to end slavery but to preserve the Union. He knew that he had to keep the border states under Union control. He was also determined to keep Britain out of the war. (The South was hoping that Britain, desperate for Southern cotton, would officially enter the war on the Confederate side.) Lincoln had a plan for how to keep the border states in and Britain out, but he needed a clear victory before presenting his new policy.

In September, after the win at ANTIETAM, Lincoln announced that on January 1, 1863, an **EMANCIPATION PROCLAMATION** order would go into effect. This military order would free all enslaved people in any area that was in rebellion and would go into effect unless those rebelling states gave up the fight before that date. Lincoln timed the proclamation with the victory so that it was seen as an act of strength, coming from a victorious army. He did not have the constitutional power to end slavery, but he did, as commander in chief, have the power to confiscate property that aided the enemy. In this case, he used the Southerners' insistence that enslaved people were property against them and declared that all enslaved people in the rebelling states would be free men and women.

This accomplished both of his goals: It kept the institution of slavery intact in the border states while signaling to abolitionists in Britain that the aim of the war was shifting toward emancipation. These abolitionists, who had successfully petitioned to end British enslaving systems in 1833, pressured the British government to stay out of the Civil War. Lincoln and the Union army had no way to enforce the Emancipation Proclamation, but word spread across the South, and the tide of people walking off of plantations seeking both freedom and the opportunity to join the Union side increased dramatically.

BLACK MEN READY to FIGHT

The Emancipation Proclamation also cleared the way for Black troops to serve in the Union army. From the start of the war, abolitionists like Frederick Douglass had argued that Black soldiers could help the North win as well as prove their worth and earn full citizenship. Lincoln resisted, afraid of how the border states would react. But many Black men and women did not wait to be freed: Freedom was theirs if they crossed Union lines. Union camps soon filled with **CONTRABAND**. As early as July 1862, Black people in New Orleans, Kansas, Missouri, and South Carolina began to

> **CONTRABAND**
> people who escaped slavery and worked behind Union lines supporting the Union cause in many ways

form unofficial military units. They were officially brought into the army in January 1863. The most famous of the Black units was the 54TH MASSACHUSETTS INFANTRY REGIMENT. This group of more than 1,000 volunteers came from Canada, the Caribbean, and all parts of the U.S.

About 180,000 Black men were enrolled in 175 UNITED STATES COLORED TROOPS (USCT) regiments by the end of the Civil War. This constituted 10 percent of the entire Union army.

The HOME FRONT

Because so many men were away fighting, women in the North and the South took on more responsibility in farming, business, and manufacturing. Women also supported the war effort as nurses; battlefield nurse CLARA BARTON later founded the AMERICAN RED CROSS.

High demand for supplies bolstered the Northern economy. Food shortages and inflation damaged the Southern economy and hurt Southern morale.

Both the Union and Confederate governments imposed an INCOME TAX and issued new currency; in the North, this money was called GREENBACK money.

The need for soldiers led to the institution of a draft on both sides. Because rich men could buy their way out of it, riots ensued in New York City, and more than 100 people died in the July 1863 draft riots.

FREDERICKSBURG and CHANCELLORSVILLE

After firing McClellan, Lincoln put AMBROSE BURNSIDE in charge. The Rebels and General Lee forced the Union to retreat in the December 1862 BATTLE OF FREDERICKSBURG. It was one of the worst defeats of the Union army, who lost more than 12,500 soldiers. Burnside resigned. GENERAL JOSEPH HOOKER took his place.

In May 1863, Hooker led the Union army in an attack on Chancellorsville, but once again Lee's army forced them to retreat. It was considered Lee's greatest victory. Hooker was replaced by GEORGE MEADE.

STONEWALL JACKSON DIED FROM BATTLE WOUNDS DURING THE ATTACK.

Remember the not-so-great Union generals **McClellan**, **Burnside**, and **Hooker** with this mnemonic device:

MAKE BETTER HEROES.

The BATTLE of GETTYSBURG

Lee took another chance on invading the North. In June 1863, Lee's army entered Pennsylvania and searched for supplies in the town of Gettysburg, unaware that Union cavalry was there as well. It was an accidental encounter that blew up into the most famous battle of the Civil War.

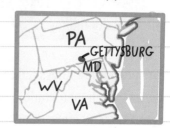

TIMELINE

July 1: After the Rebels pushed the outnumbered Union forces back into the town, the Union troops regrouped on CEMETERY HILL and CULP'S HILL, strategic positions on high ground. Both sides called for reinforcements.

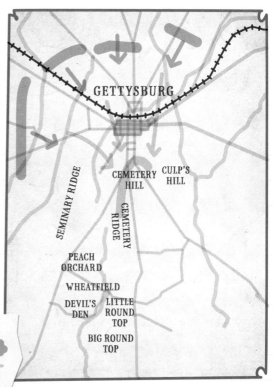

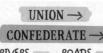

UNION →
CONFEDERATE →
RIVERS — ROADS —
RAILROAD +++

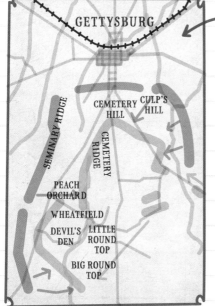

July 2: Lee ordered the Confederate army to gain the high ground on the hills BIG ROUND TOP and LITTLE ROUND TOP, but the Union held on to these positions after heavy fighting.

July 3: When the Union line appeared to be weakened, Lee ordered GENERAL GEORGE PICKETT to attack the center of the Union line. In PICKETT'S CHARGE, the Confederates marched directly into heavy Union fire.

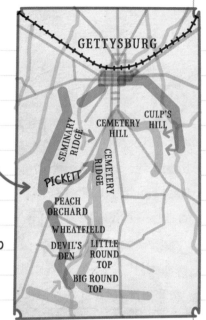

July 4: Lee and his army began to retreat to Virginia.

The BATTLE OF GETTYSBURG was a major victory for the Yankees and a turning point in the Civil War. Pickett's Charge became known as the "high-water mark of the Confederacy" because victory would never again be so close for the Confederates. Gettysburg is also famous as the site of Lincoln's GETTYSBURG ADDRESS. On November 19, 1863, during the dedication of a soldiers' cemetery there, Lincoln gave a two-minute-long speech on the importance of the Union's cause.

> The first line of the **GETTYSBURG ADDRESS**, "Four score and seven years ago, our fathers brought forth, upon this continent..." is a clue to the year in which it was delivered. A "score" is 20, so four score and seven = 4 x 20 + 7 = 87 years. 1863 – 87 = 1776.

> Vicksburg, Mississippi, also fell to the Union on July 4, 1863, which meant that the North controlled the entire Mississippi River.

The VIRGINIA CAMPAIGN

After all the disappointing Union commanders, in early 1864, Lincoln put Ulysses S. Grant in charge of all military operations so the Union armies could act as one. Grant decided that the war would be an attack on Southern morale and resources. That is, the Union would practice **TOTAL WAR**.

> **TOTAL WAR**
> war that also uses/ attacks civilians and nonmilitary resources

In the BATTLE OF THE WILDERNESS on May 5 and 6, 1864, Grant, knowing that his army was larger than Lee's, pushed into Virginia despite heavy losses. From June 9, 1864, to March 25, 1865, Lee was forced to defend Richmond and was vastly outnumbered in the SIEGE OF PETERSBURG. Grant broke through the Confederates' lines and forced Lee to abandon his fortifications. Lee's army had dwindled down to just 27,000 men, compared with Grant's force of 120,000.

SHERMAN in the DEEP SOUTH

In September 1864, GENERAL WILLIAM TECUMSEH SHERMAN marched with Union forces to Atlanta and destroyed the city. He continued on his MARCH TO THE SEA, capturing the city of Savannah, then moving north into the Carolinas. In this terrifying campaign, Sherman's army destroyed plantations and burned fields. He wanted to destroy the economy and morale of the South. He did—and he stirred up long-lasting resentment.

The ELECTION of 1864

Until mid-1864, Lincoln had been in a bad position for reelection. After victories in Gettysburg and the South in the summer and fall of 1864, he won in a landslide against George McClellan. It was seen as a mandate (command) for emancipation. On January 31, 1865, Congress passed the THIRTEENTH AMENDMENT, banning slavery in the United States (except when used as punishment for someone who is convicted of a crime). It was quickly ratified by the states.

The END of the WAR

On April 2, 1865, the government of the CSA fled, burning the city of Richmond behind them so that it wouldn't be of any use to the Union army. Lee reluctantly decided he had no choice but to surrender.

On April 9, 1865, Lee and Grant met at APPOMATTOX COURT HOUSE. Grant offered the following terms of surrender: The Confederate soldiers would be fed and allowed to return home with their property and horses. Lee accepted. The last of the Confederate army surrendered on May 26. The Civil War was over with a victory for the Union—and now it was time to rebuild the country.

CHECK YOUR KNOWLEDGE

1. Which side did each border state take during the Civil War?

2. What did the North and South learn from the First Battle of Bull Run?

3. Why didn't President Lincoln like General McClellan?

4. What did the Emancipation Proclamation do?

5. What is total war?

6. What does the Thirteenth Amendment signify?

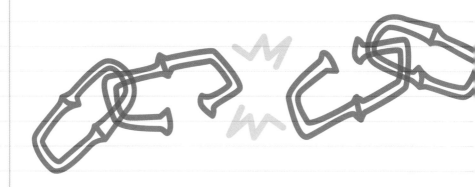

ANSWERS

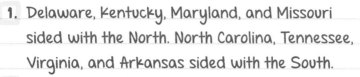

CHECK YOUR ANSWERS

1. Delaware, Kentucky, Maryland, and Missouri sided with the North. North Carolina, Tennessee, Virginia, and Arkansas sided with the South.
2. They saw that the war would be more difficult and dangerous than expected.
3. McClellan was too hesitant to attack Confederate forces.
4. It declared that enslaved people in areas controlled by the Confederate army were freed (but the Union army could not actually enforce it).
5. Total war involves attacks on civilians and resources, not just soldiers.
6. The legal end to slavery in the United States (though unpaid labor remained a legal punishment for someone who is convicted of a crime)

☆ Chapter 23 ☆
RECONSTRUCTION

RECONSTRUCTION

Reconstruction was the name of the era after the Civil War ended, lasting from 1865 to 1877. The nation struggled to find a balance between uniting the country and assisting the newly freed Black population of the South, who were collectively called freedmen.

The FREEDMEN'S BUREAU

Two months after the RATIFICATION of the THIRTEENTH AMENDMENT and a month before the war ended, Lincoln and Congress established the FREEDMEN'S BUREAU, an agency whose goal was to help the newly "freed men" by providing education, food, housing, and medical aid. The bureau was understaffed and lacked funding, but managed to set

> The Freedmen's Bureau was under General O. O. Howard, and Howard University was named in his honor.

> The Thirteenth Amendment (the first of the Reconstruction Amendments) ended slavery, but had a loophole that allowed prisoners to be used as unpaid labor.

up schools and universities for formerly enslaved people. The goal of the bureau was to help the people who had been freed but who had few of the resources they needed to navigate their new lives.

LINCOLN'S ASSASSINATION

On April 14, 1865, only a month after the Freedmen's Bureau was established and just days after Lee and Grant met at Appomattox to negotiate the South's surrender, President Lincoln and his wife attended a play at FORD'S THEATRE in Washington. During the play, Lincoln was shot in the head by Confederate sympathizer JOHN WILKES BOOTH and died the following morning. President Lincoln was the first American president to be **ASSASSINATED**. Booth's coconspirators attacked the secretary of state, William Seward, and severely wounded him, and were also supposed to kill Vice President Andrew Johnson. Lincoln's death destroyed any hope for an orderly Reconstruction.

> **ASSASSINATE**
> to kill an important person, usually for political reasons

JOHNSON'S RECONSTRUCTION and BLACK CODES

Lincoln's vice president, former Democrat ANDREW JOHNSON, was sworn into office. Although Johnson followed Lincoln's agenda for Reconstruction per his presidential duties, he did not believe in racial equality, and his interpretation of Reconstruction was lenient toward the South. Every Southern state except Texas created new governments, and Johnson approved them. The new legislatures in Southern states passed new laws called BLACK CODES, **DISCRIMINATORY** laws that denied **CIVIL RIGHTS** to Black people and prevented the Freedmen's Bureau from doing its work in those states.

DISCRIMINATORY
treatment against people based on the group or class to which they belong, such as race

CIVIL RIGHTS
rights that protect the ability to participate in activities granted to citizens, without discrimination; personal liberties

Everyone was shocked by Johnson's leniency, even Southerners who had been prepared to pay a price for the rebellion. Northerners were shocked that the war seemed to have been for nothing. Republicans in Congress refused to let Southern Democrats take their seats the next time Congress came into session. Johnson's inaction drove many to vote for the **RADICAL REPUBLICANS**, who then took control of

RADICAL
extreme

Reconstruction after winning a veto-proof majority of votes in both houses of Congress in the midterm elections. Congress gave the Freedmen's Bureau more powers and passed the CIVIL RIGHTS ACT OF 1866, which confirmed that former enslaved people were citizens and overturned the DRED SCOTT DECISION of 1857.

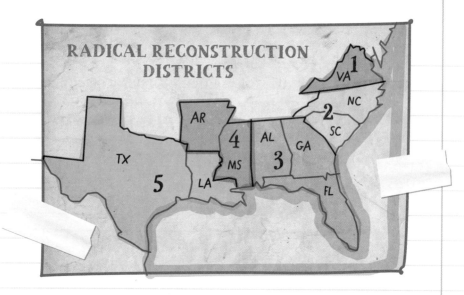

RADICAL RECONSTRUCTION DISTRICTS

The FOURTEENTH AMENDMENT

The FOURTEENTH AMENDMENT to the Constitution was passed in June 1868. It ensured that any person (except Indigenous Americans!) born or naturalized in the U.S. was a citizen with full rights, such as **DUE PROCESS**. All of the states had to accept these amendments to reenter the Union. This led to:

riots in the South   an influx of Black voters

an unsuccessful attempt by Johnson to oppose it

RADICAL RECONSTRUCTION

In March 1867, Congress passed the RECONSTRUCTION ACTS, which divided the South into five military districts that would be controlled by a military commander until the Southern states were readmitted to the Union.

IMPEACHMENT

> **TENURE**
> term or period in an
> office or position

Aware that Johnson opposed Radical Reconstruction, Congress also passed the **TENURE** OF OFFICE ACT, which limited executive power by requiring the president to secure congressional approval before he could remove members of his cabinet. During the summer of 1867, when Congress wasn't in session, President Johnson fired his secretary of war, Edwin Stanton. Congress voted to impeach Johnson for doing it without their approval (and, unofficially, for disagreeing with Congress). In February 1868, Johnson was tried in the Senate, but he was acquitted by just one vote. He didn't run for reelection.

FREED FROM CHARGE

The ELECTION of 1868

In the presidential election of 1868, the Democratic former governor of New York, HORATIO SEYMOUR, ran against Republican war hero Ulysses S. Grant. Having garnered the support of Republicans in the North and newly **ENFRANCHISED** Black Americans in the South, Grant won the election.

> **ENFRANCHISE**
> to set free or endow
> with a franchise, such
> as the right to vote

VIRGINIA, MISSISSIPPI, AND TEXAS WERE
NOT ALLOWED TO PARTICIPATE BECAUSE THEY
WEREN'T FULLY RECONSTRUCTED YET.

Because Black Americans turned out in high numbers to vote in the presidential election, Republicans feared that Southern states would try to limit their voting in future elections. In 1869, Congress proposed the FIFTEENTH AMENDMENT, which made it illegal to deny citizens the right to vote based on race.

> The Fifteenth Amendment did not make any qualifications based on gender. That is, women still could not vote.

RECONSTRUCTION PROVES REVOLUTIONARY

The purpose of Radical Reconstruction and the Reconstruction Amendments was to revolutionize the South. Fundamental changes like the opportunity to learn to read and write and the ability to keep your family together were powerful and life changing. Before his death, Lincoln had sent a delegation to Charleston, South Carolina, to ask a group of Black leaders there what kind of support they wanted and needed. They told him the newly freed people needed rights, protection of those rights, land, and to be left alone. (They only wanted land on loan until they were able to pay for it.)

The Thirteenth Amendment freed enslaved people, the Fourteenth Amendment gave them the full rights of citizenship, and the federal military presence served to protect those rights. Though they did

REMEMBER THE AMENDMENTS:
Free citizens vote.
13th 14th 15th

not specifically ask for the vote, men of African descent enthusiastically took up the work of writing new state constitutions, running for office, and voting even before the Fifteenth Amendment made their right to do so federal law. More than 1,500 Black men were elected to local and state offices, and close to 200 held federal positions. In 1870, HIRAM REVELS became the first Black American in the U.S. Senate, representing Mississippi. In 1875, BLANCHE K. BRUCE, also from Mississippi, became the second Black senator.

LIFE for FORMERLY ENSLAVED PEOPLE

Most formerly enslaved people were living below the poverty threshold. General Sherman had proposed a plan to divide plantations among freedmen (so everyone would literally get "40 ACRES AND A MULE"), but this was opposed by Congress. Landowners needed laborers to harvest cotton—the U.S. economy depended on it—and lawmakers feared that if newly freed people had land of their own they would be unwilling to work in the cotton fields. Most newly freed people were denied access to land of their own, and many resorted to either contract work on plantations or the **SHARECROPPING** system, which often forced them into a lifetime of debt to landowners.

> **SHARECROPPING**
> a system whereby farmers receive supplies and land in exchange for providing a share of the crop to the landowner

The KU KLUX KLAN

In 1866, a secret organization called the KU KLUX KLAN (the KKK) was organized in Tennessee with the purpose of violently opposing civil rights for Black Americans and terrorizing and intimidating Black communities. Wearing disguises and hiding their faces, members attacked Black people, often targeting successful Black men in a community: business owners, elected officials, and those who exercised their right to vote. The KKK often **LYNCHED** their victims. If the local authorities weren't in the KKK themselves (and they frequently were), they often ignored the KKK's activities.

> **LYNCH**
> to execute someone (usually by hanging) without a trial

Congress investigated this increasing violence against Black people and passed the FORCE ACTS in response. These acts, signed by President Grant, allowed the military to enforce the Fourteenth Amendment and protect Black people. The acts curbed KKK activity, but the KKK resurged in the 1920s and still recruits members today.

CARPETBAGGERS AND SCALAWAGS

Northerners who came to work in the South as reformers were known as **CARPETBAGGERS**, after the luggage made of carpet that they used. Carpetbaggers were accused of trying to make a profit from Reconstruction. Southerners who supported the government were known as SCALAWAGS, or rascals. They were seen as traitors to the South.

The PANIC of 1873

In September 1873, a Philadelphia financial firm called JAY COOKE AND COMPANY went bankrupt, setting off the PANIC OF 1873. A major economic depression followed. Republicans were blamed.

The COMPROMISE OF 1877

In the election of 1876, the Republican Party ran RUTHERFORD B. HAYES, the moderate governor of Ohio, against Democrat SAMUEL TILDEN, who fought corruption as governor of New York. Although it appeared that Tilden had won, the Republicans disputed electoral votes from the newly reconstructed states. Congress appointed a commission that led to the COMPROMISE OF 1877: Hayes would become president, but in return federal troops would leave the South and provide Southerners with aid for public projects. The Compromise of 1877 essentially ended Reconstruction.

SOUTHERN "REDEMPTION"

Southern Democrats retook control of their state governments. Seen as the restorers of the "true South," they became known as **REDEEMERS**. They aimed to lower taxes, decrease the size of government—and resist racial equality. Southern states instituted POLL TAXES (requiring people to pay money to vote) and LITERACY TESTS (requiring a certain level of literacy to vote). These measures targeted millions

> **REDEEM**
> to recover or make amends for

of poor and uneducated Black men, denying them their legal right to vote and participate in government. Most white men, even the uneducated and those living below the poverty threshold, were **EXEMPTED** from both the tax and the literacy tests by GRANDFATHER CLAUSES, laws that protected men whose fathers or grandfathers voted before the

> **EXEMPT**
> freed from responsibility

Civil War (because they were white). Even though these laws were discriminatory and unequally enforced, the federal government allowed them to stand because they were not explicitly based on race. Southern states also passed measures known as JIM CROW LAWS, which legalized segregation based on race.

PLESSY v. FERGUSON

When Homer Plessy rode in a whites-only **SEGREGATED** railroad car and was arrested, he sued the railroad company. The Supreme Court ruled in the *PLESSY v. FERGUSON* (1896) decision that segregation was legal as long as facilities for Black people were "SEPARATE BUT EQUAL" to those for whites. The Civil War was over, but racial equality was still a long way away.

> **SEGREGATION**
> the enforced separation of people, specifically on the basis of race

CHECK YOUR KNOWLEDGE

1. When was Reconstruction?

2. What does the Fourteenth Amendment do?

3. Why was President Johnson impeached?

4. To what does the phrase "40 acres and a mule" refer?

5. What was the Compromise of 1877?

6. What was a grandfather clause?

7. What was *Plessy v. Ferguson*?

ANSWERS 303

CHECK YOUR ANSWERS

1. 1865–1877

2. It guarantees the rights of citizenship to everyone born or naturalized in the United States, including due process and equal protection under the law.

3. He broke the Tenure of Office Act by firing a cabinet member without Congress's approval.

4. General Sherman proposed dividing up plantations and giving formerly enslaved people 40 acres of land and a mule. Congress opposed this plan.

5. Hayes would become president, but in return, federal troops would leave the South and provide Southerners with aid for public projects. It was the end of Reconstruction.

6. A grandfather clause exempted white men whose fathers and grandfathers voted before the Civil War from new voting criteria, such as literacy tests and paying poll taxes.

7. The Supreme Court case that ruled that segregation was legal as long as facilities for Black people were "separate but equal" to those for whites.

Unit 6

Reshaping the Nation
1850-1917

The developments that started before the Civil War continued after it. There was even more **EXPANSION**, more **MINING**, and more **INDUSTRY**.
In between the Civil War and World War I, the U.S. turned into the modern nation we recognize today—but getting there took work.

☆ Chapter 24 ☆

TRAINS, BONANZAS,
★ ★ ★ ★ ★ ★ and ★ ★ ★ ★ ★ ★
BUCKAROOS

EAST MEETS WEST

In the early 1860s, the PONY EXPRESS, a mail relay system using horses, connected the East and West. Within a year of its opening, telegraph lines were built in Utah and allowed for messages to be delivered instantly. The Pony Express was rendered obsolete. But the telegraph couldn't carry people or packages . . .

The TRANSCONTINENTAL RAILROAD — DURING THE CIVIL WAR!

Between 1862 and 1864, Congress passed the PACIFIC RAILWAY ACTS. It **SUBSIDIZED** the CENTRAL PACIFIC and UNION PACIFIC railroad companies to build the first transcontinental railroad in the United States.

> **SUBSIDY**
> money given by the government to help an industry or business achieve a public goal

The work was completed by thousands of immigrants, many of whom were Chinese or Irish. The immigrant laborers were paid extremely low wages and subjected to dangerous conditions, harsh weather, and rugged terrain.

The Central Pacific line started in Sacramento, California, heading east, and the Union Pacific line started in Omaha, Nebraska, heading west. On May 10, 1869, the two railroads met in the middle at PROMONTORY, Utah, where Leland Stanford, president of the Central Pacific railroad and former governor of California, drove a GOLDEN SPIKE into the railroad to connect the two lines.

> The **golden spike** was a giant nail used to attach the metal rail of a railroad to the wooden ties (the slats that run perpendicular to the rails) underneath.

TRAIN-ING the NATION

The railroad routes built during the late 1800s led to an explosion in the population of the West. Steel, cattle, and coal industries also grew, and locomotive technology expanded. To make rail travel more uniform, in 1883 the railroad industry created four standard American time zones. (Before that, individual communities kept their own time according to the sun's position.) The railroad affected the life of every American.

COWBOYS
and the
"WILD WEST"

Post—Civil War prosperity in the Northeast created a demand for beef, so RANCHERS (particularly in Texas) raised a lot of cows, using the abundant amount of grass in the Great Plains.

Cows need COWHANDS, or COWBOYS. Cowboys adopted the techniques and clothing of the Mexican vaqueros. When they arrived in a town, they had a reputation for being wild. The need for local lawmen or **VIGILANTES** to control cowboys and outlaws led to the myth of the WILD WEST—even though the West was no more wild than the rest of the country.

> **VIGILANTE**
> a person without legal authority who takes the law into their own hands

One of the most famous peace officers of the western frontier was **WYATT EARP**. He was also a farmer, buffalo hunter, and gambler, and his participation in a gunfight at the O.K. Corral made him an iconic figure of the Wild West.

HOME on the RANGE

The HOMESTEAD ACT, passed in 1862, made federally claimed land in the West available to any **HOMESTEADERS** who wanted to farm it, including women and Black Americans. It gave settlers 160 acres of land (that often belonged to Indigenous people with treaty rights to it) to get started. Originally seen as a desert that couldn't be farmed, the Great Plains proved valuable to farmers who were determined to make use of the land.

The FARMERS ORGANIZE

Population growth

More demand for food

More need for farming

More profits for farmers

More farmers

More food

Too much food

Lower prices

By the mid-1860s farmers were losing money. They blamed high shipping fees, high costs for supplies, and high interest payments.

In 1867, Oliver Hudson Kelley led farmers in creating the NATIONAL **GRANGE** OF THE PATRONS OF HUSBANDRY, an organization that provided social services and set up cost-cutting **COOPERATIVES** for farmers, although the cooperatives weren't successful. The National Grange also lobbied for state regulation of railroad fees and prices.

> **GRANGE**
> a place where grain is stored; an association of farmers

> **COOPERATIVE**
> an organization in which people share costs and profits

SILVER AND GOLD

In 1873, the nation put its currency on the GOLD STANDARD, meaning that the amount of paper money available was determined by the amount of gold in the treasury. Gold was scarce, so less money was in circulation; prices fell because each individual dollar was worth more. The FREE SILVER movement appealed to farmers because as prices fell, their profits did, too. The Free Silver movement advocated adding silver into the mix to produce more money, which would lead to INFLATION.

POPULISM and the ELECTION of 1892

SECOND PRESIDENT ASSASSINATED—THE ASSASSIN WANTED ARTHUR TO BE PRESIDENT!

Following Presidents JAMES GARFIELD and CHESTER A. ARTHUR, GROVER CLEVELAND was elected in 1884. During Cleveland's presidency, Congress passed the INTERSTATE COMMERCE ACT in 1887, regulating the railroad industry.

In 1892, during PRESIDENT BENJAMIN HARRISON's term, the political activism of farmers and the Free Silver movement led to the formation of the **POPULIST PARTY**, a new political faction with a platform of federal regulation, Free Silver, and workers' rights. In the 1892 presidential election, the Populist Party ran James B. Weaver, but Grover Cleveland decided on another (nonconsecutive) run for president and won. Then the PANIC OF 1893 set off an economic depression that devastated the country and strengthened the Populist cause.

> **POPULIST**
> having to do with populism, the political philosophy of focusing on "average" people

Remember: The **PANIC OF 1837** took place during the Jackson and Van Buren administrations.

AAAAHHHH!!!

The **PANIC OF 1873** took place during the Grant presidency.

The **PANIC OF 1893** took place during Cleveland's presidency.

WAIT, WHICH PANIC IS THIS?!

The ELECTION of 1896

In 1896, an anti-silver candidate, WILLIAM McKINLEY, ran on the Republican presidential ticket. WILLIAM JENNINGS BRYAN, a Free Silver politician, ran on the Democratic ticket and was endorsed by the Populist Party. McKinley won the 1896 presidential election, and the Populist Party fell apart.

The END of the FRONTIER

Free land for homesteaders began to run out. The U.S. government was under pressure to make more land available. The federal government decided to open up land in what is now Oklahoma and was then called "Indian Territory," the land where many Indigenous nations were forcibly relocated by the Indian Removal Act. This land was supposed to be a permanent place for Indigenous people to settle, and the displaced nations had set up a thriving community there. Even so, this was the last place that the U.S. considered "unsettled." At noon on April 22, 1889, thousands of settlers rushed into the territory to stake their claims to land. According to the historian FREDERICK JACKSON TURNER, the **FRONTIER**, considered the last of the unsettled land, was finished.

> **FRONTIER**
> the border of a settled territory and the area of land near or beyond the border

YEE-HAW!

Oklahomans are known as **SOONERS** because although the land that would eventually become Oklahoma officially opened up on April 22, some farmers and ranchers rushed into the territory sooner to claim the best land.

CHECK YOUR KNOWLEDGE

1. Why was the Pony Express first needed, and why did it later become obsolete?

2. Which two railway companies collaborated on the first transcontinental railroad?

3. Which industries were most affected by the railroad expansion?

4. Why were time zones invented?

5. Why was the West known for being "wild"?

6. What was the gold standard?

7. Who were the Sooners?

8. To whom did the territory now called Oklahoma belong when the federal government opened it up to settlers?

ANSWERS 313

CHECK YOUR ANSWERS

1. It was needed to communicate with the West, and it was made obsolete by telegraphs.

2. Union Pacific and Central Pacific

3. Steel, cattle, and coal

4. In order to coordinate train schedules

5. Cowboys and outlaws led to a need for local policing, and thus to the myth of the Wild West—even though the West wasn't more wild than the rest of the country.

6. A system where the amount of paper money available was determined by the amount of gold in the treasury

7. Eager farmers and ranchers who rushed into the Oklahoma territory to claim land before it was officially open

8. It belonged to the displaced Indigenous nations that were forcibly relocated there during the Trail of Tears.

☆ Chapter 25 ☆

COLLISION OF

⭐ ⭐ ⭐ ⭐ ⭐ ⭐ ⭐ ⭐ ⭐ ⭐ ⭐

CULTURES

LAND CONFLICT... AGAIN

Even as the Civil War raged in the East, federal expansion policy prompted Americans to settle the West, creating conflict with the Indigenous people. Once the war was over, westward migration increased, and many of the troops who had fought in the Civil War turned their attention to what would be a period of Indian Wars.

Conflict between the U.S. government and Indigenous Americans continued throughout the 1860s. In 1863, the U.S. Army burned Navajo villages to force the people to make the **"LONG WALK,"** a painful 300-mile trek to their appointed reservation in New Mexico, which killed many Navajo along the way. In 1864, the Colorado militia opened fire on a Cheyenne camp in the **SAND CREEK MASSACRE**. Although the Cheyenne, led by **CHIEF BLACK KETTLE**, retaliated, they eventually agreed to stop fighting.

These troops included Black men who became known, among Indigenous peoples, as Buffalo Soldiers because of their thick, dark hair.

INDIGENOUS CULTURE
on the PLAINS

The original inhabitants of the plains of North America were hunting-farming societies. Beginning in the 17th century many of these groups, now expert horsemen, became fully nomadic hunting cultures. These include the Blackfoot, Cheyenne, Kiowa, Ojibwe, Lakota, and Comanche, among others. Though these peoples shared the plains and often traded with more sedentary Plains peoples like the Iowa, Omaha, Osage, Pawnee, and Dakota, relations were not always peaceful, because they competed for many of the same resources.

> **LAKOTA OR SIOUX?**
> In Anglo-American history, the Lakota are incorrectly called the "Sioux" (pronounced SUE). It comes from the Ojibwe and means "little snakes." The Lakota, who were enemies of the Ojibwe, prefer to be called **LAKOTA**.

The nomadic groups traveled long distances hunting buffalo and living in small extended family groups while having close ties to other bands who spoke the same language. The size of their mobile villages was fluid and depended on the season. Councils, not individual people, made decisions for the group. Land was held in common and could not be bought or sold. American expansion was a clear threat to these people, so they began to attack railroad work crews, isolated homesteaders, and migrants headed west on any number of trails. This provoked a federal response.

RESISTANCE to RESERVATIONS

The U.S. government built military forts to defend travelers and settlers in the West. In 1866, a group of Oglala Lakota warriors led by RED CLOUD began a series of attacks against those forts to defend their territory and discourage continued settler migration. In treaty negotiations, the U.S. government agreed to abandon its forts and created **RESERVATIONS**. The Indigenous societies were forced to accept the treaties. The Lakota were removed (often forcefully) from their ancestral lands, with their removals overseen by the Bureau of Indian Affairs.

> **RESERVATION**
> land reserved by a government for a specific group of people, often Indigenous people

The idea behind the RESERVATION SYSTEM was that a specific group would live in a designated area where they could continue to hold land in common and practice their traditions. This would allow settler expansion to proceed peacefully. There were two main problems: The territories set aside were rarely large enough to support the group assigned to it, and many groups refused to go. That refusal, and the settlers' greed for the resources on the ancestral lands of Indigenous people, provoked a more violent federal response.

CUSTER'S LAST STAND

In 1874, soldiers led by LIEUTENANT GENERAL GEORGE ARMSTRONG CUSTER discovered gold in the Black Hills region of the Lakota reservation, as established by the Second Treaty of Fort Laramie. The government asked to buy the land, but CHIEF SITTING BULL (of the Hunkpapa band of Lakota) refused to sell. As gold hunters flooded the region, Sitting Bull and CHIEF CRAZY HORSE (of the Oglala Lakota) encouraged Indigenous people to resist.

By 1876, three large groups of federal forces were tracking these bands across the plains to force them onto reservation lands. General Custer led one of these groups. On June 25, when Custer's scouts spotted a large encampment of Lakota, Cheyenne, and Arapaho on the banks of the Little Bighorn River, Custer took about a third of the 1,200 men under his command to get a closer look. When Custer saw the large village, he sent for reinforcements. While the men with him rested in the midday sun waiting for men and ammo, Indigenous warriors

> Most of the men in Custer's regiment did, in fact, survive the encounter at Little Bighorn.

quietly surrounded them. None of this group, including Custer, survived to tell what happened next, but Indigenous warriors compared the attack to a buffalo hunt. The rest of Custer's regiment discovered the battlefield the next day.

RESISTANCE to REMOVAL

Although Little Bighorn was a major victory for the Cheyenne and Lakota, it was also their last stand. The federal government sent in more troops and hunted the Indigenous resisters, now broken into smaller, more mobile bands. Fleeing into the mountains and away from their villages when under attack, Lakota heard their horses slaughtered and watched as their villages were burned to the ground. In 1877, Crazy Horse accompanied his band onto a reservation. In 1881, after fleeing to Canada and living there for several years, Sitting Bull surrendered and was sent to a reservation, where he was later killed by reservation authorities.

Isolated resistance continued, though. In 1877, CHIEF JOSEPH disobeyed the forced removal order and attempted to lead the Nez Percé from present-day Oregon to Canada, instead of to their designated reservation in Idaho. He eventually gave in after the U.S. Army threatened to attack. GERONIMO led Apache resistance from the 1870s until his surrender in 1886.

Buffalo were virtually hunted into extinction between 1850 and 1880. The new settlers hunted buffalo for tongues and hides, and left the rest of the body to rot on the plains. The railroads wanted fewer buffalo because large herds caused delays in schedules, and ranchers wanted to raise their cows with less competition on the plains. The underlying and sometimes stated purpose of federal and local programs that promoted buffalo hunting was to starve the Indigenous people dependent on this food source so that they would have to go live on reservations. The population of what may have been 60 million buffalo in 1800 was reduced to less than 400 by 1900!

ASSIMILATION EFFORTS

Some Americans called openly for the elimination of Indigenous groups actively resisting reservations, whereas others thought that assimilation was a better solution. (This echoed President Thomas Jefferson's approach, but it did not keep the Cherokees from being forced to leave their homelands under the Indian Removal Act.)

> **ALLOTMENT**
> a portion or share, as of land

The first assimilation strategy employed by the government was to transform the Plains peoples' relationship to the land. Congress passed the DAWES GENERAL ALLOTMENT ACT in 1887, splitting Indigenous American land into privately owned **ALLOTMENTS** to be used for farming, which was in direct contrast to their traditional communal ownership of land. Like the Homestead Act, allotments were 160 acres (often insufficient for a family). If the land wasn't used for farming, the federal government could reclaim it and sell it to American settlers.

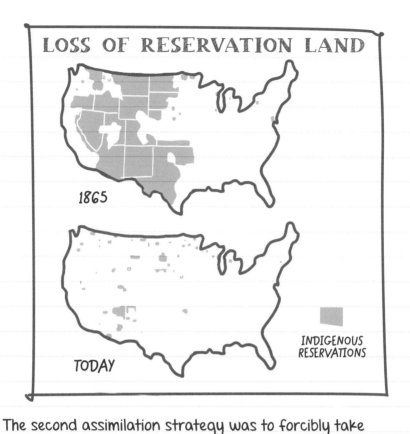

LOSS OF RESERVATION LAND

1865

TODAY

INDIGENOUS
RESERVATIONS

The second assimilation strategy was to forcibly take
Indigenous children away from their parents and educate
them to be culturally American. Captain Richard H. Pratt,
founder of the CARLISLE SCHOOL,
the first boarding school created for
this purpose, was explicit that his intent
was to "kill the Indian, save the man." As part of this cultural
genocide, students were stripped of their traditional clothing,
given American names, and punished for speaking their
Indigenous languages. By 1926, over 80 percent of school-
age Indigenous children were living away from their families
in more than 350 boarding schools across the nation. They

OLYMPIAN JIM THORPE
GRADUATED FROM HERE.

suffered physical and emotional abuse far away from their loved ones, to whom some of these students never returned. The consequences of the psychological damage done to the Indigenous children is still being felt generations later.

INDIGENOUS POPULATION in CRISIS

Many Indigenous Americans hoped to reclaim their crumbling culture and their stolen lands. Some turned to a religious movement led by a prophet named WOKOVA, a Paiute medicine man. Based on a vision, Wokova taught that if the Plains people lived good lives and performed the traditional GHOST DANCE properly, the American settlers would disappear, and the buffalo would return. The Ghost Dance movement spread, and fears that it represented a new united coalition of Indigenous peoples against the government led to yet another tragedy.

On December 9, 1890, American troops attacked and killed up to 300 Lakota (mostly children and older adults) who were gathered for a Ghost Dance in the WOUNDED KNEE MASSACRE. This was the last major clash between the U.S. government and Indigenous Americans. Over the course of the 19th century the Indigenous population of the United States had fallen from 600,000 in 1800 to less than 230,000 in 1890.

CHECK YOUR KNOWLEDGE

1. Why were reservations created?

2. Why did Indigenous Americans sign treaties forcing them onto reservations?

3. What happened to the buffalo population in the 1800s?

4. What was the "Long Walk"?

5. Who won at the Battle of the Little Bighorn?

6. How did the U.S. government make money from the Dawes Act?

7. Why did the U.S. government take Indigenous children away from their families?

8. What was the Ghost Dance movement?

ANSWERS 323

CHECK YOUR ANSWERS

1. To move Indigenous communities onto smaller parcels of land, and open up more land for settlers

2. They were forced to and forcibly removed from their land.

3. It was hunted into near extinction.

4. It was the journey the Navajo were forced to make from their homeland to their reservation.

5. Crazy Horse and Sitting Bull led the Lakota and Cheyenne to a victory.

6. If land in reservation allotments was not used for farming it was sold to settlers.

7. They were sent to boarding schools to be assimilated and "Americanized."

8. A religious movement led by Wokova who preached that if Plains people lived good lives and performed the Ghost Dance, settlers would disappear and buffalo would return

☆ Chapter 26 ☆

The SECOND INDUSTRIAL

★ ★ ★ ★ ★ ★ ★ ★ ★ ★ ★

REVOLUTION

The SECOND INDUSTRIAL REVOLUTION

In the late 1800s, industry was revolutionized for a second time, creating a SECOND INDUSTRIAL REVOLUTION. After the Civil War, the U.S. became one of the leading industrial powers in the world, and businesses such as steel and railroads grew by leaps and bounds. Business tycoons, notably the RAILROAD BARONS (those who rose to prominence in the railroad industry) flourished, and life changed for people of every income level.

INVENTIONS GALORE

Industrial growth, especially in the railroad sector, fueled a demand for new technology, and each new innovation led to others. Many of America's most significant technological developments came about in the late 19th century.

AMERICAN INVENTIONS GALORE

BEEP! BEEP!

1851: ISAAC SINGER improved on the original 1845 SEWING MACHINE design, enabling the garment industry to begin replacing at-home clothing construction.

1866: The first TRANSATLANTIC TELEGRAPH wire was put in place.

1867: The first commercially successful TYPEWRITER was invented by Christopher Sholes, Carlos Glidden, and Samuel W. Soule.

1876: ALEXANDER GRAHAM BELL invented the TELEPHONE and started the Bell Telephone Company, launching the telecom industry.

1876: THOMAS EDISON opened a lab in Menlo Park, New Jersey, and went on to patent more than 1,000 inventions. In 1879, he developed a version of the electric lightbulb that was cheap to make and made available to many.

1886: GEORGE WESTINGHOUSE founded the Westinghouse Electric Company, which expanded the power grid created by Edison.

1888: The ADDING MACHINE, an early calculator patented by William Seward Burroughs, facilitated business transactions, and the KODAK CAMERA brought snapshot photography to the mainstream thanks to George Eastman.

1903: ORVILLE AND WILBUR WRIGHT made the first airplane flight at KITTY HAWK, NORTH CAROLINA, on December 17.

1908: HENRY FORD devised the Model T car. Created by his innovative assembly line system, the car was affordable enough for many middle-class Americans to own.

ASSEMBLY LINE → If everyone on the line does one job over and over (specialization and division of labor), people working together can produce more in a shorter time period. Those workers are also paid less because they have fewer skills.

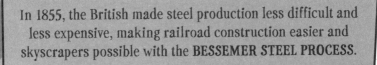

In 1855, the British made steel production less difficult and less expensive, making railroad construction easier and skyscrapers possible with the BESSEMER STEEL PROCESS.

With new inventions also came a higher demand for fuel. After Edwin L. Drake's 1859 discovery of CRUDE OIL (which could be turned into kerosene for lighting lamps and used as fuel) underground in Pennsylvania, the petroleum industry began to skyrocket.

The CORPORATION

As businesses grew, many of them became too expensive or risky for one person to own. Instead, CORPORATIONS owned them and SHAREHOLDERS controlled them, meaning less risk, as well as the promise of **DIVIDENDS**. Selling **STOCK** was an easy way for corporations to raise **CAPITAL**, and banks could make a profit through involvement in corporate finances.

DIVIDENDS
sums of money paid to shareholders of a corporation from its earnings

STOCK
a share of a corporation, entitling the owner to a portion of the company's profits

CAPITAL
in this context, financial assets

HORIZONTAL and VERTICAL INTEGRATION

Some individual businessmen were so successful that they gained worldwide recognition, like JOHN D. ROCKEFELLER. Rockefeller founded an oil refinery in 1863, which became the STANDARD OIL COMPANY of Ohio in 1870. Before long, Standard Oil controlled almost the entire American petroleum industry, because Rockefeller created a **MONOPOLY** by driving his competition out of business.

In 1882, he founded the Standard Oil **TRUST**, a corporate board that bought stock in and controlled many companies in the industry. Standard Oil then owned its competition and could set prices across the industry. Once Rockefeller controlled the industry, he found ways

> **MONOPOLY**
> when one company or person controls an entire market
>
> **TRUST**
> a group of companies controlled by a single corporate board

to make even more profit, including demanding that railroads charge him less to transport his products. The railroads complied; if they didn't, they would lose too much business.

Another famous businessman of the time was the Scottish-born steelmaker ANDREW CARNEGIE, who began his career as a railroad employee and, after making smart investments in steel and iron, founded the CARNEGIE STEEL COMPANY. Carnegie controlled every step of the manufacturing process, a tactic known as VERTICAL INTEGRATION: He owned not only the steel mills, but also the mines, the transportation,

VERTICAL INTEGRATION (Carnegie)

HORIZONTAL INTEGRATION (Rockefeller)

and the warehouses. He was able to cut costs and ensure a better product. Unlike Rockefeller, Carnegie did not intend to take over his competition (that tactic is known as HORIZONTAL INTEGRATION).

ROBBER BARONS and PHILANTHROPISTS

GILDED
covered in gold, but not made of it

There was so much inequality that the period between 1869 and 1896 became known as the **GILDED AGE**, because it looked like gold on the outside but was something crude on the inside. People like Rockefeller were called ROBBER BARONS, meaning that while they lived like nobility, they were also unethical men who had used trickery and exploitation to become wealthy while their laborers suffered and saw very little of the profits. In July 1890, Congress passed the SHERMAN ANTITRUST ACT. Based on the concept that competition is necessary in free markets, it made trusts and monopolies illegal. It was difficult to enforce, and many trusts continued to operate anyway.

Carnegie published an article that came to be known as "The Gospel of Wealth." He said that it was the wealthy's responsibility to society to act philanthropically.

Regardless of how they obtained their wealth, Carnegie and Rockefeller both were **PHILANTHROPISTS**, giving

PHILANTHROPIST
someone who gives to charity

330

away large amounts and founding establishments such as Carnegie Hall and the Rockefeller Institute.

LIFE in the FACTORY

Although many businessmen prospered, factory workers faced long hours, low pay, and unhealthy conditions. At this time, factory workers were not only adults but children as well. As automation increased and skilled labor was less necessary, workers themselves became part of the machine—and many bosses treated them as such.

UNIONS

Although unions and trade guilds had existed before, they grew in size and scope. The first national union, the KNIGHTS OF LABOR, was founded in Philadelphia in 1869. Originally established as a secret society to protect its members from employer retaliation, the organization went public, under the leadership of Terence V. Powderly, in the 1880s. Unlike most unions, the knights of Labor welcomed women, Black people, and unskilled laborers—but Asians were still excluded.

With its large membership, the knights tried to use the tactic of **COLLECTIVE BARGAINING** to secure pay equality and other workplace rights. In 1886,

> **COLLECTIVE BARGAINING**
> the idea of workers acting together, or collectively, giving workers the power to persuade the management to make a compromise

SAMUEL GOMPERS founded the AMERICAN FEDERATION OF LABOR (AFL), a coalition of many smaller unions of skilled workers, which became a much more influential organization.

GOING on STRIKE

Although **STRIKES** helped unions fight businesses, they also sometimes damaged the reputation of the unions, some of which came to be seen as violent **ANARCHIST** groups.

STRIKE
when employees refuse to work, usually in an attempt to negotiate a change in working conditions

ANARCHIST
opposed to government and/or law

The Haymarket Affair, Chicago, Illinois, 1886:
When the McCormick Harvester Company hired strikebreaking workers, a scuffle followed, killing a union member. This led to a protest at Haymarket Square in which several civilians and eight policemen were killed, and public opinion turned against the strikers.

The Homestead Strike, Homestead, Pennsylvania, 1892:
At Andrew Carnegie's Homestead steel mill, a strike led to a fight that resulted in ten deaths. The state militia was called in.

The Pullman Strike, Pullman, Illinois, 1894:
When EUGENE DEBS, the president of the American Railway Union, led a strike at the Pullman Palace Car Company over pay cuts, President Cleveland called in soldiers to put an end to the strike, which had shut down many railroads across the country.
Debs went to prison.

CHECK YOUR KNOWLEDGE

1. How did the Bessemer Steel Process affect the steel industry?

2. Why are assembly lines important?

3. Why was crude oil in higher demand in the mid-1800s than it had been before?

4. How did the Standard Oil Trust help create a monopoly for Standard Oil?

5. Why was Rockefeller seen as a "robber baron"?

6. What were the terms of the Sherman Antitrust Act?

7. Why were the Knights of Labor originally a secret society?

8. How did strikes affect labor unions' reputations?

ANSWERS

CHECK YOUR ANSWERS

1. Steel got cheaper and easier to make.
2. They allow faster, cheaper production through division of labor.
3. New inventions needed fuel.
4. The trust owned Standard Oil's competitors and could control prices across the industry.
5. He lived like nobility and gained his wealth through unethical trusts and monopolies, while the many people who worked for him suffered and were paid poorly.
6. It made trusts and monopolies illegal, to allow fair business competition.
7. To protect their members from being retaliated against by employers
8. Unions became unfairly associated with anarchist movements because some strikes turned violent.

ANY THOUGHTS?

I GIVE IT A WEEK.

☆ Chapter 27 ☆

NEW IMMIGRANTS,
✶ ☆ ✰ ✰ ✰ ✶ ✰ ✶ ✰ ✰ ✰ ✶
NEW CITIES

The NEW IMMIGRANTS

The 1880s was another period of increased immigration to the U.S. During the first major wave of immigration, most immigrants had come from Western and Northern Europe. The "new immigrants" were largely from Eastern and Southern Europe, as well as Asia and Mexico.

The reasons for both waves of immigration were mostly the same. Immigrants strived to escape the overcrowding, religious and political persecution, and economic problems of their homelands. They hoped for a better life in the U.S.

ELLIS ISLAND

After immigrants completed the often treacherous journey to the U.S., they had one last hurdle to cross: the immigration processing center, where their health, legal status, and destination were confirmed. Many immigrants had their names misspelled, shortened, or otherwise "Americanized." The most famous immigration processing center was ELLIS ISLAND in New York Harbor. Most of those who came through Ellis Island were Europeans who had crossed the Atlantic Ocean. Immigrants from Asian countries usually crossed the Pacific Ocean and entered the U.S. through the Bay Area's ANGEL ISLAND, and Mexican immigrants tended to arrive through an immigration center in El Paso, Texas.

The **STATUE OF LIBERTY**, installed in New York Harbor in 1886, was a gift to the U.S. from France. The poem on the base of the statue includes the famous lines
"Give me your tired, your poor,
Your huddled masses yearning to breathe free"
(from "The New Colossus," by **EMMA LAZARUS**).
To many immigrants, the first sight of the statue represented a new beginning and the American dream.

BECOMING "AMERICAN"

Like previous immigrants, the new immigrants tended to settle in ethnically divided neighborhoods where they could continue speaking the language and practicing the religion, cuisine, and traditions of their homelands. However, the new immigrants were more likely to be of different races, and the diversity they brought to cities was often seen as a negative by the people who already occupied the land. Some

U.S. citizens feared the immigrants would "take" jobs away from citizens by working for less, whereas others thought that the

ASSIMILATE
to blend in

immigrants should **ASSIMILATE** into American culture as quickly as possible. NATIVISM, an opposition to immigration, was on the rise again. Racism against immigrants of color increased and would become formalized.

In 1882, Congress passed the CHINESE EXCLUSION ACT, which banned immigration from China for ten years (the act was renewed twice, for a total of 30 years). Congress also limited immigration from Japan and (unsuccessfully) attempted to restrict all immigration by people who were illiterate. Convicts and people with certain illnesses were banned from coming to the U.S.

Although immigrants were encouraged to **AMERICANIZE**, the notion of being "American" could not be defined. As immigrants assimilated, the meaning of what it meant to be American changed. America was becoming a **"MELTING POT"**: a blending of cultures.

URBANIZATION

Most immigrants moved to cities. As machinery reduced the need for farm labor, those workers also began coming to cities in the North for factory work, as did many Black Americans from the South. It was a time of great URBANIZATION, or growth of cities.

337

Many immigrants, including women and children, ended up working in factories or **SWEATSHOPS** under harsh conditions for very low pay.

> **SWEATSHOP**
> a factory defined by its poor working conditions and low wages

Immigrant farmers could not always afford to purchase their own land and often had no choice but to accept the work.

CITY LIFE

For the growing MIDDLE CLASS, turn-of-the-century cities were places of innovation and excitement:

The steel industry and the invention of the **ELEVATOR** (patented by **ELISHA OTIS**) allowed buildings to be taller; building up rather than out conserved city space. The first **SKYSCRAPER** was a ten-story building constructed in Chicago in 1884.

Next time you're in an elevator, look for a logo. The **OTIS ELEVATOR COMPANY** is still a major producer of elevators.

Public transportation enabled travel. San Francisco installed its **CABLE CARS** in 1873, and Richmond, Virginia, introduced **TROLLEYS**, electric cars to replace horse-drawn streetcars. Boston opened up its subway system in 1897, and New York City's followed in 1904.

Construction of **CENTRAL PARK** was completed in 1873. Designed by **FREDERICK LAW OLMSTED**, the park was built when New York recognized the importance of having a green space; other major parks were built during this same time period.

However, cities were still in need of development. The working class often lived in dangerous tenements that were unhygienic and overcrowded. Areas with many tenements became SLUMS—places filled with poverty—which led to increased crime. City sewage systems were not equipped to handle so many people. Earthquakes and fires could destroy large sections of cities at a time because of unsafe building standards. Many middle class people could afford to move to the SUBURBS, now easier to reach because of better transportation.

REFORMING the CITIES

Local governments did little to address the problems of the cities, especially for immigrants. However, individual activists tried to make a difference. Photojournalist Jacob Riis took photos of slums to expose their terrible conditions. Others set up SETTLEMENT HOUSES to provide social services to people living below the poverty threshold. New York's NEIGHBORHOOD GUILD, founded in 1886 by Charles Stover and Stanton Coit, was the first. The most famous settlement house was Chicago's HULL HOUSE, founded in 1889 by JANE ADDAMS and Ellen Gates Starr.

CHECK YOUR KNOWLEDGE

1. What was new about the new immigrants?

2. Why did the new immigrants make the trip to the U.S.?

3. What was the point of immigration processing centers?

4. Why did some people want to stop immigrants from coming to the U.S.?

5. How does the concept of a "melting pot" apply to the assimilation of immigrants in the U.S.?

6. What were the causes of urbanization during the Second Industrial Revolution?

7. How did certain areas of American cities become slums?

8. What led to the growth of the suburbs?

9. Why did Jacob Riis take photographs of people in the slums?

10. Why were settlement houses necessary?

ANSWERS ⇒ 341

CHECK YOUR ANSWERS

1. They were from Southern and Eastern Europe rather than Northern and Western Europe. There were also Asian and Mexican immigrants.

2. Economic problems, religious and political persecution, overcrowding, poverty, and the hope of a better life

3. To determine the health, destinations, and legal status of each immigrant

4. They were afraid immigrants would "take" jobs by working for less.

5. When immigrants become part of American culture, they also add their own heritage to the mix and expand what it means to be American.

6. Immigrants usually moved to cities and many people (especially Black Americans) were moving North, because fewer farmworkers were needed to do the same amount of work.

7. Too many people lived there without adequate public services.

8. Bad urban housing, transportation improvements, and the growth of the middle class

9. To educate others about the unsafe conditions

10. The government was not providing for people living below the poverty threshold.

Chapter 28

★ ★ ☆ ★ ☆ ★ ★ ★ ☆ ★ ☆ ★

PROGRESS! (ivism)

★ ★ ☆ ★ ☆ ★ ★ ★ ☆ ★ ☆ ★

CONSUMERISM and LEISURE TIME

> **CONSUMERISM**
> increasing consumption; focus on consumption and purchasing

Industrialization led to long hours in the factories, but unlike farmers, factory workers (and the wealthy) had days off. In the late 1800s, as LEISURE TIME became more common, so did activities such as

{ shopping in **DEPARTMENT STORES,** which encouraged **CONSUMERISM** via advertisements }

{ amusement parks, such as CONEY ISLAND in New York }

{ VAUDEVILLE, circuses, and other theater }

{ WORLD'S FAIRS, where consumers, merchants, and innovators came together }

CORRUPTION in the GILDED AGE

Political parties used illegal means (like bribes and extortion) and legal means (like persuading those living below the poverty threshold to vote a certain way by promising them jobs) to control elections. These organizations were called POLITICAL MACHINES, and their leader was the BOSS. The most famous political machine was New York's Democratic TAMMANY HALL, led by WILLIAM MAGEAR "BOSS" TWEED, who is said to have stolen millions of dollars from the city.

The PROGRESSIVE MOVEMENT

Some people, known as SOCIALISTS, believed that government should take complete ownership of corrupt businesses. Others, known as PROGRESSIVES, thought the government should regulate, not control. They aimed to democratize American society, and many of their reforms were to give the people a greater say in government. The PROGRESSIVE MOVEMENT in the 1890s aimed to fix social and economic problems, particularly in cities.

MUCKRAKERS

The Progressives gained support for their cause from journalists known as MUCKRAKERS, who exposed the "muck" of society. Famous muckrakers included IDA TARBELL, who exposed the oil trusts in her book *THE HISTORY OF THE STANDARD OIL COMPANY* (1904); UPTON SINCLAIR, who wrote about the meatpacking industry's awful labor conditions in his novel *THE JUNGLE* (1906); and JACOB RIIS, who displayed tenement life in his book of photographs *HOW THE OTHER HALF LIVES* (1889). Another muckraker, LINCOLN STEFFENS, exposed political machines.

REFORMERS and THEIR PROJECTS

Many of the most active Progressives in the country were middle-class women who were well educated but were expected to stop working outside the home when they got married. By the turn of the century, families tended to be smaller, and technology (like the vacuum cleaner) helped with housework, freeing up more of women's time to create change. Many reform movements grew.

POLITICAL REFORM

Supported by President Arthur, the Pendleton Civil Service Act (1883) created a civil service exam to evaluate job candidates on the basis of merit, putting an end to the spoils system at the federal level.

CONTINUED

POLITICAL REFORM (continued)

Wisconsin held the first PRIMARY ELECTION
in 1903, prompting voters to become
more involved in national politics.

Oregon introduced VOTER INITIATIVES (for citizens
to propose laws), REFERENDA (to approve laws), and
RECALLS (to remove officials before the end of their
term), allowing voters more control over state politics.

Adopted in 1913, the SIXTEENTH AMENDMENT established
a federal income tax, which gave government
funding to do, in the Progressives' view, great things.

Ratified in 1913, the SEVENTEENTH AMENDMENT gave the
people the right to elect their senators directly rather
than through the often corrupt state legislatures.

EDUCATION REFORM

Progressives like JOHN DEWEY advocated changes
in public education to place greater emphasis on
understanding rather than on rote memorization.

Settlement houses offered
some of the first
kindergarten classes.

Compulsory education laws
were designed not only to
educate children but to
eliminate child labor.

ANTI-ALCOHOL REFORM
(TEMPERANCE)

Organizations like the WOMAN'S CHRISTIAN **TEMPERANCE** UNION and the ANTI-SALOON LEAGUE worked to prohibit alcohol, which they saw as the cause of social problems.

TEMPERANCE
abstaining from drinking alcohol

PROHIBITION
period in American history when alcohol was illegal

Temperance activist CARRIE NATION charged into saloons and destroyed liquor bottles with an ax.

Ratified in 1919, the EIGHTEENTH AMENDMENT began **PROHIBITION**, the period during which the production, sale, and transport of alcohol were illegal in the U.S.

LABOR REFORM

Since children could be paid less than adults, CHILD LABOR was commonly used. Many people advocated placing limits on child labor, but congressional limits were deemed unconstitutional.

In 1905, a Socialist union called the INDUSTRIAL WORKERS OF THE WORLD was established, and it welcomed women, minorities, and others who could not join the American Federation of Labor (AFL).

Following the 1911 TRIANGLE **SHIRTWAIST** COMPANY factory fire in New York, which killed nearly 150 workers (mostly young women) who were locked inside by the company owners to prevent theft, the INTERNATIONAL LADIES' GARMENT WORKERS Union advocated for increased workplace safety.

In 1912, Massachusetts created the first minimum wage law.

SHIRTWAIST
a common term for a lady's shirt during the early 20th century

WOMEN'S RIGHTS

Once slavery was banned, many former abolitionists turned their attention to women's **SUFFRAGE**. In 1869, the NATIONAL AMERICAN WOMAN SUFFRAGE ASSOCIATION (NAWSA) was formed, and its leaders were Elizabeth Cady Stanton, Susan B. Anthony, Anna Howard Shaw, and Carrie Chapman Catt.

SUFFRAGE
the right to vote

In 1920 the NINETEENTH AMENDMENT was ratified, which prohibited state and federal governments from denying citizens the right to vote based on gender. At last, women had the right to vote—but it was not universally enforced. States passed laws that stopped Black women from voting, and Indigenous and Asian women were not legally considered citizens, so the amendment did not protect them.

FINALLY!!!

SUSAN B. ANTHONY

One of most famous women reformers of the time was Mary Harris Jones, better known as **MOTHER JONES**, who helped organize numerous labor strikes.

Antidiscrimination Movements

The American Jewish Committee and the ANTI-DEFAMATION LEAGUE fought antisemitism, hostility or prejudice against Jewish people; the SOCIETY OF AMERICAN INDIANS advocated for Indigenous American rights; and the Mexican American **MUTUALISTAS** assisted those living in the BARRIOS (labor camps or predominantly Spanish-speaking neighborhoods). Other groups facing discrimination included Catholics, Asians, and Black people.

> **MUTUALISTAS**
> community-based
> aid groups

Within the Black community, two major schools of activism emerged. One was led by BOOKER T. WASHINGTON, who believed that education and financial stability were the keys to equality; that is, if the Black community persevered, equality would automatically follow. Washington struck the ATLANTA COMPROMISE with Southern white leaders, which said that Black people should be resigned to white political rule as long as they could receive education and economic equality. On the opposite side of the spectrum was W.E.B. DU BOIS, who believed that legal equality for Black people would put an end to injustice.

Du Bois used the term "The Talented Tenth" to describe a class of leaders in the Black community that he believed would help create social change.

In 1881, Washington founded the TUSKEGEE INSTITUTE, an agricultural and industrial school in Alabama, and in 1909, Du Bois helped found the NATIONAL ASSOCIATION FOR THE ADVANCEMENT OF COLORED PEOPLE, or NAACP (pronounced "N-double-A-C-P"). It remains one of the most influential civil rights organizations in the U.S.

Another significant Black American figure of the time was GEORGE WASHINGTON CARVER. A member of the Tuskegee faculty, Carver revolutionized Southern agriculture by developing hundreds of uses for peanuts and other crops that were alternatives to cotton.

CHECK YOUR KNOWLEDGE

1. What is a political machine?

2. What is the main difference between Socialist beliefs and Progressive beliefs?

3. Who was Ida Tarbell?

4. Why were many reformers middle-class women?

5. What happened during the Triangle Shirtwaist Company factory fire?

6. When was suffrage granted to women?

7. What did Booker T. Washington and W.E.B. Du Bois disagree about?

ANSWERS 351

CHECK YOUR ANSWERS

1. Political machines are political groups that use illegal and legal means to control election outcomes.

2. Socialists believed that government should take complete ownership of corrupt businesses. Progressives thought the government should regulate, not control.

3. A muckraker who exposed the oil trusts in her book *THE HISTORY OF THE STANDARD OIL COMPANY*

4. They were well educated and had time but were expected not to work outside the home.

5. Nearly 150 workers (mostly young women) were killed because they were locked inside by the company owners to prevent theft.

6. Suffrage was granted to women in 1920. (Though Black women were often prohibited from voting, and Asian and Indigenous women were not considered citizens, so it did not apply to them.)

7. They disagreed about whether the Black community ought to focus on economic freedom or political freedom first.

☆ Chapter 29 ☆

EXPANSIONISM
★ ★ ☆ ★ ☆ and ★ ☆ ★ ☆ ★
IMPERIALISM

Despite progress, many Americans still clung to old ideas, like Manifest Destiny (the belief that the U.S. was "destined" to expand across the North American continent). Even though the continental U.S. had taken shape and it seemed there was nowhere else to go, some Americans wanted to expand overseas.

> **SOCIAL DARWINISM** was a major factor in imperialism. It was a popular idea that technologically advanced societies should rule over and control less advanced societies.

> **IMPERIALISM** the policy of gaining authority over other nations or of acquiring colonies

In Europe, **IMPERIALISM** was at its height as European powers took over nations in Asia and Africa. Many Americans believed that imperialism would bring prosperity and prestige to the U.S. and would allow Americans to spread Western ideals. Since Washington's Farewell Address, the U.S. had steered clear of foreign problems, as Washington had advised—but its agenda was about to change.

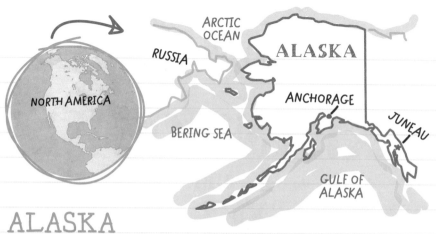

ALASKA

Shortly after the Civil War, Secretary of State WILLIAM SEWARD purchased Russia's claim to ALASKA for $7.2 million. Considering how cold Alaska was, many people considered this a foolish purchase, calling it "SEWARD'S FOLLY" and referring to Alaska as "Seward's Ice Box." As it turned out, Alaska was rich with natural resources, and the U.S. officially annexed it in 1884.

The U.S. in the PACIFIC

The U.S. was becoming increasingly interested in the Pacific to open foreign markets to trade and American business interests. In 1854, COMMODORE MATTHEW PERRY first used gifts and then later displays of military force to pressure Japan to enter into trade relations with the U.S. Japan did not have a navy with which to defend itself, so it had little choice but to enter the agreement. Japan was beginning a period of major modernization, and trade was seen as lucrative.

In 1867, the U.S. annexed the MIDWAY ISLANDS, islands midway between America and Asia where American ships

THE PACIFIC

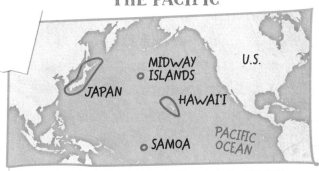

MIDWAY ISLANDS

SAMOA

HAWAIIAN ISLANDS

could stop en route. Still, the U.S. wanted even more of a presence in the Pacific.

HAWAI'I

Since about the beginning of the 19th century, the Hawaiian Islands, which were unified, had been a source of sugar for the U.S. Most of the sugar planters were Americans who had moved there and forced the king of Hawai'i to grant them political power. In 1891, QUEEN LILIUOKALANI came to power and attempted to limit American influence. At about the same time, Congress imposed tariffs on foreign imports, including Hawaiian sugar. The planters lost a lot of money and wanted to overthrow the Hawaiian government so that Hawai'i could become part of the U.S. and the tariffs would be lifted.

THEY OVERTHREW QUEEN LILIUOKALANI

In 1893, planters staged a revolt with the help of the U.S. Marines and the U.S. ambassador to Hawai'i, forming their own government. The Hawaiian people and their leadership did not support the coup. The new government asked to be annexed by the United States. President Benjamin Harrison agreed, but the treaty he signed was not ratified before he left office. President Cleveland, who succeeded him, opposed annexation without the support of the Hawaiian people. It wasn't until 1900, during President McKinley's administration, that Hawai'i became a territory of the U.S. In 1899, the U.S. annexed part of SAMOA, a group of islands 2,500 miles south of Hawai'i.

The OPEN DOOR POLICY

In the second half of the 1800s, European nations and Japan persuaded the weaker nation of China to grant them SPHERES OF INFLUENCE, or areas within China to control. Since the U.S. didn't have a sphere of influence there, in 1899, Secretary of State John Hay suggested an OPEN DOOR POLICY of equal access for multiple imperial powers, including the U.S., to trade with China. There wasn't any reason for the other nations to agree—until the BOXER REBELLION of 1900, in which a Chinese antiforeign secret society known as the Boxers killed a number of foreigners living in China. Once the Boxers were defeated, the imperial powers agreed to Hay's policy and cooperated with one another.

However, Japan soon began ignoring the policy, which started the RUSSO-JAPANESE WAR with Russia. The 1905 TREATY OF PORTSMOUTH ended the Russo-Japanese War, but Japan had become an even greater power, and U.S.-Japanese tensions began to rise.

CHECK YOUR KNOWLEDGE

1. What were the major arguments for imperialism in the U.S.?

2. What was Seward's Folly?

3. How did Commodore Perry persuade Japan to enter into trade relations with the U.S.?

4. Why did the U.S. want territories in the Pacific in the late 1800s?

5. Who was Queen Liliuokalani?

6. Why did President Cleveland oppose President Harrison's plan to annex Hawai'i?

7. What is a sphere of influence?

8. What persuaded other nations to agree to an Open Door Policy with China?

ANSWERS 357

CHECK YOUR ANSWERS

1. People wanted to spread Western ideals, open trade, and increase the prestige of the U.S.

2. Secretary of State William Seward purchased Alaska from Russia for $7.2 million. Most people at the time thought there was nothing but cold up there, so they called the move "Seward's Folly."

3. Commodore Perry used a combination of gifts and threats to persuade Japan to enter into trade relations with the U.S.

4. U.S. ships needed a place to stop on their way to trade with Japan.

5. Queen Liliuokalani was the queen of Hawai'i who tried to limit American influence.

6. President Cleveland opposed annexation without the support of the Hawaiian people.

7. Areas in China that were controlled by foreign nations

8. The Boxer Rebellion of 1900 persuaded other nations to agree to an Open Door Policy with China.

☆ Chapter 30 ☆

SPANISH-AMERICAN WAR

REBELLION in CUBA

While U.S. influence was expanding, Spanish influence was shrinking. Many of Spain's colonies in the Americas declared independence, and those remaining were eager to be free of Spanish rule. In 1895, Cuban revolutionary JOSÉ MARTÍ returned from exile to lead the fight for Cuban independence. This worried many in the U.S., who were concerned about trade with Cuba and the island's proximity to Florida. However, neither President Cleveland, who was in his second term at the time, nor his successor, President McKinley, wanted to interfere.

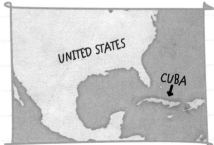

UNITED STATES

CUBA

YELLOW JOURNALISM

The fighting in Cuba became very violent, and Spanish troops treated Cuban prisoners terribly. The American public was shocked, but shock sold newspapers. In a tactic known as YELLOW JOURNALISM, Joseph Pulitzer and William Randolph Hearst exaggerated and sensationalized the stories, stirring up public fury. They were in competition with each other, and scandals sold well.

REMEMBER the *MAINE*!

McKinley wished to avoid war. However, uprisings in Havana, the capital of Cuba, put Americans in the area in danger. McKinley sent the ship USS *MAINE* to Havana in January 1898 to protect them. With no warning, the ship exploded on February 15. Although evidence later suggested that it was an accident, Spain was blamed, and "REMEMBER THE *MAINE*!" became a rallying cry for war.

On April 20, Congress recognized Cuban independence and demanded that Spanish troops leave the island. In the TELLER AMENDMENT, the U.S. said that it had no interest in controlling Cuba. On April 25, 1898, Congress declared war on Spain. The SPANISH-AMERICAN WAR had begun.

DEWEY in the PHILIPPINES

The Philippines were another holding of the Spanish Empire, and like the Cubans, the FILIPINOS wanted independence and revolted in the 1890s. When COMMODORE GEORGE DEWEY led an American fleet to the Philippines on April 30, 1898, he had the support of the Filipino people because they thought Americans were helping them win independence. On May 1, in the first battle of the Spanish-American War, Dewey destroyed the Spanish ships in Manila Harbor. It turns out that the U.S. made a secret deal with Spain to win the battle and take control of the city, keeping Filipino forces out of the city center (a betrayal that prompted the Philippine-American War).

The ROUGH RIDERS

HAVANA
ATLANTIC OCEAN
CUBA
CARIBBEAN SEA
SAN JUAN HILL
GUANTÁNAMO

Although the navy did much of the fighting, the army also played a role in the Spanish-American War. Many volunteers signed up to fight, including the FIRST U.S. VOLUNTEER CAVALRY, a diverse regiment of cowboys, students, and others organized by THEODORE "TEDDY" ROOSEVELT that became known as the ROUGH RIDERS. On July 1, 1898, the Rough Riders captured the hills around Santiago, Cuba. They helped the Americans win the BATTLE OF SAN JUAN HILL.

"TEDDY" ROOSEVELT

The TREATY of PARIS (AGAIN [AGAIN])

On August 12, only a few months after fighting had begun, an **ARMISTICE** was declared. The Spanish Empire was over, and the fighting had cost very few American lives. (In fact, many more Americans died of tropical diseases than of battle wounds.) In the 1898 TREATY OF PARIS, signed on December 10, Spain ceded control of Cuba, Puerto Rico, Guam, and the Philippines to the U.S.

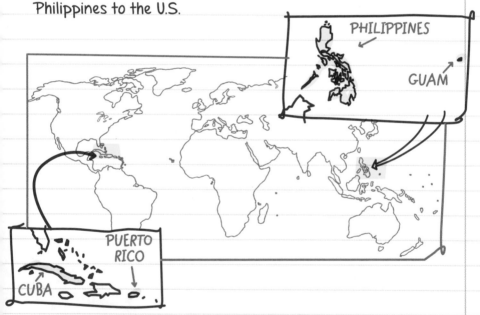

Remember: The **1763 TREATY OF PARIS** ended the Seven Years' War, the **1783 TREATY OF PARIS** ended the Revolutionary War, and the **1898 TREATY OF PARIS** ended the Spanish-American War.

EXPANSIONISM EXPANDS

The United States, instead of Spain, was now the colonizing power of the Pacific. Many Americans, including the founders of the ANTI-IMPERIALIST LEAGUE, thought that the island countries should be given their independence (what they were fighting Spain for in the first place!)—to do otherwise would be **ANATHEMA** to American democratic ideals and betray America's own history of fighting for independence from British colonialism. Others argued that colonies would provide the U.S. with markets, resources, naval stopovers, and places to spread those democratic ideals. The U.S. chose imperialism. And though each country was handled differently, all were denied independence. Here's what happened:

> **ANATHEMA**
> something hated

Cuba became an American **PROTECTORATE**, an independent country with American oversight and military protection. When Cuba rewrote its constitution in 1901, the PLATT AMENDMENT specified that the U.S. still had a right to make decisions for the Cuban government and that the U.S. could maintain a military presence at GUANTÁNAMO BAY.

> **PROTECTORATE**
> a country that is protected and controlled by another, more powerful country

THE LIST CONTINUES

The Philippines became an American colony, prompting their president, Emilio Aguinaldo, to lead another fight for independence. This was the Philippine–American War, in which the Philippines fought for independence against their new colonizer, the U.S. This second struggle in the Philippines was much more challenging for the U.S., but the U.S. managed to capture Aguinaldo in 1901. In 1946, the Philippines became independent by allowing the U.S. to retain military bases there and agreeing to trade agreements favorable to the U.S.

Puerto Rico and Guam became territories, meaning that they were governed by the U.S. and remained under U.S. control. In 1917, Puerto Ricans gained citizenship.

CHECK YOUR KNOWLEDGE

1. Why did the Cuban revolution worry many people in the U.S.?

2. Why did American newspapers sensationalize the conflict in Cuba?

3. Why were people supposed to remember the *MAINE*?

4. What event started the Philippine-American War?

5. Who were the Rough Riders?

6. What happened to the Spanish Empire during the Spanish-American War?

7. Why did the Anti-Imperialist League oppose expansion?

8. What were some arguments for expansion?

9. What happened to the island nations that Spain ceded to the United States?

ANSWERS 365

CHECK YOUR ANSWERS

1. Cuba is very close to Florida, and many American businesses traded with Cuba.

2. To sell newspapers

3. To remember why the U.S. needed to fight Spain

4. When the Philippines revolted against Spain for independence, the U.S. made a secret alliance with Spain, and betrayed Filipino forces in the first battle of the Spanish–American War.

5. They were Teddy Roosevelt's First U.S. Volunteer Cavalry.

6. It fell apart after Spain's defeat, and the U.S. took control of their former territories.

7. They thought imperialism was opposed to American democratic values.

8. Colonies would provide the U.S. with markets for trade and allow the spread of democratic ideals.

9. Cuba became an American protectorate. Puerto Rico and Guam became territories that remained under U.S. control. The Philippines fought the U.S. for independence, and won.

☆ Chapter 31 ☆

A MAN and HIS PLAN:
★ ★ ☆ ★ MORE ☆ ★ ★ ★
IMPERIALISM

Hero of the Spanish–American War TEDDY ROOSEVELT became governor of New York and then vice president during PRESIDENT McKINLEY's second term. When McKinley was assassinated by an anarchist in 1901, Roosevelt, who was 42, became the youngest person to be a U.S. president.

Roosevelt became known as the first conservationist president, founding the U.S. Forest Service. For his work helping to negotiate the Treaty of Portsmouth to end the Russo-Japanese War, Roosevelt also won the Nobel Peace Prize.

 Roosevelt was the inspiration for the **TEDDY BEAR**. He loved to hunt, but during a hunting trip in 1902, he decided not to shoot a bear captured by others in his party. A toy maker heard this story and named the stuffed bear toy he was making after the president.

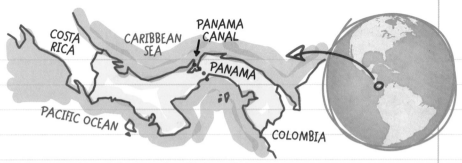

The PANAMA CANAL

The distance between U.S.-controlled land in the Pacific (the Philippines and Hawai'i) and in the Atlantic/Caribbean (Cuba and Puerto Rico) made it difficult for U.S. ships to travel from place to place. The **ISTHMUS** of PANAMA seemed like the perfect place for a canal connecting the two oceans.

> **ISTHMUS**
> a narrow piece of land connecting two larger land masses

The narrow piece of land was owned by Colombia. Knowing that the people of Panama were planning a revolution against Colombia, Roosevelt sent a warship to block Colombian troops from reaching the uprising. The Panamanian revolution was successful. Roosevelt quickly recognized the new nation and negotiated a 99-year lease on the 10-mile-wide CANAL ZONE. The 1903 HAY–BUNAU-VARILLA TREATY established the canal zone and the right of the U.S. to protect it.

Construction of the PANAMA CANAL began in 1904. The work was dangerous, mostly because of malaria and yellow fever carried by mosquitoes, and many workers died before construction was completed ten years later. On August 15, 1914, the *ANCON* was the first ship to make the crossing.

SPEAK SOFTLY and CARRY a BIG STICK

Roosevelt believed that the U.S. had the right and the responsibility to act in Panama as it did. Roosevelt was famous for saying that one ought to "SPEAK SOFTLY AND CARRY A BIG STICK." That is, as the U.S. took greater charge of the Western Hemisphere, Roosevelt saw the nation's role as that of a police officer and reminded other nations of the power of the American military (the "big stick").

The ROOSEVELT COROLLARY

The Monroe Doctrine had warned European nations not to interfere in the Western Hemisphere. At that time, the U.S. didn't have the military power to support that warning. By 1900, that was no longer the case. When several Latin American nations defaulted on debts to European countries, Roosevelt worried that those countries would begin to interfere in the Western Hemisphere.

> **COROLLARY**
> a conclusion that follows naturally from another proposition

To avoid European interference, he released the **ROOSEVELT COROLLARY** to the Monroe Doctrine: It said that the U.S. would only intervene in Latin American countries if those countries couldn't pay their debts or posed a threat to the United States. The U.S. used this to justify imperialistic interference in many Latin American countries, often for economic and political advantage.

ROOSEVELT and the SQUARE DEAL

Roosevelt viewed the presidency as a "bully pulpit," or powerful platform, to advance his political agenda. He was the first president to enforce the Sherman Antitrust Act, fighting trusts that he singled out for working against the public good, a practice that earned him the name "trustbuster."

In 1902, during a UNITED MINE WORKERS strike, Roosevelt was the first president to threaten to use the army to break a strike *on behalf of the union* (he persuaded the company to agree to **ARBITRATION**).

> **ARBITRATION**
> deciding on a question by presenting it to an "arbitrator," a third party; usually used to avoid going to court or having a strike

In his bid for reelection in 1904, Roosevelt ran on the platform that every American deserved a "Square Deal," and easily won. His Square Deal program included:

controlling corporations and fighting corruption

protecting consumers (he passed the Meat Inspection Act and the Pure Food and Drug Act of 1906)

conserving natural resources

TAFT: A PROGRESSIVE?

Roosevelt wanted Republican WILLIAM HOWARD TAFT to succeed him as president. In 1908, Taft defeated the

Democratic nominee William Jennings Bryan, and Eugene V. Debs, who ran on the Socialist ticket. Taft supported the SIXTEENTH AMENDMENT (to establish federal income taxes) and the SEVENTEENTH AMENDMENT (to establish the direct election of U.S. senators). However, Taft didn't lower tariffs or support conservation.

DOLLAR DIPLOMACY

Whereas Roosevelt's big stick was the military, Taft preferred a big wallet. He encouraged DOLLAR DIPLOMACY, using business investments and international loans to increase American influence in Latin America and East Asia. Taft was reluctant to resort to violence, but did sometimes use the military to protect American investments, which led to resentment in South and Central America.

The PROGRESSIVE PARTY

A rift developed between Roosevelt and Taft, and Roosevelt chose to run again for president in 1912, even though the Republican Party still supported Taft. Roosevelt formed the PROGRESSIVE PARTY (also known as the BULL MOOSE PARTY because of the strength Roosevelt attributed to it), but he succeeded only in splitting the Republican vote. As a result, the Democrat WOODROW WILSON was elected president.

 A BULL MOOSE IS JUST A MALE MOOSE, NOT SOME WEIRD MUTANT BULL-MOOSE THING.

> Don't forget that the priorities and values of the Democratic and Republican political parties have changed since these parties were established in the late 1700s.

PROGRESSIVISM UNDER WILSON

Except when it came to segregation, which he supported, Wilson was progressive in his policies. During his two terms, progressive advances included:

The CLAYTON ANTITRUST ACT of 1914, which further limited the ability of companies to form monopolies and increased government regulatory power.

The FEDERAL RESERVE ACT of 1913, which created the FEDERAL RESERVE BOARD (the FED) to oversee the federal banks and control interest rates.

The UNDERWOOD TARIFF of 1913, which decreased tariffs.

The creation of the FEDERAL TRADE COMMISSION in 1914, which enforced trade laws.

The KEATING-OWEN ACT of 1916, which limited child labor (though it was later struck down).

The MEXICAN REVOLUTION and PANCHO VILLA

President Wilson was more opposed to imperialism than his predecessor. His policy of MORAL DIPLOMACY involved doing business only with countries that were free and democratic.

However, when the Mexican Revolution began in 1910, Wilson decided to use military force. Because of the many economic ties between the U.S. and Mexico, the revolution affected the U.S.

1911:
The reformer Francisco Madero overthrew dictator Porfirio Díaz.

1913:
General Victoriano Huerta overthrew Madero.

1914:
Wilson refused to recognize Huerta's government and sold weaponry to Venustiano Carranza, Huerta's rival. With help from the U.S., which granted him diplomatic recognition, Carranza took power.

Then, in January 1916, FRANCISCO "PANCHO" VILLA, a prominent Mexican Revolutionary general who had sought **DIPLOMATIC RECOGNITION** from the U.S. for years, protested Carranza's administration by killing 15 Americans in Chihuahua, Mexico. When this didn't provoke conflict, he crossed into New Mexico and killed about 20 people in Columbus, a border town.

> **DIPLOMATIC RECOGNITION**
> when a nation is acknowledged by other governments and other countries

Wilson sent GENERAL JOHN J. PERSHING and his troops, who chased Pancho Villa for a year, until World War I called them away. The Mexican Revolution ended in 1920.

CHECK YOUR KNOWLEDGE

1. How did Roosevelt get the Canal Zone lease?

2. What did Roosevelt mean by "speak softly and carry a big stick"?

3. What is the Roosevelt Corollary?

4. How did Taft use dollar diplomacy?

5. What did the Federal Reserve Act of 1913 do?

6. How did President Wilson's views about Latin America differ from those of Taft and Roosevelt?

7. Why did General Pershing stop chasing Pancho Villa?

ANSWERS

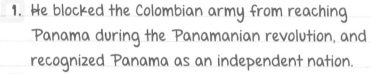

CHECK YOUR ANSWERS

1. He blocked the Colombian army from reaching Panama during the Panamanian revolution, and recognized Panama as an independent nation.

2. Roosevelt meant that the U.S. should act like a police officer and remind other nations of America's military power.

3. The Roosevelt Corollary to the Monroe Doctrine stated the U.S. would intervene in Latin American disputes to avoid European interference.

4. Taft used business investments and loans, rather than the army, as his first tool to influence Latin America.

5. The Federal Reserve Act of 1913 created the Federal Reserve Board (the Fed) to oversee the federal banks and control interest rates.

6. Wilson said he was opposed to imperialism and preferred Moral Diplomacy.

7. World War I started, and he was needed elsewhere.

Unit 7

Modern America and the Great War

1900s-1930s

It's impossible to separate American history from world history. George Washington instructed politicians to avoid foreign entanglements, and they did for a while. The beginning of the 20th century put an end to that. It was hard to hide on the other side of an ocean. The U.S. affected and was affected by the rest of the world.

☆ Chapter 32 ☆

☆☆☆☆ THE ☆☆☆☆
GREAT WAR

When WORLD WAR I, initially called the Great War, erupted across multiple European nations and swept up their colonial holdings in the fighting as well, many Americans argued that it was not any of their business. For a time, that was true. The causes of the war had little to do with the United States, but the United States was forever changed by this war.

EUROPEAN EMPIRES READY for WAR

As competition for resources and land increased in Europe and around the world, European powers undertook MILITARISM. Building a standing army and spending money on new war technology led to an arms race.

Many European countries were also forging ALLIANCES—basically picking teams and promising that when one country went to war, their allies would come to their defense.

This policy of militarism and these alliances were meant to protect the interests of the European powers who had built empires around the world. Other countries, jealous of these powerful empires' imperial holdings, wanted a bigger share of the world pie, and **IMPERIALISM** spread, especially into Africa.

At the same time, there was a rise in **NATIONALISM** across Europe among groups who were subjects of these same powerful empires. These people, proud of their distinct cultures and languages, craved independence. Bosnia wanted to break away from the Austro-Hungarian Empire (Austria-Hungary). The Irish in the British Empire, the Armenians in the Ottoman Empire (Turkey), and the Polish in the Russian Empire also wanted to break away from colonial rule.

Remember the **MAIN** reasons for World War I using this mnemonic device:

MILITARIES
ALLIANCES
IMPERIALISM
NATIONALISM

These tensions made peace in Europe so fragile that anything could have set off conflict. It was a powder keg ready to explode.

The SPARK

Millions of Slavic people who lived under the AUSTRO-HUNGARIAN EMPIRE wanted to become part of Serbia. On June 28, 1914, a Serbian nationalist named GAVRILO PRINCIP assassinated ARCHDUKE FRANZ FERDINAND (heir to the throne of the Austro-Hungarian Empire) and his wife, Sophie, in SARAJEVO. A month later, on July 28, 1914, Austria declared war on Serbia. Within weeks, nations had taken their sides, and within months the shape of the war was determined. By early August 1914, a full-scale war had developed in Europe. These lists show the two sides and the number of estimated deaths from each country:

The CENTRAL POWERS	The ALLIED POWERS, or the ALLIES
Austria-Hungary 2 million	Serbia 750,000
Germany 2.7 million	Russian Empire 3.3 million
The Ottoman Empire 3 million	France 2 million
Bulgaria 400,000	British Empire 1.5 million
	Italy 1 million
	Romania 600,000

Estimates for the total number of people who died during the war range from 16 million to 35 million. Historians estimate that almost half of the deaths were civilian. Many other countries suffered war deaths as well, but no other countries suffered to the degree that these first groups did. The United States, after joining the war later, in 1917, lost about 117,000 people.

EUROPE
1914

ATLANTIC OCEAN

NORTH SEA

NORWAY

SWEDEN

DENMARK

BALTIC SEA

GREAT BRITAIN

NETH.

BELG.

GERMANY

RUSSIA

LUX.

FRANCE

SWITZ.

AUSTRIA-HUNGARY

ITALY

PORTUGAL

SPAIN

ROMANIA

SERBIA

BULGARIA

BLACK SEA

OTTOMAN EMPIRE

GREECE

CENTRAL POWERS

ALLIED POWERS

MEDITERRANEAN SEA

A MODERN and DEADLY WAR

Modern weapons caused far more casualties at a faster rate than ever before. New weapons included machine guns, poison gas, submarines, armored tanks, and airplanes.

Pilots who shot down lots of enemy planes were called **ACES**. The most famous German ace was Manfred von Richthofen, also known as the Red Baron. The most famous American ace was Eddie Rickenbacker.

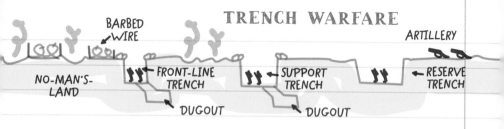

TRENCH WARFARE

BARBED WIRE

ARTILLERY

NO-MAN'S-LAND

FRONT-LINE TRENCH

SUPPORT TRENCH

RESERVE TRENCH

DUGOUT

DUGOUT

The armies used a new style of fighting, called TRENCH WARFARE: Soldiers stayed in dug-out trenches for long stretches of time, with a NO-MAN'S-LAND between them. The soldiers would sometimes fire at one another, but there were few gains for either side, causing a four-year **STALEMATE**.

STALEMATE
a situation in which nothing can be done or won by either side; also called an impasse

With no working farms or factories, starvation was another big problem. In addition, successful blockades of food supplies prevented food imports from getting to needy countries.

And an unusual flu (identified first in Spain) caused a **PANDEMIC** in 1918 that killed more people than died in combat. As much as 5 percent of the world's population died from a disease that easily mutated and traveled around the world with the movement of troops.

PANDEMIC
an epidemic, or widespread disease, that affects an entire country or continent, or even the entire world

The U.S. GETS OFF the FENCE

President Wilson, and the American people, were reluctant to get involved in this deadly war. In fact, Wilson won reelection in 1916 using the slogan "HE KEPT US OUT OF WAR." So, what made the United States finally get involved?

U.S. industries traded with both sides during the war, but Britain's blockade of Germany meant more trade with the Allied forces. U.S. banks made huge loans to the Allies and needed to make sure the Allies won if they wanted those loans paid back. The Germans retaliated against the British blockade by targeting Allied ships with submarines called UNTERSEEBOOTS, or U-BOATS.

"UNDERSEA-BOATS"

On May 7, 1915, a U-boat sank the British ship *LUSITANIA*, killing 1,000 people, including over 100 Americans. Ammunition and unlawful goods were stored in the cargo, but the *Lusitania* was a passenger ship, and the civilian deaths seemed inhumane. Anti-German sentiment rose in the U.S., but Wilson was determined to remain neutral. Wilson also wanted a seat at the negotiation table after the war. He persuaded Germany to promise not to target passenger ships. This became a pattern: Germany would sink a ship, the U.S. would chastise Germany, and Germany would pledge to stop. However, in January 1918, Germany announced that it would resume "unrestricted submarine warfare."

A month later, British intelligence intercepted a telegram from a German official named Arthur Zimmermann. The ZIMMERMANN NOTE proposed an alliance between Germany and Mexico against the U.S. Mexico declined the invitation, but the telegram was published by American newspapers, and anti-German sentiment boiled over.

In March 1917, a month after the Zimmermann Note was made public, the Russian Revolution began. CZAR NICHOLAS II, forced to step down, was replaced by a democratic government. This meant the U.S. could join the war without siding with an oppressive monarchy.

Within the year, a political group called the **BOLSHEVIKS**, led by Vladimir Ilyich Lenin, seized power in Russia and set up a **COMMUNIST** government promising "Land, Peace, Bread" to the people while making peace with Germany.

Historians argue that President Wilson was an idealist and really wanted to participate in the treaty negotiations at the end of

COMMUNISM
an economic system where the government owns the means of production and distributes resources equitably

the war. The only way to get a seat at that table was to take part in the war itself. On April 2, 1917, Wilson asked Congress to declare war. After three months of debate, the U.S. entered the fight.

WAR PREPARATIONS

To prepare for war, the federal government had to mobilize an army, reorganize industries to manufacture war supplies, rally public support, and silence dissent.

ARTISTS OF THE ERA SATIRIZED THE SMALL SIZE OF THE U.S. MILITARY IN POLITICAL CARTOONS LIKE THIS.

Even with a large number of volunteers—including women and Black people—the U.S. military was too small to handle such a big war. In May 1917, the SELECTIVE SERVICE ACT started a DRAFT for all men between the ages of 21 and 30. Black soldiers were segregated from white soldiers in the American forces but fought shoulder to shoulder with French soldiers. Some of these Black Americans were awarded the French Croix de Guerre (Cross of War) medal for their bravery.

The WAR INDUSTRIES BOARD directed the distribution and production of war supplies. Meanwhile the COMMITTEE ON PUBLIC INFORMATION (CPI) created propaganda about German atrocities to promote anti-German feelings. It worked, but generated harassment of German Americans.

RALLYING PUBLIC SUPPORT

The CPI also played a major role in getting the public to:

> Buy WAR BONDS—which was like making a loan to the government to be paid back with interest after the war.

> Save resources like food and fuel through voluntary programs. (When you pledged to do this, the FUEL ADMINISTRATION and the FOOD ADMINISTRATION gave you posters to put in your windows as proof of your patriotism.)

> Plant VICTORY GARDENS so that a higher percentage of the food from larger farms could go to soldiers.

SILENCING DISSENT

Though most Americans supported the war effort once war was declared, there were still many who opposed the war. The government responded by passing two new laws:

The **ESPIONAGE ACT**, which created penalties for spying, and the **SEDITION ACT**, which made it illegal to express negative opinions about the government or interfere with the war effort

As a result, many **PACIFISTS**, who oppose war altogether, and **SOCIALISTS**, who thought the everyday people were paying the price to protect American business interests, were jailed. In the 1919 Supreme Court case *SCHENCK v. UNITED STATES*, the court ruled that those limitations on free speech were valid in a time of war.

U.S. ENGAGEMENT TURNS the TIDE

> **CONVOY**
> a group traveling together, often for safety

The U.S. immediately helped the Allies by introducing the **CONVOY** system, sending cargo ships across the Atlantic accompanied by warships to protect them from U-boat attacks. (The U.S. army was small, but our navy was not.)

When the American army, called the AMERICAN EXPEDITIONARY FORCES (AEF), led by GENERAL JOHN PERSHING arrived in France, it provided an influx of energy to the Allies. The introduction of manpower boosted morale and shifted the momentum of the war.

> Many believe that the AEF soldiers were called **DOUGHBOYS** because the buttons on their uniforms looked like dough.

President Wilson proposed the FOURTEEN POINTS, a plan to avoid another world war. Among other things, this plan:

Argued that no country should:
- maintain an oversized military
- negotiate secret alliances/treaties
- claim new imperial colonies
- interfere with ocean travel and trade

Proposed the boundaries and borders of the participating countries could be renegotiated and adjusted fairly.

Suggested that the populations seeking independence from the Ottoman Empire, the Russian Empire, and the Austro-Hungarian Empire be granted AUTONOMY.

AUTONOMY
self-government

Insisted that a LEAGUE OF NATIONS— an organization of countries working together to resolve disputes—be established.

By 1918, the Central powers were falling apart. Germany had underestimated the U.S. forces, and their navy was close to mutiny. At the same time, the deadly 1918 INFLUENZA PANDEMIC was taking over the globe and devastating military camps and hospitals on all sides.

Germany agreed to armistice, and a cease fire went into effect at 11 a.m. on November 11, 1918. The Great War was over.

THAT'S 11/11 AT 11!

The TREATY of VERSAILLES

In 1919, the BIG FOUR—President Wilson, Prime Minister David Lloyd George of England, Premier Georges Clemenceau of France, and Prime Minister Vittorio Orlando of Italy—met at Versailles, near Paris. (No Central powers were invited.) Wilson wanted to end the war with minimal animosity. But the victorious European nations wanted Germany to take full blame, lose its colonies, lose its military, and pay **REPARATIONS**.

> **REPARATIONS**
> financial compensation paid to someone who has been wronged

The Treaty of Versailles addressed some of Wilson's Fourteen Points. It redrew boundaries in Europe and split up the Austro-Hungarian and Ottoman Empires. But this failed to solve ethnic divisions and maybe even made them worse. Germany was punished so harshly that recovery from the war was all but impossible. Wilson campaigned for the Treaty of Versailles, but Congress rejected it. They worried that the LEAGUE OF NATIONS would rob Congress of power by deciding when and where the American military would fight. Wilson's greatest ambition was realized when the League of Nations was established, but the U.S. never joined.

A GLIMPSE OF THE FUTURE

American society was changed by this war. With so many young men drafted into the army, women, immigrants, and Black people had access to better jobs than ever before. Labor agents from the North even came south with railroad tickets in hand to entice Black laborers to move north, causing massive migration within the country.

After the war, Americans wanted to return to **ISOLATIONISM**. The Senate, which must approve treaties negotiated by the president,

> **ISOLATIONISM**
> the policy of isolating one's country from the affairs of other nations by declining to enter into alliances or other international agreements

rejected the Treaty of Versailles and never entered the League of Nations. Despite this, it was clear that the United States had taken its place on the world stage. To engage in world trade, the country had to engage in the world.

CHECK YOUR KNOWLEDGE

1. Which country was the first to declare war in the conflict that would become World War I?

2. Why was the attack on the *LUSITANIA* significant?

3. Why were there far more casualties than in previous wars?

4. Why did the U.S. finally enter the Great War?

5. What other major global event occurred at the end of World War I?

6. What was the point of the League of Nations?

7. Why did Congress reject the Treaty of Versailles?

ANSWERS

CHECK YOUR ANSWERS

1. Austria (against Serbia)
2. American civilians were killed, and anti-German feeling in the U.S. increased.
3. Modern weapons like machine guns and poison gas caused more deaths at a faster rate.
4. One reason was that the U.S. had made loans to the Allied forces and needed them to win so they could pay back the loans.
5. The 1918 influenza pandemic
6. To use diplomacy to prevent another global war
7. They believed the League of Nations would take power away from them.

☆ Chapter 33 ☆

The ROARING
★ ★ ★ ★ ★ ★ ★ ★ ★ ★ ★ ★ ★
TWENTIES

BACK to NORMAL ... OR NOT

World War I and the influenza pandemic challenged Americans' sense of certainty and stability and proved disruptive to traditions both abroad and at home. Many wanted what presidential candidate WARREN G. HARDING coined, in 1920, as a "RETURN TO NORMALCY." Though Harding won the presidential contest, there was no chance the U.S. could step back in time. Over the decade, Americans tried to shake off the war with high spirits and consumer spending, but there were deep underlying problems:

PROBLEM 1: THE ECONOMY
When soldiers returned home, the government didn't need extra workers to make supplies for them anymore; this led to high unemployment.

PROBLEM 2: LABOR

Wages and prices had been kept down during the war; after the war, prices went up, but not wages, leading to strikes. Women, immigrants, and Black people who had access to jobs during the war were often pushed out of those jobs to favor the soldiers returning from the war.

PROBLEM 3: NATIVISM AND RACISM

With the lack of jobs, racism and anti-immigrant feelings increased. ("They're taking our jobs!")

The RED SCARE

Americans were afraid the Communist takeover in Russia would repeat itself in the U.S. and put an end to CAPITALISM, an economic and political system where industry is controlled for profit. This led to the RED SCARE, a fear of Communists, called REDS, and other "radicals." When bombings took place across the country, Communists were blamed, and ATTORNEY GENERAL A. MITCHELL PALMER led the PALMER RAIDS ← BUT NO MAJOR DISCOVERIES WERE EVER MADE on suspected Communists, **SOCIALISTS**, and anarchists, often without warrants. Labor unions were deemed Communist organizations, and when workers began to strike, violent government intervention was seen as justified.

> **SOCIALISM**
> an economic system in which property and the means of production are regulated by the state and equally distributed among citizens

The trial and execution of NICOLA SACCO and BARTOLOMEO VANZETTI suggested that the Red Scare had a nativist foundation: The two Italian-born anarchists were sentenced to death for killing two men during a robbery. They probably didn't get a fair trial.

HARDING'S REPUBLICANISM and TEAPOT DOME

President Harding, a former Republican senator from Ohio, was a strong believer in small government. As president he instituted high tariffs and income tax reductions, especially for the wealthy. Harding appointed his friends from Ohio, many of whom were unqualified and corrupt, to important government positions. Harding's friend and Secretary of the Interior Albert Fall was convicted of accepting bribes from oil executives for rights to drill on government land in Teapot Dome, Wyoming, which became known as the TEAPOT DOME SCANDAL.

When Harding died of a heart attack on August 2, 1923, his vice president, CALVIN COOLIDGE, became president.

CALVIN COOLIDGE

Coolidge was seen as quiet and honest. He believed in laissez-faire economics and tried to keep the government out of the economy. He was reelected in 1924 on the strengths of his beliefs in minimal government, high tariffs, and low taxes. Coolidge is known for the KELLOGG-BRIAND PACT of 1928, which made war illegal. More than 60 nations signed the agreement. (But think about it: How do you enforce something that says you can't fight?)

In 1924, the year Coolidge was reelected, **NELLIE T. ROSS** of Wyoming and **MIRIAM A. FERGUSON** of Texas were elected the nation's first women governors. In 1916, **JEANNETTE RANKIN** of Montana had become the first woman elected to the U.S. Congress.

CONSUMERISM

Prosperity seemed to be on the rise again, and new consumer goods, often inspired by new war technology and made cheaper by new production methods, flooded the stores. The radio, previously used only by the military, is one example. Consumers could buy the things they wanted using INSTALLMENT PLANS if they didn't have the money to buy goods outright.

The automobile is an example of consumerism, which refers to large amounts of goods sold to individual people instead of businesses.

ALL THAT JAZZ

People had shorter workdays, more leisure time, and a live-for-today attitude. Young people moved to the cities. The excitement and modernity of this time period gave it the nickname the ROARING TWENTIES.

RADIOS became a part of every home, and radio networks made sure that Americans listened to the same programs (and ads).

The FILM INDUSTRY grew. Hollywood became the center of a major industry. "Talkies"—as opposed to silent movies—were introduced.

Americans followed the lives of celebrities, from sports stars (like BABE RUTH) to pilots (like CHARLES LINDBERGH and AMELIA EARHART).

Women were voting, were better educated, and were working (mostly as nurses, teachers, secretaries, and clerks).

Other new aspects of popular culture were ART DECO architecture, crossword puzzles, and dances like the Charleston.

JAZZ was a big part of pop culture. It was developed by Black musicians in New Orleans, who were influenced by music from West Africa, the Dominican Republic, Haiti, and France. Jazz was so popular that this decade is also called the JAZZ AGE.

The HARLEM RENAISSANCE

During World War I, many Black people moved from the South to the North to work in factories in the GREAT MIGRATION. They brought jazz and the blues with them to the North. The Great Migration was met with resistance, especially by the KKK, which was no longer limited to the South. To fight back, organizations like the NAACP worked to secure civil rights. A reformer, MARCUS GARVEY, founded the UNIVERSAL NEGRO IMPROVEMENT ASSOCIATION (UNIA) and advocated a large-scale return to Africa. The plans fell short, but he did encourage BLACK NATIONALISM and a sense of racial dignity.

> DON'T CONFUSE WITH THE GREAT MIGRATION FROM ENGLAND TO THE PRESENT-DAY U.S., FROM 1629 TO 1640.

> The KKK was virtually wiped out after the Force Acts under the Grant administration. It returned after D. W. Griffith released his film *The Birth of a Nation* in 1915, which portrayed the KKK as heroic.

Black communities thrived in New York City's HARLEM, a neighborhood where overdevelopment had driven down the price of real estate. Harlem became home to many Black artists and gave rise to

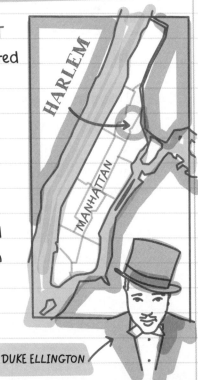

HARLEM

MANHATTAN

DUKE ELLINGTON

the HARLEM RENAISSANCE—an intellectual and cultural revival of Black art, literature, fashion, music, and politics. Prominent names of this movement include writers like LANGSTON HUGHES and ZORA NEALE HURSTON and jazz artists such as DUKE ELLINGTON.

Black Americans weren't the only people fighting for their civil rights in the 1920s. The **LEAGUE OF UNITED LATIN AMERICAN CITIZENS** (LULAC) was founded, and the **INDIAN CITIZENSHIP ACT** was passed, granting full citizenship to Indigenous Americans.

BACKLASH

Rapid modernization also created a backlash, especially in rural areas.

More NATIVISM

The government set limits on the number of immigrants who could come to the U.S. The EMERGENCY QUOTA ACT of 1921 mostly targeted Southern and Eastern European immigrants. THE IMMIGRATION ACT of 1924 included the ASIAN EXCLUSION ACT, and targeted restrictions on Asian immigrants specifically.

FUNDAMENTALISM

This religious movement centered on the belief in a literal interpretation of the Bible, particularly regarding **CREATIONISM**.

CREATIONISM
the belief that people were created by God exactly as described in the Judeo-Christian Bible

In 1925, a teacher named JOHN SCOPES broke Tennessee law by teaching his students about evolution. During his trial (the "Scopes Monkey Trial"), WILLIAM JENNINGS BRYAN represented the prosecution, and CLARENCE DARROW (and the American Civil Liberties Union) defended Scopes. Scopes was originally found guilty of violating the law, but the state supreme court overturned the ruling on a technicality. The law itself was eventually ruled unconstitutional. However, it was not repealed until 1967.

PROHIBITION

Prohibition (a ban on alcohol) began in 1920. It was hard to enforce because people could make their own alcohol or buy it in underground bars called SPEAKEASIES. Outlaws known as BOOTLEGGERS also smuggled alcohol. Some worked with gangsters like AL CAPONE. Prohibition made organized crime worse. It was repealed by the TWENTY-FIRST AMENDMENT in 1933.

The LOST GENERATION

Many intellectuals and creative people—including writers like ERNEST HEMINGWAY and F. SCOTT FITZGERALD—grew disenchanted with the violence of World War I, consumerism, and the U.S. in general. Many lived as **EXPATRIATES**.

EXPATRIATE
someone who chooses not to live in their home country

CHECK YOUR KNOWLEDGE

1. What caused unemployment after WWI?

2. What were the Palmer Raids meant to uncover?

3. Why were the twenties "roaring"?

4. What are the musical origins of jazz?

5. How did Harlem become a thriving neighborhood of Black artists?

6. What was the verdict in the Scopes Monkey Trial?

7. How did Prohibition support the spread of organized crime?

8. Which parts of American culture were members of the "Lost Generation" upset about?

ANSWERS 401

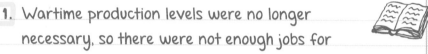

CHECK YOUR ANSWERS

1. Wartime production levels were no longer necessary, so there were not enough jobs for all the soldiers returning home.

2. They were meant to uncover Communists, Socialists, and anarchists, but no major discoveries were made.

3. The economy was doing better, and American culture was experiencing a period of excitement, leisure, and consumerism.

4. Jazz originated with Black musicians in New Orleans who were influenced by music from West Africa, the Dominican Republic, Haiti, and France.

5. Affordable real estate attracted many artists to settle in the area.

6. The state supreme court of Tennessee overruled the original guilty verdict on a technicality, but the law itself was eventually ruled unconstitutional.

7. With alcohol illegal, people who wanted to drink depended on bootleggers and gangsters to smuggle it in.

8. They were disillusioned by consumerism and war.

☆ Chapter 34 ☆

The GREAT

✦ ☆ ✦ ☆ ✦ ☆ ✦ ☆ ✦ ☆ ✦

DEPRESSION

STOCK
MARKET
CRASH

During the boom of the 1920s, many
people hoped to grow their wealth by
speculating in the STOCK EXCHANGE, a
market for shares of companies. If a
company does well, the value of the stock
increases and the owner can then sell the
stock for a profit.

During the BULL MARKET of the 1920s, people
bought stocks eagerly, because their values

were increasing, even though the companies were not worth any more than they had been. Some people bought stocks using borrowed money, which they hoped to pay back with the profit from their stock. People were also "buying on margin," which meant they paid only 10 percent of the stock price initially. They hoped the price would rise quickly so they could resell for a profit.

In the middle of 1929, the value of stocks reached a high point, and some people decided to sell their shares. The more stocks people sold, the fewer stocks people wanted to buy, decreasing the value of the stocks. On October 29, 1929, a day known as BLACK TUESDAY, the stock market CRASHED to almost zero value. Many people lost all their money in a single day.

BUY!

During a **BULL MARKET**, stock prices rise or are expected to rise, so people tend to purchase stocks; during a **BEAR MARKET**, stock prices fall or are expected to fall, so people tend to sell stocks.

SELL!

The GREAT DEPRESSION

Black Tuesday was the beginning of the GREAT DEPRESSION, the worst economic crisis in U.S. history. Many people had bought stocks on the EASY CREDIT of the 1920s, but when they **DEFAULTED** on their loans, banks and stockbrokers lost

DEFAULT
to fail to pay a debt

money, too. However, the stock market crash was only one cause of the Great Depression. Other causes include:

The illusion of wealth that swept the country in the previous decade had led to overproduction in factories and agriculture. In reality, few people could afford to purchase the goods produced. The surplus (an excess) caused prices to fall, which caused profits to fall, which led companies to lay off their workers. Because of high unemployment, even fewer people could afford the goods, causing the cycle to **SNOWBALL**.

SNOWBALL
to grow or become larger or more intense at an accelerating rate

Anyone who deposited money into a bank account lost it if the bank went out of business. When people with savings in banks saw that loans were being defaulted on, they panicked and withdrew as much money as possible, causing a "run" on the banks. This put more banks out of business, making it impossible for other businesses to take out loans; layoffs followed, and this process snowballed, too.

Tough economic times in other countries (a result of the Great War) reduced the market for exports.

HOOVER'S ECONOMICS

The president at the start of the Great Depression was
HERBERT HOOVER. During the election of 1928, the Republican
Party was credited with the perceived prosperity of the
1920s, so when the Republican Party nominated Hoover, he
was virtually assured a victory.

Hoover was a strong believer in laissez-faire economics and
small government. Hoover's stance on the Depression was
that it was not the job of the federal government to take care
of people; instead, the crisis would take care of itself as part
of what many thought was a normal cycle of the economy.

High unemployment, hunger, and
homelessness were on the rise across

24 PERCENT OF AMERICANS
(12 MILLION PEOPLE)
WERE UNEMPLOYED.

the country. Children left school to work or ran away because
they felt they were a burden on their parents. Families fell
apart. Even when the nation pleaded with the government
to act, Hoover refused. The
SHANTYTOWNS that sprang
up to house people evicted from
their homes became known
as HOOVERVILLES.

SHANTYTOWN
a neighborhood of informal
houses, usually made from
discarded materials

Eventually, Hoover gave in. In 1931, he authorized
spending on public works (such as the Boulder Dam, now
the HOOVER DAM) to create jobs, and in 1932, he agreed to

the creation of the Reconstruction Finance Corporation, which made loans to banks and businesses.

The BONUS ARMY

Hoover's reputation was damaged even more when, in the summer of 1932, World War I veterans who were due to receive bonus pay in 1945 marched on Washington to demand early payment. When Hoover and the Congress refused, some of the protesters stayed in a D.C.-area Hooverville. Under Hoover's direction, GENERAL DOUGLAS MacARTHUR led the military to drive out the "BONUS ARMY" using tanks and tear gas. Several Great War veterans were killed, and the public was shocked.

FRANKLIN DELANO ROOSEVELT

Hoover ran for president again in 1932, even though he knew that his chances of winning were slim. His Democratic rival, FRANKLIN DELANO ROOSEVELT (FDR), was a distant cousin of Teddy Roosevelt, and he was paralyzed from the waist down from polio. Roosevelt had an excellent record of helping the people of New York, where he was governor, and a strong group of advisers known as the BRAIN TRUST helped him with policy. His campaign promised a "NEW DEAL" for Americans, and he won the election easily.

WHAT DO YOU THINK?

I TRUST YOU...WHAT DO YOU THINK?

The FIRST NEW DEAL

In his first inaugural address, FDR famously told the nation that "THE ONLY THING WE HAVE TO FEAR IS FEAR ITSELF," and he quickly set out to destroy that fear. Roosevelt became president on March 4, 1933, and he called a special session of Congress that is known as the HUNDRED DAYS. He instituted a BANK HOLIDAY, closing all banks in the nation for a few days while the EMERGENCY BANKING RELIEF ACT was passed, and reopened only the ones that were stable. He then gave the first of his many radio addresses to the nation—a FIRESIDE CHAT—in which he explained the new banking policy and eased fears. Beginning during the Hundred Days and continuing until 1935, President Roosevelt instituted the programs that made up the FIRST NEW DEAL, which included the founding of these agencies: ←

CALLED THE "ALPHABET AGENCIES" FOR ALL THE INITIALISMS

FEDERAL EMERGENCY RELIEF ADMINISTRATION (FERA), which helped the unemployed

AGRICULTURAL ADJUSTMENT ADMINISTRATION (AAA), which subsidized farmers for occasionally destroying their crops. This kept food supplies low and prices high (this policy was controversial, as hunger remained a problem for many people and yet food was being thrown away).

PUBLIC WORKS ADMINISTRATION (PWA), which sponsored public works and created jobs

PUBLIC WORKS work like building roads, schools, and infrastructure that is done by the government for the public

CIVILIAN CONSERVATION CORPS (CCC), which was similar to the PWA but focused on conservation projects

FEDERAL DEPOSIT INSURANCE CORPORATION (FDIC), which insured bank deposits so people would not lose their money if banks failed

TENNESSEE VALLEY AUTHORITY (TVA), which brought electricity to the Tennessee Valley through new dams and created jobs in the area

NATIONAL INDUSTRIAL RECOVERY ACT (NIRA), which set labor standards (such as minimum wage and a ban on child labor)

SECURITIES AND EXCHANGE COMMISSION (SEC), which regulated the stock market

The SECOND NEW DEAL

In the 1934 midterm elections, and then during the 1936 presidential election, the nation showed strong support for the Democratic Party and Roosevelt, who won in a landslide victory. Although some conservatives thought the New Deal was a Socialist abuse of presidential power, and some liberals (notably Senator Huey Long of Louisiana) thought it didn't go far enough toward redistribution of wealth, most people needed more assistance. The Depression was still in full force.

So when the New Deal began to expire, Roosevelt instituted a SECOND NEW DEAL. More than the first set of programs, these initiatives attempted to generate true social change rather than simply help people get by. The new WORKS PROGRESS ADMINISTRATION (WPA) was much like the PWA but went further to employ artists and young people. The REVENUE ACT OF 1935 raised taxes on the rich, and the WAGNER ACT made sure that labor unions had the right to fair negotiations. Perhaps most importantly, the SOCIAL SECURITY ACT (August 1935) gave birth to the modern system of **WELFARE** in America: People pay Social Security taxes throughout their working lives and, in return, receive payment back when they retire or if they are unable to work.

> **WELFARE**
> assistance from the government, usually in the form of money

The DUST BOWL

In addition to the Depression, Americans were hit with another misfortune during the 1930s: In 1931, a severe drought struck the Great Plains, which turned the area into a DUST BOWL that lasted more than a decade. For years, farmers had cleared land in such a way that the natural grass lost the roots that would connect it to topsoil. When winds came through, the dry dirt, unanchored by grass, was swept into dust storms. Farmers from Oklahoma in particular left the area to become MIGRANT WORKERS in California. The Oklahoma natives living below the poverty threshold were known as OKIES.

John Steinbeck's Great Depression-era novel *THE GRAPES OF WRATH* is about this experience.

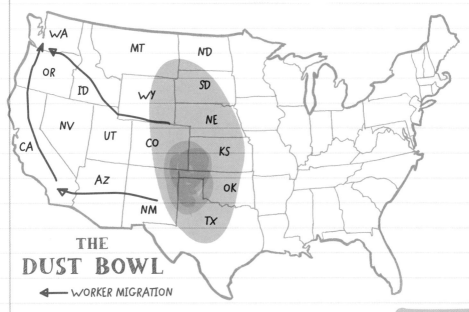

THE DUST BOWL

◄— WORKER MIGRATION

LABOR STRENGTH

In 1935, the Supreme Court struck down the NIRA (which protected laborers with minimum wage standards and a ban on child labor) as an unconstitutional restriction of commerce. Congress quickly responded by passing the NATIONAL LABOR RELATIONS ACT, also known as the WAGNER ACT, guaranteeing certain rights to unions. The AFL remained strong, and the newly founded CONGRESS OF INDUSTRIAL ORGANIZATIONS (CIO) increased its membership by welcoming women, people of color, and unskilled laborers. Unions began using SIT-DOWN STRIKES, which were strikes that took place within the factories. Remarkably, unions and labor organizations grew at a time when America had a surplus of labor.

NEW DEAL COALITION

Another aspect of Roosevelt's presidency was his ability to attract new voters. Especially during the 1936 presidential elections, many Black Americans switched over to the Democratic Party, thanks to FDR's progressive policies. It was the first time, as a demographic group, that they stepped away from the "Party of Lincoln" (from which the current Republican Party developed). Roosevelt relied on his wife, ELEANOR ROOSEVELT, and a "BLACK CABINET" (a group of Black men) to advise him on matters affecting the Black population.

Unfortunately, to keep the support of the white Southern Democrats, FDR also deliberately limited universal access to some of his most important programs. **REDLINING** made it harder for Black families to use federal programs to buy houses, and domestic service jobs mostly held by Black laborers (being a cook, maid, or chauffeur, for example) were not eligible to participate in Social Security.

> **REDLINING**
> the practice of denying services to people living in certain areas, often based on race

At the same time, Eleanor Roosevelt rose to prominence in national life and became a sign of the advancement of women's rights. FDR appointed the first woman cabinet member, **FRANCES PERKINS**, as secretary of labor.

> Eleanor Roosevelt was a controversial first lady and an American politician, diplomat, and activist in her own right. She was outspoken and active in fighting for the rights of women, Black and Asian Americans, and war refugees. She famously arranged a concert by the Black singer Marian Anderson at the Lincoln Memorial after the Daughters of the American Revolution banned her from singing at Constitution Hall.

ESCAPISM

Although some art that emerged during the Great Depression took a serious look at American life (like *THE GRAPES OF WRATH* and Woody Guthrie's folk music), the 1930s were also the height of **ESCAPISM**. People watched movies and listened to music and radio to get away from daily life.

Soap operas, radio dramas, big band and swing music, and movies such as *THE WIZARD OF OZ*, *KING KONG*, and *GONE WITH THE WIND* helped many Americans make it through the decade.

HOW WAS YOUR DAY?

HARD.

ESCAPISM
escaping from daily life, usually through entertainment

The END of the DEPRESSION

In 1937, it seemed as though the New Deal was working. Roosevelt decided that it was time to cut the **DEFICIT**, which had grown during the Depression. However, to do so, he needed to decrease spending on recovery programs—and when he did this, he miscalculated the stability of the economy.

DEFICIT
the amount by which more money is spent than is coming in

Roosevelt's decision to decrease spending, combined with limiting loans, led to another dip in the nation's economy, known as the ROOSEVELT RECESSION. Full recovery did not occur until World War II began. Most of the New Deal programs expired or were canceled as the economy improved, but some of them—such as Social Security, the FDIC, and the SEC—remain central aspects of the relationship between American citizens and the federal government.

CHECK YOUR KNOWLEDGE

1. Why was there a large surplus in manufactured goods at the start of the Depression?

2. What caused the runs on the banks at the start of the Depression?

3. How did Hoover think the Depression would end?

4. How did President Roosevelt's approach to the economy differ from Hoover's?

5. How did public works projects help the economy?

6. How does Social Security work?

7. Why did movies like *THE WIZARD OF OZ* appeal to audiences in the 1930s?

ANSWERS 415

CHECK YOUR ANSWERS

1. Most people were not actually rich in the 1920s, despite the economic boom. The commonly held belief that the whole country was wealthy led to overproduction of goods.

2. When they saw banks were defaulting, people withdrew all their money, causing banks to go out of business.

3. He thought it would be resolved as part of the cyclical nature of the economy.

4. FDR actively intervened to end the Depression.

5. They created jobs.

6. People pay a tax on their salaries when they are working, and receive a share back when they retire or are unable to work.

7. People were looking for an escape from their daily lives.

HEY, WHERE DID EVERYONE GO?

DIDN'T YOU HEAR? THERE'S ANOTHER WAR!

Unit 8

World War II
1930s-1945

The world was fragile after the events of World War I, the 1918 pandemic, and the Great Depression. Once again tensions were growing. Land and resources were in high demand, and countries were forming alliances with each other. Xenophobia was on the rise, and across the world powerful nations were blaming their problems on innocent groups of people.

World War II was officially fought on two fronts—continental Europe and the Pacific. And for many American citizens, the U.S. home front was also a war zone.

☆ Chapter 35 ☆
WORLD WAR II BEGINS

TOTALITARIANISM

After World War I, poverty, instability, and dissatisfaction in Europe led to the rise of **TOTALITARIAN** dictators, who promised they could create change if only they had complete control of EVERYTHING.

Totalitarian leaders did bring stability to their countries—at the cost of individual liberty.

> **TOTALITARIANISM**
> a system in which the government acts as absolute ruler with complete control over every element of life

Italy had been one of the Big Four nations to negotiate the Treaty of Versailles, but economic failure led to chaos. In 1922, BENITO MUSSOLINI, the leader of a **FASCIST** totalitarian movement, forced the king of Italy to grant him power. He named himself dictator under the title IL DUCE (the leader).

> **FASCISM**
> a form of totalitarianism that emphasizes nationalism and conformity

The USSR formed in 1922 when the Russian Socialist Federative Soviet Republic (RSFSR) united with three smaller Soviet republics.

"USSR" OR "SOVIET UNION"

In the UNION OF SOVIET SOCIALIST REPUBLICS, after the death of Lenin in 1924, JOSEPH STALIN took control. He began to **EXTERMINATE** any countrymen who he thought might challenge his power.

EXTERMINATE
put to death

In Germany, the debt from reparation payments for World War I and from having to shut down the military had pretty much brought about an economic collapse and destroyed the nation. ADOLF HITLER and the NATIONAL SOCIALIST GERMAN WORKERS' PARTY—the NAZIS (from the German word NATIONALSOZIALISTISCHE)—won the 1932 German elections, and Hitler was appointed CHANCELLOR.

He promoted the idea of **ARYAN** superiority and blamed the economic and social problems plaguing Germany on the Jewish population. Hitler named himself **FÜHRER** and took control.

ARYAN
of Northern European heritage; non-Jewish

FÜHRER
German for "leader"

Meanwhile, in Japan, HIDEKI TŌJŌ, a military leader, was elected prime minister in 1941. Tōjō became a dictator and soon had more influence than the emperor of Japan.

419

TOTALITARIAN EXPANSIONISM

Each totalitarian leader believed that his country was superior to all others and had the right to conquer.

JAPAN SOUGHT COLONIES WITH NATURAL RESOURCES TO EXPAND.

JAPAN invaded China, starting with MANCHURIA. Then, in 1937, Japan invaded Nanjing and perpetrated the NANJING MASSACRE, a violent attack on the city and its people.

ITALY left the League of Nations and conquered ETHIOPIA in 1935. In 1939, Italy conquered ALBANIA.

GERMANY annexed the RHINELAND, a coal-rich area that the Treaty of Versailles had declared a neutral **BUFFER ZONE** in 1936. In 1938, Germany conquered AUSTRIA.

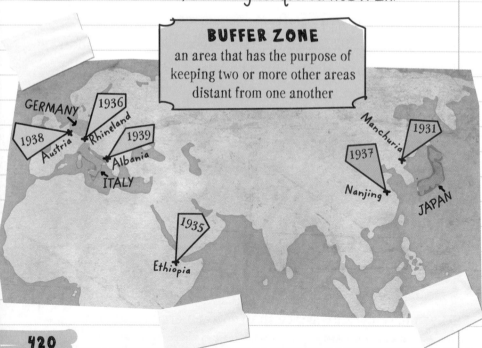

BUFFER ZONE
an area that has the purpose of keeping two or more other areas distant from one another

GERMANY 1936
1938 Rhineland
Austria 1939
Albania
ITALY

Manchuria 1931
1937
Nanjing JAPAN

1935
Ethiopia

APPEASEMENT at MUNICH

Germany's next target was
the SUDETENLAND, an area of Czechoslovakia with a large
German population. Czechoslovakia turned to France and
England for help. In September 1938, British prime minister
NEVILLE CHAMBERLAIN proposed that Hitler could have the
Sudetenland if he promised not to invade anywhere else. This
APPEASEMENT was supposed to prevent another war. In
March 1939, Hitler broke his promise and conquered the rest
of Czechoslovakia. England and France warned that they'd
defend Poland, which seemed to be Hitler's next target.

The AXIS

With their similar philosophies, these dictators formed alliances.
In 1936, Hitler and Mussolini formed the Rome-Berlin Axis,
aka THE AXIS, a coalition in which the leaders of Italy and
Germany promised to support each other in the event of war.
Japan joined the pact in 1940. Stalin didn't join the Axis, but signed
a NON-AGGRESSION PACT with Germany. The two countries
agreed not to attack each other and secretly agreed to grab
the recently created Poland and divide it between them.

WORLD WAR ... ROUND 2

On September 1, 1939, Germany invaded Poland. On
September 3, Britain and France declared war on
Germany, as promised. World War II had begun.

Hitler used a BLITZKRIEG ("lightning war")—a tactic that combined speed and surprise—to conquer Poland in only a few weeks.

Once again, the world would split into two warring sides:

The AXIS POWERS
Germany
Italy
Japan

The ALLIED POWERS
Great Britain
France ← UNTIL GERMANY INVADED
The Soviet Union
AFTER GERMANY BETRAYED THEM → The U.S. ← AFTER 1941
China
(and many more countries)

The Soviet Union also attacked Poland and then moved on to the Balkan Peninsula (Hungary, Yugoslavia, Bulgaria, Albania, and Greece) and Finland. Hitler moved north, conquering Denmark and Norway in April 1940, then Belgium, the Netherlands, and Luxembourg.

WAR in WESTERN EUROPE

France was the next target. Allied troops had set up along the MAGINOT LINE at the German border, but they were forced to retreat to DUNKIRK, a French town on the English Channel, where they were trapped as the Germans invaded from the north and Italy attacked from the south. On June 14, 1940, the Germans seized Paris, and France surrendered on June 22. Thousands of French and British soldiers at Dunkirk escaped on fishing boats and went to England, where they joined the Free French Forces led by GENERAL CHARLES DE GAULLE.

It was far easier to replace military equipment than men, so it was important that they live to fight another day.

FUTURE PRESIDENT OF FRANCE

The BATTLE of BRITAIN

MEANS "AIR WEAPONS"

In the summer of 1940, Hitler began an air attack on England. During the BATTLE OF BRITAIN, the *LUFTWAFFE* (Germany's air force) tried, unsuccessfully, to incapacitate the ROYAL AIR FORCE (RAF) by bombing airfields and airstrips.

The goal was to pave the way for an invasion of Britain. When the Luftwaffe changed tactics and bombed London on the night of August 24, the RAF responded by bombing Berlin, the capital of Germany. The war intensified and the Battle of Britain became the BLITZ. Germany postponed the invasion but continued to bomb the British cities of London, Liverpool, and Manchester every night from September 1940 until May 1941. Britain, led by PRIME MINISTER WINSTON CHURCHILL, refused to surrender. Ultimately Germany retreated.

> A lot of children were evacuated from London during the bombings. This event even appears in the Chronicles of Narnia books: The main characters are sent away to live in the English countryside.

Hitler decided to change direction. Needing the resources and manpower of the Soviet Union, but worried about competition from Stalin, he decided to attack Russia in June 1941, breaking the pact the two countries had formed. The Soviets were forced to retreat, losing thousands of troops who were captured or killed. Stalin changed course as well: He joined the Allies and ordered his people to destroy their own resources and burn their own cities before the Germans could get them. This is the SCORCHED EARTH tactic. After Germany's betrayal, Stalin accepted the idea that "the enemy of my enemy is my friend."

CHECK YOUR KNOWLEDGE

1. Which conditions in Europe contributed to the rise of totalitarianism?

2. What is fascism?

3. Why did Neville Chamberlain agree to give Hitler the Sudetenland?

4. At the start of the war, who were the Axis powers? Who were the Allied powers?

5. What was the Blitz?

6. What did Stalin instruct his people to do when Germany invaded Russia?

ANSWERS 425

CHECK YOUR ANSWERS

1. Instability, low morale, and economic trouble

2. Fascism is a type of totalitarianism that emphasizes nationalism and conformity.

3. To appease Hitler, avoid further German invasions, and prevent another war

4. At the start of the war the Axis powers were Germany, Italy, Japan, and the Soviet Union. The Allied powers were Great Britain, France, China, and other European countries.

5. The German air force bombed London every single night for eight months. British forces didn't surrender, and Hitler retreated.

6. He told them to destroy their resources so the Germans couldn't get them.

☆ Chapter 36 ☆

The U.S.

★ ★ ☆ ★ ★ ★ ☆ ★ ★ ★ ☆ ★ ★

HOME FRONT

The other key turning point of 1941 came when the United States finally declared war on the Axis powers. Just as in World War I, the American public was reluctant to get involved, but again, the nation was provoked into engaging in the conflict.

ISOLATIONISM v. REALITY

The U.S. tried to stay neutral. Between 1935 and 1937, Congress passed the NEUTRALITY ACTS, making it illegal for Americans to sell weapons or loan money to foreign nations. When FDR was elected for a third term (the first time any president had served more than twice) in 1940, he knew, based on intelligence reports and communication with Prime Minister Churchill, the nation was on the brink of war.

Congress had expanded the American military at FDR's request, and in 1940, it passed the SELECTIVE TRAINING AND SERVICE ACT, the first PEACETIME DRAFT in American history. In March 1941, the LEND-LEASE ACT made it legal to sell or lend weapons and supplies to the Allies. That August, after German attacks on American destroyers, FDR and Churchill issued the ATLANTIC CHARTER. It said that neither country had any territorial ambitions in the war and that all people had the right to determine and live under a government of their own choosing.

> The Atlantic Charter was a little hypocritical, given that the British Empire was so large that "the sun never set on the British Empire" and the U.S. controlled Puerto Rico, Cuba, Guam, and the Philippines.

PEARL HARBOR

Meanwhile, HIDEKI TŌJŌ, the prime minister in control of Japan, set his sights on capturing islands in the Pacific. Japan had previously launched very successful invasions of mainland Asia.

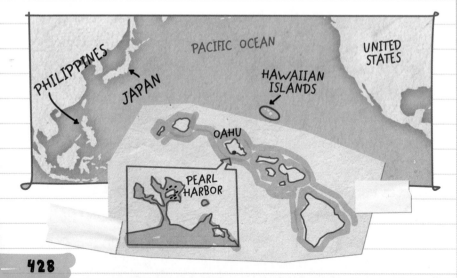

On DECEMBER 7, 1941, Japan launched a surprise attack on the U.S. naval base at PEARL HARBOR, Hawai'i. The intent was to disable the U.S. Naval fleet housed there. It was a devastating attack that sank or heavily damaged eight U.S. battleships along with three cruisers and several other ships. A total of 2,403 American civilians and servicemen were killed, and 1,178 were wounded.

FDR, who had been inching the country away from its isolationist tendencies, seized the moment and took advantage of the universal American outrage the attack caused. The next day, he asked Congress to declare war on Japan. Three days later, Germany and Italy declared war on the U.S., so Congress declared war back.

In his call for war, FDR referred to December 7, 1941, as "A date which will live in **INFAMY**."

INFAMY
being well known for bad reasons

MOBILIZATION
on the HOME FRONT

Industries produced tanks, ammunition, and other war-related products under the direction of the government. All that work ended the Great Depression, creating an employment rate of almost 100 percent. New government agencies formed, just like in World War I:

The WAR PRODUCTION BOARD decided which goods factories would produce. Americans were encouraged to **RATION** food and grow victory gardens.

RATIONING control of how much of something is available to each individual in a group

The OFFICE OF PRICE ADMINISTRATION controlled inflation.

The NATIONAL WAR LABOR BOARD resolved labor conflicts.

The REVENUE ACT OF 1942 raised taxes; the government also raised money by selling WAR BONDS.

OPPORTUNITIES and DISCRIMINATION

World War II provided opportunities for women and people of color:

Posters of ROSIE THE RIVETER were used to encourage women to work in factories and the defense industry.

Women enlisted in high numbers as WACs (Women's Army Corps), WAVES (Women Appointed for Volunteer Emergency Service) in the navy, or as WASPs (Women's Airforce Service Pilots), but as noncombatants.

Threats by Black labor leader A. PHILIP RANDOLPH to protest in Washington, D.C., led Roosevelt to sign EXECUTIVE ORDER 8802 (the FAIR EMPLOYMENT ACT), prohibiting racial discrimination in factories supplying the war effort.

Black Americans worked in defense factories in the North.

Though initially Black enlistees were given only menial jobs and filled military ranks as laborers, ultimately they were allowed into combat, though in segregated units. Famous Black units included the TUSKEGEE AIRMEN.

Indigenous Americans fought, and they also created unbreakable secret codes based on the Navajo language.

The government recruited Mexican American laborers called BRACEROS to work in agriculture.

ON THE FLIP SIDE:

Women and workers of color were still paid much less than white men doing the same jobs.

Greater Black and Mexican American presence in cities led to tension and uprisings, including the 1943 "ZOOT SUIT RIOTS" in LA, named after the clothing style worn by many young Latino men at the time.

After the war ended, Black, Latino, and Indigenous people, even those who fought in the war, still faced discrimination.

JAPANESE INTERNMENT
in the U.S.

Japanese Americans represented only about 3 percent of the population on the West Coast, and yet they faced severe discrimination. Japanese Americans born in Japan (ISSEI) were not allowed to become naturalized citizens or own land. Their children (NISEI) who were born in the United States were citizens but still faced discrimination.

Lawmakers on the West Coast, already responsible for years of laws that discriminated against Japanese people, took advantage of the fear and outrage that Americans felt toward Japan after the attack on Pearl Harbor to further **MARGINALIZE** this group. They ordered Japanese Americans to "evacuate" the coastal states, and most other states refused to take them in.

> **MARGINALIZE**
> to set aside as unimportant

So, FDR signed EXECUTIVE ORDER 9066 on February 19, 1944. This order forced more than 110,000 Americans of Japanese descent into "internment camps" ← BY LEGAL DEFINITION THEY WERE CONCENTRATION CAMPS. that sprang up practically overnight. Entire families were relocated. Their land was seized, resold by the government, and never returned; many people lost everything they owned. In 1944, in the case of *KOREMATSU v. UNITED STATES*, the Supreme Court upheld FDR's order as necessary, though two separate investigations revealed that Japanese Americans posed no threat.

The camps were poorly built out of unseasoned wood. Whole families lived in one or two rooms of connected barracks. Dozens of families shared common toilet, bathing, and laundry facilities as well as a mess hall. Japanese Americans were imprisoned by their own government.

In time, the government saw that Japanese Americans were valuable in the war effort. But, having justified their imprisonment by saying that the group posed a security risk,

> In 1942, the 442 Regimental Combat Team was created and composed of Japanese Americans. They served heroically during the war in Europe but were not allowed to fight in the Pacific.

the government could not release them without admitting its mistake. Instead, a LOYALTY QUESTIONNAIRE was created to determine who could be released to rejoin American society and join the war effort. People who passed the test might be released to return to college, pick crops, or join the military in segregated forces. Some men who passed the test refused to join the army until their families had also been released from camps, and those men spent years in jail as draft resisters. People who failed the test, whether because of confusion or anger, were kept in the camps.

In December 1944, PUBLIC PROCLAMATION NO. 21 lifted the executive order and declared that the camps would close, and Japanese Americans were able to return to their communities. A slow resettlement process began. The last camp closed in March 1946.

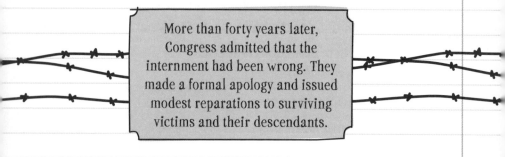

More than forty years later, Congress admitted that the internment had been wrong. They made a formal apology and issued modest reparations to surviving victims and their descendants.

CHECK YOUR KNOWLEDGE

1. How did America help the Allies before Pearl Harbor?

2. How did World War II contribute to the end of the Great Depression?

3. What was the intent behind the Japanese attack on Pearl Harbor?

4. What opportunities did World War II provide for women?

5. What drawbacks did people of color and women face despite advances made possible by World War II?

6. What was Executive Order 9066?

7. What did investigations into the need for Japanese internment reveal?

ANSWERS 435

CHECK YOUR ANSWERS

1. The Lend-Lease Act allowed weapons and supplies to be leased to the Allies.

2. The economy was improved by the high demand for war supplies and labor.

3. The intent was to disable the U.S. Naval fleet.

4. Women were encouraged to work in factories and the defense ministry. They also enlisted in noncombatant roles in the army, navy, and air force.

5. People of color and women were paid less than white men who had the same jobs. People of color faced discrimination in hiring and in the military.

6. An order that forced Japanese Americans of all ages into internment camps

7. Two separate investigations revealed that Japanese people posed no threat to national security.

☆ Chapter 37 ☆

AMERICA ENTERS
★ ★ ☆ ★ ★ ★ the ☆ ★ ★ ★ ★ ★
WAR in EUROPE
(via NORTH AFRICA)

ALLIED STRATEGY

With a draft and volunteers, the American military was ready to fight with the Allies. But where to start? The U.S. had to fight the Axis in the Atlantic and Japan in the Pacific. Stalin wanted continental Europe to be the first target. Churchill thought the inexperienced American troops would be easily defeated and stretched too thin. He suggested that Americans head to German-occupied North Africa. In December 1941, FDR agreed to Churchill's plan, leaving Stalin to handle Europe.

FIRST, NORTH AFRICA

The fighting in North Africa stretched throughout several countries. In June 1942, the German AFRIKA KORPS, led by the "DESERT FOX," GENERAL ERWIN ROMMEL, pushed into Egypt. In the BATTLE OF EL ALAMEIN, the British stopped the German advance, preventing them from capturing the

strategically located SUEZ CANAL, the British-controlled
water route between the Mediterranean and Red Seas.
Later that year, GENERAL DWIGHT D. EISENHOWER set up
headquarters in Gibraltar, and in 1943, the Allies helped
drive the Afrika Korps out of North Africa.

THEN, ITALY

The Allies reentered Europe from the south. In July 1943,
they landed on Sicily, an Italian island. Led by GENERAL
GEORGE S. PATTON, they moved on to mainland Italy. By
then, after losses in Africa and shortages in Italy, Italian
leaders had overthrown Mussolini, and the new government
surrendered to the Allies. Hitler didn't accept defeat. He
sent more Axis troops. In January 1944, the Allies surprised
German troops at Anzio, a city on the western coast of
Italy, and, after several months, defeated them. By June
1944, Rome was liberated.

MEANWHILE, BACK in the USSR

After their invasion of the Soviet Union in September 1942, German troops advanced to the industrial city of STALINGRAD. But when winter came, the cold was so severe that much of the German army starved or froze to death. Still, Hitler refused to withdraw. In January 1943, German commander General von Paulus defied the Führer's wishes and retreated. The Soviets suffered massive losses, but their victory was a turning point in the war because it showed Hitler's totalitarianism was weakening. The Germans tried to seize Leningrad (modern-day St. Petersburg), but the Russians pushed them west.

> Just as harsh weather conditions in Russia stymied the German army, weather was a factor in the defeat of Napoleon's army in 1812. Russia has been a challenging country to conquer because of its natural safeguards.

D-DAY

After freeing Italy, the Allied forces were finally ready to enter German-occupied France. In June 1944, General Eisenhower, who was then the Supreme Allied Commander in Europe, started OPERATION OVERLORD. Hitler expected any invasion to be near the town of Calais.

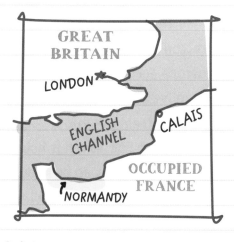

Early on June 6, 1944—which came to be known as D-DAY—
Allied forces landed, but not at Calais. PARATROOPERS (who
arrived by parachutes) and AMPHIBIOUS troops (trained
to operate on both land and sea) arrived in NORMANDY in
France. There were thousands of casualties, but the invasion
was successful.
American General
Omar Bradley led
the troops inland.
On August 25, Paris
was liberated.
Other Western
European nations
soon followed.

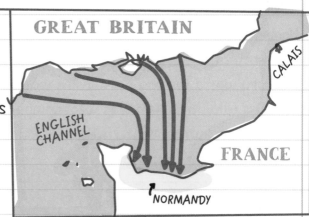

BATTLE of the BULGE

Hitler made a final attempt to turn the tide. On December 16,
1944, he attacked the Belgian
region of ARDENNES. The
attack forced Allied lines
to move back in one spot,
turning their line into a bubble
shape (a bulge, which is how
this attack came to be known
as the BATTLE OF THE BULGE).
By January, the Allies had
stopped the German advance.

The HOLOCAUST

Hitler rose to power by convincing his people that Jews were to blame for Germany's hardships.

In September 1935, Germany passed the NUREMBERG LAWS, stripping Jews of citizenship. On November 9, 1938—KRISTALLNACHT (the "night of the broken glass")—Jewish businesses, synagogues, and other property were destroyed in riots. The HOLOCAUST (literally, "burned whole") had begun. Jews were moved into **GHETTOS** and forced to wear identifying yellow labels in the shape of the Star of David, a Jewish symbol. Antisemitism (discrimination against Jews) became the law in Germany.

> **GHETTO**
> a segregated area in a city, often occupied by one group with a shared racial, ethnic, or religious identity

In January 1942, Hitler and the Nazis came up with a plan they called the FINAL SOLUTION: They planned to kill every Jew in a **GENOCIDE** in concentration camps. The young and healthy were forced to work in camps until they died; others were killed immediately in gas chambers. Six million Jewish people were killed, along with about five million others who didn't fit in with Hitler's idea of a perfect Aryan society, including gay people, Romani people, disabled people, and anyone who opposed the Nazis.

> **GENOCIDE**
> a killing of a race, ethnicity, or religious group of people

When Allied soldiers freed camp prisoners later, they were shocked to see the depth of Nazi brutality.

PRESIDENT TRUMAN

In the election of 1944, Roosevelt became the only person to be elected president for the fourth time in a row. But his health was fading. On April 12, 1945, FDR died, and Vice President HARRY S. TRUMAN took charge.

> The S wasn't short for a middle name. It stood for his two grandfathers, who both had S names. Apparently that wasn't such an odd thing to do with a middle initial in some places. And Harry was his full first name.

VICTORY in EUROPE

After other air raids on German cities, the Allied forces launched a major attack on Dresden in February 1945. As Soviet troops entered Berlin, Hitler went into hiding. On April 30, 1945—two days after Mussolini was killed by Italian partisans—Hitler committed suicide so he wouldn't have to face Germany's defeat. On May 7, after the Soviet army captured Berlin, the Germans surrendered to the Allied forces. May 8 was declared V-E DAY in honor of the Victory in Europe. But World War II wasn't over yet. It was time to defeat Japan and end the war.

CHECK YOUR KNOWLEDGE

1. Why did Churchill think the Allies ought to focus on North Africa before Europe?

2. How did Hitler react to the surrender of Italy?

3. How was the siege of Stalingrad a turning point in the war?

4. Whom did Hitler blame for Germany's problems in the 1930s?

5. Which groups other than Jews were to be exterminated as part of the Final Solution?

6. Where did Allied forces land to commence Operation Overlord?

7. How did the Battle of the Bulge get its name?

ANSWERS 443

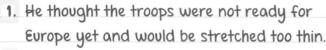

CHECK YOUR ANSWERS

1. He thought the troops were not ready for Europe yet and would be stretched too thin.

2. He did not accept it and sent his soldiers to fight for Italy. (They lost.)

3. Hitler's officers disobeyed his command not to retreat, showing that totalitarianism was weakening.

4. Jews

5. Disabled people, gay people, Romani people, and anyone who opposed the Nazis

6. Normandy

7. It is named after the bulge shape created in the Allied line when the Axis attacked at one point.

☆ Chapter 38 ☆

☆ WAR in the ☆
PACIFIC

JAPANESE VICTORIES

In December 1941, on the same day the Japanese bombed Pearl Harbor, they attacked American bases in Guam, Wake Island, and the Philippines and took over Manila, the capital of the Philippines. They also invaded Thailand, Hong Kong, Malaya, and Burma.

> NOW PART OF MALAYSIA

MYANMAR TODAY

ASIA
JAPAN
PACIFIC OCEAN

JAPAN

PACIFIC OCEAN

HIROSHIMA

NAGASAKI

TOKYO

EAST CHINA SEA

JAPANESE ATTACKS AND INVASIONS

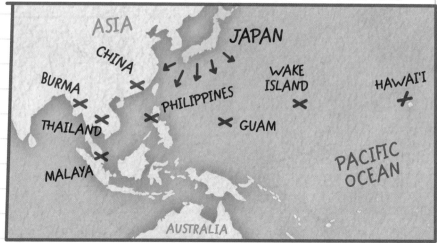

After months of conflict, American general Douglas MacArthur, his family, and some key aides were ordered to leave the Philippines to defend Australia. The Philippines surrendered to Japan. The troops still in the Bataan province of the Philippines were captured and forced on a brutal walk of over 60 miles to the Bataan Peninsula prison camps, where hundreds of Americans and thousands of Filipinos were killed; the event came to be known as the BATAAN DEATH MARCH.

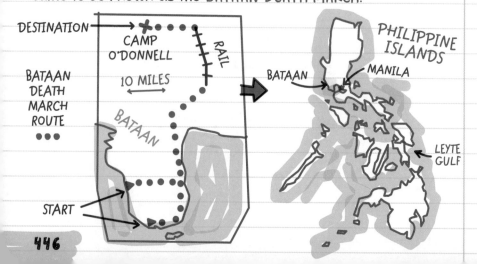

TURNING the TIDE

In April 1942, Americans launched air raids on Tokyo, which wasn't militarily significant but did boost American morale. In the BATTLE OF THE CORAL SEA, they blocked Japan from reaching Australia, helped by ADMIRAL CHESTER NIMITZ of the U.S. Pacific Fleet, who intercepted Japanese communications. Code cracking also helped the Allies prepare for the BATTLE OF MIDWAY on June 4, 1942. In a major American victory and turning point, the American navy destroyed four Japanese aircraft carriers.

The U.S. used Navajo CODE TALKERS— Navajo soldiers who communicated in codes based on the Navajo language. It was impossible for the Japanese or other outsiders to figure out the codes, and the code talkers made an invaluable contribution to the war.

MacArthur and Nimitz adopted a strategy called ISLAND HOPPING to secure air bases in order to launch larger attacks on Japan: capture small islands, use each as a base to capture other islands, hop closer to the Philippines and Japan. It was time-consuming but effective. From August 1942 to February 1943, the marines fought to capture the island of GUADALCANAL. In the October 1944 BATTLE OF LEYTE GULF, the Allies destroyed almost the entire Japanese navy. Allied forces liberated Manila in March 1945 and headed for Japan.

ISLAND HOPPING

REACHING JAPAN

The Allied forces targeted two Japanese islands:
IWO JIMA in February 1945 and OKINAWA in April.
In a desperate attempt to gain the upper hand, the
Japanese used KAMIKAZES—suicide pilots—to attack
Allied ships, but the Allied forces still advanced.

The A-BOMB

Japan was unwilling to surrender, and the Allies considered
a full-scale invasion. However, the U.S. had also conducted
the first successful test of an ATOMIC BOMB on July 16, 1945,
after three years of work on the "MANHATTAN PROJECT,"
led by scientist J. ROBERT OPPENHEIMER. (FDR founded the
Manhattan Project after Albert Einstein and other scientists
had warned him that an atomic weapon was being developed
by Germany.) Even though he knew that a single atomic bomb
could cost thousands of civilian lives, President Truman saw
it as a justifiable way to end the war and to save countless
Americans. Truman issued the POTSDAM DECLARATION: If
Japan did not surrender, the U.S. would inflict "prompt and
utter destruction."

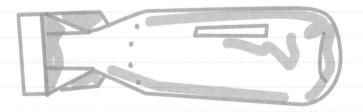

This seemed like just another threat, so Japan did not surrender. On August 6, 1945, the B-29 bomber *ENOLA GAY* dropped an atomic bomb on the city of HIROSHIMA. At least 75,000 people were killed in an instant. Japan remained firm. On August 9, the U.S. dropped another atomic bomb on the city of NAGASAKI, killing over 20,000 civilians. Many of those who survived the bombings later died from radiation and horrific burns or lived with severe health problems and disabilities.

The WAR ENDS

On August 15, 1945, Japan surrendered. August 15 was Victory over Japan Day, or V-J DAY. *3 MONTHS AFTER V-E DAY* (Some consider August 14 to be V-J Day because of time differences between the U.S. and Asia.) On September 2, Japan signed the surrender documents. World War II was finally over.

WHAT MAKES A NUCLEAR WEAPON NUCLEAR?

The power comes from reactions in the NUCLEI of atoms of RADIOACTIVE elements, which emit energy. When the particles collide, the result is so strong that a tiny amount of material can create a huge explosion. Atomic bombs, or "A-bombs," get their power by splitting the nucleus. Even more powerful hydrogen bombs, or "H-bombs," invented in the 1950s, fuse multiple nuclei together.

CHECK YOUR KNOWLEDGE

1. What happened to the Allied troops who stayed in the Philippines when MacArthur left?

2. What was a major communications advantage the Allies had over the Japanese?

3. What is "island hopping" and how does it work?

4. What islands were the first two Allied targets in Japan?

5. What inspired FDR to found the Manhattan Project?

6. What did President Truman think about the morality of using an atomic weapon?

7. What Japanese cities did the U.S. drop atomic bombs on?

8. What happened to many people in Hiroshima and Nagasaki who survived the initial blast of the atomic weapons?

CHECK YOUR ANSWERS

1. They were forced to make the Bataan Death March.

2. Japanese codes had been broken, but the Navajo-based American codes had not.

3. "Island hopping" is the strategy of taking one island at a time and using it as a base to attack the next.

4. Iwo Jima and Okinawa

5. Einstein alerted him to the possibility that the Germans could develop the technology first.

6. He thought its potential to save American lives that might be lost to the war outweighed the devastation the bombings would cause for Japanese citizens.

7. Hiroshima and Nagasaki

8. Many later died from burns and radiation or lived with severe health problems and disabilities.

Unit 9

Post-World War II Era
1945-1990

The post-World War II era was full of exciting change. Television became the main form of entertainment. Rock and roll swept the nation. Black Americans and women fought for equal rights. Also significant: America entered the Korean and Vietnam Wars, the Cold War began, and everyone was afraid of Communism and nukes.

Chapter 39

AMERICA
★ ★ ★ ★ ★ ★ ★ ★ ★ ★ ★ ★
AFTER the WAR

The WORLD AFTER the WAR

As the only major world power to have had minimal fighting on the home front, the U.S. came out of the war better off than its allies and enemies in almost every way. (The only fighting that took place on U.S. soil was the attack on Pearl Harbor.) The economy had been helped by the war and continued to grow.

YALTA and POTSDAM

In February 1945, three months before Germany surrendered and six months before Japan surrendered, it was clear the Allies were going to win the war. The BIG THREE—Churchill, FDR, and Stalin—met at the YALTA CONFERENCE and discussed what should happen once the war was over. The first priority was to prevent future German aggression. The leaders decided to divide Germany into four parts. The city of Berlin would also be divided in four. The U.S., the U.K., France, and the Soviet Union would each control a section.

The
BIG
THREE

CHURCHILL   FDR   STALIN

The three also agreed at Yalta that all territories freed from Nazi control would have the right to hold democratic elections. (Stalin, whose country had been devastated by German aggression in both world wars, was given rights to a "sphere of influence" in Eastern Europe.) The USSR agreed to commit troops to the war against Japan. Everyone agreed to put suspected Nazi war criminals on trial, and they made plans for a new peacekeeping group, the UNITED NATIONS, to replace the failed League of Nations.

> The next time these countries met was at the POTSDAM CONFERENCE, in July 1945: FDR had died, Germany had surrendered, and Stalin had failed to move his troops out of Eastern Europe. Meanwhile, President Truman hinted to Stalin that the U.S. had a new, powerful bomb, but Japan was still defiant.

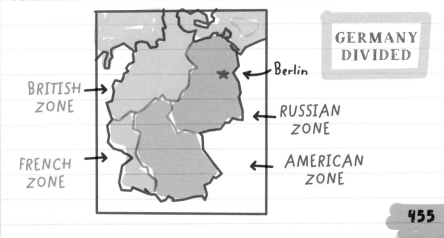

GERMANY DIVIDED

BRITISH ZONE →

Berlin

→ RUSSIAN ZONE

FRENCH ZONE →

← AMERICAN ZONE

The UNITED NATIONS

The UNITED NATIONS (or UN) formed on June 26, 1945, when 50 countries signed its charter in San Francisco. The UN's goal is to preserve world peace through **DIPLOMACY**.

> **DIPLOMACY**
> the managing of international relations through a country's representatives

After the Holocaust, many Jews sought a homeland to call their own. One of the UN's first tasks was to create Arab and Jewish states from a British-controlled area in the Middle East called Palestine. In 1948, by UN mandate, the state of ISRAEL was officially formed. The region that was formerly called Palestine had a mainly Muslim Arab population that was not happy with a new Jewish state taking control.

Neighboring Arab countries attacked the newly formed Israel in 1948, but Israel fought back hard. Thousands of Palestinian Arabs fled the area and sought refuge in the West Bank and the Gaza Strip, two Arab-controlled lands. Arab forces attacked again in 1967, and this time Israel gained control of the West Bank, the Gaza Strip, and parts of Syria and Egypt.

The conflict between Palestine and Israel continues to this day.

The NUREMBERG TRIALS

In November 1945, in Nuremberg, Germany, the NUREMBERG TRIALS began, trying Nazis for CRIMES AGAINST HUMANITY and war

> **TRIBUNAL**
> a court

crimes. In the first round of trials, 19 Nazis were found guilty and 12 were sentenced to death. More than 100 were found guilty before the process ended. A similar **TRIBUNAL** (the International Military Tribunal for the Far East) was held in Tokyo, where General Hideki Tōjō and six other Japanese leaders were convicted and executed.

The IRON CURTAIN

Even though the U.S. and the Soviet Union fought on the same side during World War II, their political differences were too great to maintain an alliance. Without a common enemy, they became enemies of each other. Although Stalin had promised free, democratic elections in the Eastern European nations, he set up Communist **SATELLITE** governments there under his control.

> **SATELLITE** describes something that is subordinate to another authority

There was mutual distrust. Each side thought the other was trying to sway countries to their political beliefs and thus strengthen its position in the world. The tension between Communist governments (USSR and Eastern Europe) and capitalist governments (U.S. and Western Europe) became known as the COLD WAR, which consisted of threats and intimidation, as opposed to a "hot" war with actual fighting. In a speech in 1946, Winston Churchill said that an IRON CURTAIN had descended on Eastern Europe, separating it from the rest of the world.

The TRUMAN DOCTRINE

President Truman decided that the U.S. would fight the Cold War through CONTAINMENT (in other words, stop communism from spreading). Truman persuaded Congress to allocate money to help defeat Communist rebels in Greece and Turkey to prevent the spread of Communism to two more countries. Holding back Communism through containment and giving assistance to groups committed to fighting Communism was the TRUMAN DOCTRINE.

The MARSHALL PLAN

In June 1947, Secretary of State GEORGE MARSHALL came up with his MARSHALL PLAN to rebuild Europe. The U.S. hoped to contain Communism, boost European economies, and continue U.S. trade with Europe. The U.S. gave about $13 billion in aid to Western European nations between 1948 and 1951. Economic aid was supposed to protect countries that were unstable and low-income and prevent Communists from taking over. The U.S. also provided economic assistance to Asian countries, including Japan, which it had occupied immediately after WWII and continued to during this time.

The BERLIN AIRLIFT

The U.S., the U.K., and France announced that they would combine their shares of Germany and Berlin into a single democratic nation. Truman believed that a unified Germany was the key to Europe's recovery. Stalin saw this as a threat, not only to the Soviet-controlled part of Germany, but also to Europe in general if the Germans regained power.

> **BLOCKADE**
> to seal off access to a specific location, in order to prevent supplies, food, aid, or people from entering or leaving

Stalin began the Berlin **BLOCKADE**— a strategy to cut off the city's access to the West. Truman organized the

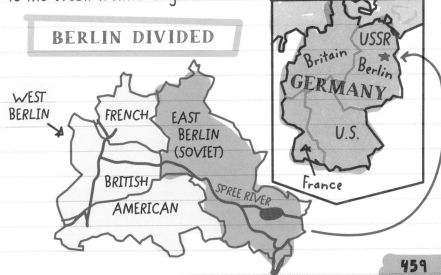

BERLIN DIVIDED

WEST BERLIN

FRENCH

EAST BERLIN (SOVIET)

BRITISH

AMERICAN

SPREE RIVER

USSR

Britain

Berlin

GERMANY

U.S.

France

BERLIN AIRLIFT: U.S. and British planes brought food and supplies to West Berlin until Stalin ended the blockade. Still, Berlin remained divided into East and West Berlin.

By the end of 1949, Germany was also divided into two nations: the Federal Republic of Germany (democratic, West Germany) and the German Democratic Republic (Communist, East Germany).

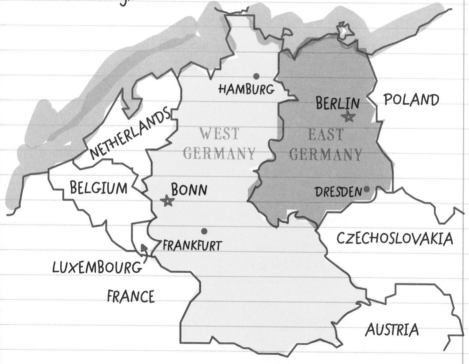

NATO and the WARSAW PACT

In 1949, the U.S. and Canada joined with Western Europe to form an alliance, the NORTH ATLANTIC TREATY ORGANIZATION (NATO). It was a defensive alliance   FIRST PEACETIME MILITARY ALLIANCE meant to prevent a Soviet assault on Western Europe. In 1955, the USSR and seven other satellite states in Europe established their own alliance, the WARSAW PACT.

The FAIR DEAL

Truman also had to pay attention to the needs of Americans at home. He began preparing a slate of domestic reforms in 1945. This extension of the New Deal was called the FAIR DEAL, but Truman had only limited success in getting Congress to pass it. These were some of his goals:

a higher minimum wage

better Social Security

job creation

better public housing

national health insurance

WHAT'S THE DEAL?

Remember: The SQUARE DEAL was Teddy Roosevelt's domestic program that focused on conservation, control of corporations, and consumer protection.

The NEW DEAL was a series of economic programs enacted by FDR during his first term in office.

The FAIR DEAL was a series of domestic reforms proposed by Harry Truman.

Truman also established a COMMITTEE ON CIVIL RIGHTS in 1946. He asked Congress to write laws ending POLL TAXES, which kept poor people from voting, and to pass anti-lynching laws. With little support from a conservative Congress, Truman made significant and permanent changes to federal policy when he ended discriminatory hiring practices in the federal government and desegregated the U.S. military by executive order.

The ELECTION of 1948

The Republican Party was sure they'd win. Truman hadn't succeeded with the Fair Deal, and the Democratic Party was divided: Some Southern Democrats, angry about Truman's support of civil rights, formed a new party, called the States' Rights Democratic Party, or the DIXIECRATS. Other Democrats formed a new PROGRESSIVE PARTY to try to reconcile with the Soviets.

The Republican candidate, THOMAS DEWEY, was so far ahead in the polls that the *CHICAGO DAILY TRIBUNE* newspaper released a special edition with a huge "DEWEY DEFEATS TRUMAN" on the front page before the votes were tallied. But Truman had gone on a **WHISTLE-STOP TOUR**, convincing Americans that the failure of the Fair Deal was the fault of the Republican Congress. Truman won a second term.

> **WHISTLE-STOP TOUR**
> a campaign trip from town to town, referring to the train stations where candidates would make a quick stop before continuing on

CHECK YOUR KNOWLEDGE

1. Why was the U.S. in a better position after World War II than its allies were?

2. What did the Allies decide when they met at the Yalta Conference?

3. What is the goal of the United Nations?

4. The defendants at the Nuremberg Trials were accused of what?

5. What made the Cold War "cold"?

6. What was the thinking behind the policy of containment?

7. What were the components of Truman's Fair Deal?

8. What inspired the Dixiecrats to break away from the Democrats?

ANSWERS 463

CHECK YOUR ANSWERS

1. There had been no fighting on U.S. soil, other than Pearl Harbor, and the U.S. economy was thriving.

2. They decided they needed a better peacekeeping group, they would fight against Japan, and they would divide Germany into occupied zones.

3. To preserve peace through diplomacy

4. Crimes against humanity and war crimes

5. They fought using threats and intimidation instead of active fighting.

6. Truman believed that it was best to prevent Communism from spreading.

7. The Fair Deal promised a higher minimum wage, job creation, health insurance, better Social Security, and better housing.

8. They were opposed to Truman's civil rights programs.

☆ Chapter 40 ☆

The KOREAN WAR ☆

COMMUNISM IN ASIA

When Japan invaded China in 1937, China was in the midst of a civil war about who would lead it. Once Japan was defeated and forced to leave China, the civil war picked up again. In 1949, MAO ZEDONG led the Communist Party to drive CHIANG KAI-SHEK's NATIONALISTS out of power. The Nationalists fled to TAIWAN, where they set up a government that the West recognized as the legitimate Chinese ruling body. On the mainland, the PEOPLE'S REPUBLIC OF CHINA was established on October 1, 1949. Many Americans thought that their government should have done more to stop a Communist nation and ally of the USSR from forming.

In 1949, the Soviets detonated an atomic bomb, which meant that the U.S. no longer had a nuclear monopoly.

The 38th PARALLEL

From 1910 to 1945, Korea was an occupied colony of Japan. When Japan surrendered at the end of WWII, the U.S. proposed sharing control of Korea with the Soviet Union. They divided Korea on the 38TH PARALLEL. The Soviets helped Communists take power in NORTH KOREA, and the U.S. supported the democratic government in SOUTH KOREA.

On June 25, 1950, North Korean troops crossed the border to try to take over South Korea and unite Korea under one Communist government. This was another civil war in Asia over what type of government would be established in the newly independent country. Having lost China to Communism, Truman decided to take a stand in Korea, even though that country shared a huge border with China. Truman sent military assistance to South Korea and asked for help from the United Nations without ever officially declaring war.

The KOREAN WAR

The United Nations put together soldiers from 16 different nations, but the majority were American. The forces were led by U.S. General Douglas MacArthur. MacArthur forced the North Korean troops to retreat, and the UN forces pushed them all the way back to the North Korean border with China. This was like poking a sleeping bear. China entered the war on the side of North Korea. On November 25, 1950, the Chinese army entered North Korea, and American troops retreated.

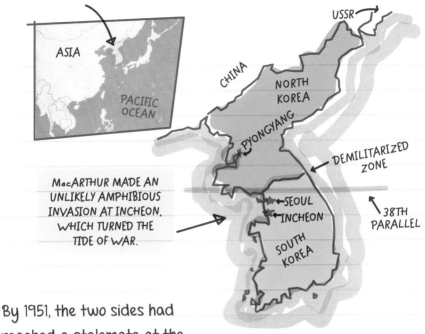

MacARTHUR MADE AN UNLIKELY AMPHIBIOUS INVASION AT INCHEON, WHICH TURNED THE TIDE OF WAR.

By 1951, the two sides had reached a stalemate at the 38th parallel. General MacArthur wanted to go nuclear against China, but Truman refused. MacArthur publicly criticized Truman, and Truman fired him. Peace talks between the UN and North Korea began in July 1951, but progress was slow.

"I LIKE IKE"

THIS WAS EISENHOWER'S

I LIKE IKE

MAIN POLITICAL SLOGAN

Americans were angry about what seemed like pointless fighting in Korea. The Republican nominee, DWIGHT D. EISENHOWER (known as "Ike"), promised

FROM WWII!

to end the war and easily defeated Democrat ADLAI STEVENSON in the 1952 presidential election. He was the first Republican to defeat a Democrat in a presidential election since 1928.

467

The FORGOTTEN WAR

It took more than a year, but a cease-fire finally ended fighting on July 27, 1953. A DEMILITARIZED ZONE (DMZ) was established not far from the 38th parallel as a no-man's-land and **DE FACTO** border between North Korea and South Korea. Thirty-three thousand American service members died, as did nearly 3 million Koreans and Chinese, the majority of whom were civilians. Still, it is often referred to as the "Forgotten War."

> **DE FACTO**
> in effect

WE STILL DON'T HAVE A PEACE TREATY WITH NORTH KOREA.

McCARTHYISM

Fear of Communism was strong in the U.S., setting off another Red Scare. The HOUSE UN-AMERICAN ACTIVITIES COMMITTEE (HUAC) was established in 1938 to investigate "un-American activity"— meaning any behavior that seemed Communist-like.

> **BLACKLIST**
> a list of people who are not welcome

President Truman investigated accusations of **ESPIONAGE** among government workers.

The HUAC targeted the movie industry; people who were charged were **BLACKLISTED** by movie studios if they refused to reveal information.

Communist groups were required to register with the government.

In 1951, a State Department employee named **ALGER HISS** was jailed for perjury in connection with giving information to the Soviets.

JULIUS and **ETHEL ROSENBERG** were executed in 1953 for selling atomic secrets to the Soviet Union.

In 1950, JOSEPH McCARTHY, a Republican senator, took charge of the hunt for Communists. He made reckless accusations (mostly against leftists) and claimed to have a list of Communists working for the State Department, even though he never showed it. McCARTHYISM now refers to the practice of making unfounded accusations of treason and the use of accusations to prevent criticism. During televised hearings in 1954, McCarthy couldn't back up his accusations and lost all his credibility. As a result, he was censured by the Senate for distorting facts and violating senatorial ethics.

YOU CAN WATCH THESE ONLINE NOW.

ARMS RACE

Using stolen technology, the Soviet Union built an atomic bomb in 1949. In 1950, the U.S. began working on a HYDROGEN BOMB, which was many times more powerful. The H-bomb was tested successfully in 1952; by 1955, the Soviets had developed their own H-bomb. Both sides raced to stockpile the most weapons.

The U.S. and USSR were developing missile technology and became locked in a SPACE RACE, starting when the Soviet Union launched the first artificial satellite, SPUTNIK 1, in 1957. The next year, the U.S. launched a satellite and founded the NATIONAL AERONAUTICS AND SPACE ADMINISTRATION (NASA).

BRINKMANSHIP

Eisenhower was a moderate Republican who balanced the budget and supported the 1956 FEDERAL HIGHWAY ACT, which created the first interstate highways. He believed that containment wasn't strong enough for the Cold War. His secretary of state, JOHN FOSTER DULLES, coined a new term for their strategy: "BRINKMANSHIP," meaning that the U.S. would issue warnings with increasing pressure (to go to the BRINK of a crisis). The greatest way to prevent nuclear war was knowing that there would be no winner; both sides would be destroyed. The MUTUAL ASSURED DESTRUCTION (MAD) doctrine was a cornerstone of U.S. and Soviet foreign policy during the Cold War.

Relations between Soviet leader NIKITA KHRUSHCHEV and Eisenhower deteriorated further when Eisenhower sent a U-2 spy plane over Russia, denied its purpose, and then refused to apologize even when the pilot was captured.

CHECK YOUR KNOWLEDGE

1. Which of the two Chinese governments did the U.S. officially recognize?

2. Why did North Korean troops cross the 38th parallel?

3. When did Congress declare war on North Korea?

4. Where was the demilitarized zone established in Korea?

5. What was considered an "un-American activity" during the Red Scare?

6. How did McCarthy lose his credibility?

7. What did the U.S. do after the Russians launched the first satellite?

ANSWERS   471

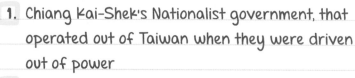

CHECK YOUR ANSWERS

1. Chiang Kai-Shek's Nationalist government, that operated out of Taiwan when they were driven out of power

2. They wanted to unite Korea under one Communist government.

3. Trick question! The U.S. never declared war.

4. Along the 38th parallel, where the line had been at the beginning of the conflict

5. Anything suspected of Communist leanings

6. He couldn't back up his accusations.

7. They founded the National Aeronautics and Space Administration (NASA).

Chapter 41

THE BABY BOOM

AMERICAN AFFLUENCE

America prospered under Eisenhower. Although he wanted to decrease the size of government, he decided not to reverse the social reforms that Truman had put in place. He even expanded Social Security, increased the minimum wage, and established the Department of Health, Education, and Welfare. Not all Americans, however, had equal access to this affluence, even if they had defended the country patriotically in the wars.

The economy boomed. Americans bought home appliances, cars, clothes, and televisions. They watched programs like *I LOVE LUCY* and *THE LONE RANGER*, where they saw advertisements for more products to buy. The "AMERICAN DREAM" was linked to owning the same things as the families on television. These shows often reinforced stereotypes about who "real"

Americans were, while failing to represent the diverse American population.

The G.I. BILL and the BABY BOOM

One reason people could afford to buy so much was the **G.I.** Bill (or the G.I. BILL OF RIGHTS or the SERVICEMEN'S READJUSTMENT ACT), which President Roosevelt had signed into law in 1944. The G.I. Bill provided veterans with loans to get an education and buy homes. Home sales helped the economy. Many veterans were also ready to start families, leading to a sudden spike in the national birth rate. The BABY BOOM was a prosperous time.

> **G.I.**
> an American soldier, from the initials for "Government Issue"

The G.I. Bill of Rights, however, like New Deal programs before it, was administered locally. This meant local officials could discriminate against Japanese, Black, and Indigenous Americans and restrict or deny their benefits. In addition to being denied loans, grants, or unemployment benefits, these groups were marginalized in other ways. Tuition to attend technical school or college doesn't benefit you if no colleges will accept you because of your race. A home loan does you no good if new suburban neighborhoods have bylaws preventing people of color from buying there.

WHITE FLIGHT

The Highway Act created new highways, enabling more people to travel and commute.

> These new highways were often built through Black communities, destroying homes, apartment buildings, Black churches, and Black-owned businesses. Convenience for some came at the cost of whole communities for others.

Builders were eager to keep up with demand and keep homes affordable, so they began creating complexes where every house looked exactly the same. Built in 1951, LEVITTOWN, on Long Island, New York, became the first mass-produced suburb. Families moved from the cities to the SUBURBS. People who couldn't afford to move had to stay in the cities. Because of WHITE FLIGHT—the process of affluent, mostly white families moving out of the cities—many INNER CITY areas became places of concentrated poverty. Taxes went to suburban infrastructures, causing a decline in the quality of public services in urban areas. Conditions deteriorated so much that the federal government had to create URBAN RENEWAL initiatives. It wasn't just city people who missed out on the prosperity. Small farmers were hurt by the growth of **AGRIBUSINESS**.

AGRIBUSINESS
large-scale corporate farming

POP CULTURE
and the GENERATION GAP

In the 1950s a new kind of American music called ROCK AND ROLL emerged. It originated from Black American music genres, including rhythm and blues, gospel, jazz, and country music. Rock and roll became immensely popular. Black musicians reached white audiences, and white musicians started playing rock and roll, too. In 1956, teenagers fell in love with ELVIS PRESLEY and his music. Rock influenced culture, style, and what it meant to be a young American. For the first time, young people were being targeted as a generation, with advertisements and fads. No surprise, many adults didn't understand the attraction.

ROCK-AND-ROLL
FASHION

CHECK YOUR KNOWLEDGE

1. How did Eisenhower's social beliefs differ from Truman's? How did that translate into his domestic policies?

2. How did television influence consumerism?

3. What did the G.I. Bill provide for veterans?

4. What was the baby boom?

5. Why were homes mass-produced for some suburbs? Which suburb was most famous for this?

6. What were the effects of white flight on urban areas in the 1950s?

7. How did agribusiness affect farmers?

8. What were the roots of rock-and-roll music?

ANSWERS 477

CHECK YOUR ANSWERS

1. Eisenhower believed in smaller government, but he didn't actually reverse Truman's policies. He even expanded some welfare programs.

2. Television presented a vision of an ideal American life, and ran advertisements for things to buy to achieve it.

3. Home loans and subsidized education

4. A spike in the national birth rate when veterans returned after World War II

5. They were produced, notably in Levittown, to meet demand.

6. Inner city areas lost valuable tax dollars and became places of concentrated poverty.

7. Agribusiness allowed for large-scale corporate farming, which hurt small farmers' businesses.

8. Rhythm and blues, or R&B; jazz; gospel; and country music

☆ Chapter 42 ☆

☆ ☆ ☆ The ☆ ☆ ☆
CIVIL RIGHTS
MOVEMENT

The MOVEMENT BEGINS

The CIVIL RIGHTS MOVEMENT was a period of **GRASSROOTS** efforts to put an end to racial discrimination, especially in the 1950s and '60s. Protests against

> **GRASSROOTS**
> from the people, as opposed to the government

segregation had begun decades earlier, but World War II helped raise more awareness—particularly among Black veterans—of the hypocrisy in fighting for freedom abroad while inequality persisted at home.

GRASS HAS ROOTS THAT GO WIDE AND DEEP,
EVEN THOUGH GRASS ISN'T VERY TALL. ➡

BROWN v. BOARD of EDUCATION

One of the first targets was segregation. The NAACP challenged this law in the early 1950s, on the basis that many "separate but equal" public schools for Black kids were inferior

479

to all-white schools in the same district. That was a violation of the Fourteenth Amendment, which says that all U.S. citizens are entitled to the EQUAL PROTECTION OF THE LAW.

The parents of a girl named Linda Brown sued her school district when she wasn't allowed to attend the all-white school near her house in Topeka, Kansas. The Supreme Court heard the arguments in the case of BROWN v. BOARD OF EDUCATION OF TOPEKA, KANSAS in 1952.

THURGOOD MARSHALL, a lawyer for the NAACP, presented arguments for the Brown family. He persuaded

THURGOOD MARSHALL became the first Black American Supreme Court justice.

✓ IT WAS A UNANIMOUS 9–0 DECISION.

the court to make a landmark ruling on May 17, 1954, that said placing Black Americans in "separate but equal" schools was unconstitutional because things that are separate are never actually equal. In a case the next year (Brown II), the Supreme Court required that all segregated public schools integrate "WITH ALL DELIBERATE SPEED." The court did not give a deadline, so some schools delayed integration for years.

The LITTLE ROCK NINE

In September 1957, an Arkansas high school was ordered by a judge to admit nine Black students. Arkansas Governor ORVAL FAUBUS was a segregationist, and he sent the Arkansas National Guard to stop the students from going in. One of the LITTLE ROCK NINE, ELIZABETH ECKFORD, was threatened with lynching. For three weeks, the students were kept out. President Eisenhower ultimately sent paratroopers to escort the students and enforce the law.

ROSA PARKS and the MONTGOMERY BUS BOYCOTT

City buses were segregated, too. Black riders were required to give up their seats if white riders wanted them. On December 1, 1955, in Montgomery, Alabama, an activist named ROSA PARKS refused to give up her seat for a white passenger. She was arrested and fined. In response, Black Americans organized the MONTGOMERY BUS BOYCOTT, which lasted for more than a year.

Most people who rode the buses were Black, so the boycott cost the city a lot of money. Boycotters organized carpools or walked, even when faced with violent retaliation from segregationists and the KKK.

During the civil rights era, Southern states resisted the Supreme Court decisions and vowed not to enforce them, in a strategy called MASSIVE RESISTANCE. Furthermore, various governors proposed to interject the state government between the federal government and its citizens in a tactic called STATE INTERPOSITION. Eisenhower, however, stood fast and used federal troops to enforce the law.

On November 13, 1956, the Supreme Court ruled that the bus segregation law was unconstitutional, and buses were desegregated.

MARTIN LUTHER KING JR.

A young reverend named DR. MARTIN LUTHER KING JR. (MLK JR.) rose to prominence during the Montgomery Bus Boycott. His talent for speechmaking made him popular. In 1957, he helped found the SOUTHERN CHRISTIAN LEADERSHIP CONFERENCE (SCLC), a key organization in the civil rights movement. MLK Jr. was influenced by A. PHILIP RANDOLPH and by MOHANDAS GANDHI, who had led protests in India against British foreign rule, using nonviolent tactics of civil disobedience.

> MOHANDAS GANDHI was also known as Mahatma, or "Great Soul." He used nonviolent protest to advocate self-rule in India against British colonizers.

SIT-INS

One of the most efficient forms of nonviolent protest was the SIT-IN: sitting in protest. On February 1, 1960, four Black college students sat at a whites-only lunch counter in Greensboro, North Carolina. Although the lunch counter staff refused to serve them, the students returned each day with more and more people. Eventually, store owners desegregated to prevent further disruption of their businesses.

An organization called the STUDENT NONVIOLENT COORDINATING COMMITTEE (SNCC) formed to help people launch sit-ins across the South. The grassroots civil rights movement was growing and making its mark.

JOHN F. KENNEDY

In the election of 1960, JOHN F. KENNEDY (JFK), a young Democratic senator from Massachusetts, challenged incumbent Republican vice president RICHARD NIXON. JFK came from a prominent political family and was a WWII navy war hero. The Kennedy-Nixon debates were the first televised presidential debates. Americans saw that Kennedy was more youthful and appealing than Nixon. Although some people thought a Catholic like Kennedy would be more loyal to the pope than to the American people, Kennedy reassured them, and he promised supporters a "NEW FRONTIER" on domestic reforms, a call for public service, vigorous federal government, and a strong anti-Communist foreign policy.

NO HAT

PILLBOX HAT

SUNGLASSES

PEARLS

SUIT

SKINNY TIE →

The election was close, but Kennedy won. He and his wife, JACQUELINE, were exciting, stylish, and popular.

JFK and Jackie were style icons.

Kennedy didn't immediately pursue the reforms he had promised, in order to avoid upsetting Southern Democrats. Civil rights leaders criticized him for not bringing about change fast enough.

FREEDOM RIDERS

In May 1961, the CONGRESS OF RACIAL EQUALITY (CORE) sent Black people and white people to ride together as FREEDOM RIDERS on interstate buses to segregated bus stations in the South. They planned to refuse to obey racial restrictions. The Freedom Riders faced violent attacks from angry white people in the towns where they stopped, but they continued riding. That autumn, the Interstate Commerce Commission began enforcing desegregation in bus depots. Another nonviolent protest had worked.

OUTRAGE in BIRMINGHAM

In spring 1963, the SCLC staged a major nonviolent protest in Birmingham, Alabama. Its members urged business leaders to end segregation in restaurants, stores, and facilities. Birmingham police attacked nonviolent protesters, including children, with high-pressure water jets and police dogs. When the national news media captured images of the violence, the public was outraged.

During these protests, in April 1963, MLK Jr. was arrested and spent over a week in jail. He wrote his famous "LETTER FROM BIRMINGHAM JAIL," in which he eloquently laid out the causes for protest and the philosophy of nonviolence. He wrote,

"INJUSTICE ANYWHERE IS A THREAT TO JUSTICE EVERYWHERE."

The MARCH on WASHINGTON

JFK spoke on national television about the need for civil rights and introduced a bill on the issue. In support of this bill, MLK Jr. led a quarter of a million people in the MARCH ON WASHINGTON on August 28, 1963. The march was the scene of his "I HAVE A DREAM" speech.

The KENNEDY ASSASSINATION

On November 22, 1963, while campaigning in Dallas, President Kennedy was shot and killed by Lee Harvey Oswald. Two days later, Oswald, while in police custody, was shot and killed by Jack Ruby. Ruby was suspected of conspiring with Oswald in JFK's assassination, but a government commission later confirmed that Oswald acted alone.

A COMMUNIST SYMPATHIZER

The CIVIL RIGHTS ACT of 1964

Kennedy's vice president, LYNDON B. JOHNSON (LBJ), was sworn in as president, and he prioritized Kennedy's civil rights bill in order to honor the late president's memory. The CIVIL RIGHTS ACT OF 1964 passed quickly. It:

outlawed discriminatory voter registration practices

ended segregation in establishments that affected interstate commerce, which was broadly defined as "any place of public accommodation"

← SUCH AS HOTELS, RESTAURANTS, GAS STATIONS, ETC.

ended segregation in public places and public schools

established the **EQUAL EMPLOYMENT OPPORTUNITY COMMISSION**

gave the federal government the power to enforce the laws

FREEDOM SUMMER

Once desegregation became law, the civil rights movement tackled voting rights. In the summer of 1964, after the TWENTY-FOURTH AMENDMENT (which banned poll taxes) was ratified, the SNCC organized FREEDOM SUMMER, during which students from the North came to the South to conduct VOTER REGISTRATION drives. In Mississippi, three volunteers were murdered by the KKK. The local police department attempted to cover it up.

In early 1965, the SCLC and MLK Jr. led a protest in SELMA, ALABAMA, including a march to Montgomery, during which protesters were violently attacked by state troopers. Americans watched the event in horror on national television. President Johnson signed the VOTING RIGHTS ACT OF 1965, allowing the federal government to protect all people's right to vote. It significantly increased the number of registered Black voters.

The GREAT SOCIETY

During a State of the Union address to Congress in January 1964, President LBJ declared a WAR ON POVERTY. He

> 1 out of 5 Americans lived in poverty

proposed a sweeping plan to address economic inequality. This set of initiatives was called the GREAT SOCIETY.

Great Society programs, many of which still exist, were:

The establishment of **MEDICARE** and **MEDICAID**

Funding for public schools

Funding for environmental protection

The establishment of the
DEPARTMENT OF HOUSING AND URBAN DEVELOPMENT
and the DEPARTMENT OF TRANSPORTATION

MEDICARE
government-run and
government-subsidized health
insurance for the elderly

MEDICAID
government health insurance
for the needy

ALTERNATIVE CIVIL RIGHTS TACTICS

Some leaders—such as MALCOLM X, a member of the Black Muslim group NATION OF ISLAM—blamed the slow pace of reform on nonviolence. He proposed that Black people should use violence as self-defense against police brutality. He also believed that self-determination was the only way for Black Americans to achieve equality, and proposed that they should separate to form their own society. (He later changed his mind, instead advocating peaceful coexistence.)

Malcolm X was assassinated in 1965, but he inspired the **BLACK POWER** movement, which SNCC leader STOKELY CARMICHAEL popularized.

> **BLACK POWER**
> a movement for political and economic power to encourage cultural pride and to promote racial equality and justice

HUEY NEWTON and BOBBY SEALE founded the radical BLACK PANTHER PARTY, which carried arms and demanded equality in housing, education, and employment.

ANGER in the STREETS

Despite progress, violence against Black communities continued, sometimes by law enforcement in response to peaceful protests against injustice and sometimes in random acts of terror. Rising tensions and frustration at the slow pace of change sparked **RACIAL UPRISINGS** that broke out in cities across the U.S. every summer from 1965 to 1967. On April 4, 1968, Rev. Dr. Martin Luther King Jr. was assassinated in Memphis, Tennessee. More uprisings swept the country as communities were devastated by the news and fearful of what it meant for the future.

> "Long hot summer" refers to the summer of 1967, when there were many racial uprisings.

> **RACIAL UPRISING**
> a public outbreak of violence between two racial groups in a community, or a rebellion of a racialized community against race-based discrimination

CHECK YOUR KNOWLEDGE

1. How did World War II help raise awareness about civil rights issues among Black American veterans?

2. Why were "separate but equal schools" a violation of the Fourteenth Amendment?

3. Under what circumstances were the Little Rock Nine finally able to attend school?

4. How did Mohandas Gandhi influence MLK Jr.?

5. How did television help Kennedy get elected?

6. What were the Freedom Riders riding? Why?

7. What were Northern volunteers doing in the South during Freedom Summer?

8. Name the programs of the Great Society.

9. How did Malcom X's initial approach to civil rights reform differ from the approach of MLK Jr.?

10. What was the Black Panther Party?

11. Why were there racial uprisings?

CHECK YOUR ANSWERS

1. World War II raised awareness of the hypocrisy in fighting for freedom abroad while inequality persisted at home.
2. The schools for Black children were far inferior to those for white children.
3. The president sent paratroopers to escort them.
4. Gandhi used nonviolent tactics to advocate for self-rule in India.
5. In the first televised presidential debates, Kennedy appeared youthful compared with Nixon.
6. They were riding interstate public buses to protest illegally segregated bus depots in the South.
7. They were registering voters.
8. The War on Poverty, Medicare, Medicaid, education funding, environmentalism, the Department of Transportation, and the Department of Housing and Urban Development
9. Dr. King favored the approach of nonviolent protest. Malcolm X initially proposed that Black people should separate to form their own society rather than join white society.
10. The Black Panther Party was a radical group that carried arms and demanded equality.
11. Racial uprisings were a response to violence against the Black community, and frustration about the slow pace of change.

☆ Chapter 43 ☆

CIVIL RIGHTS GROWS

CIVIL RIGHTS for HISPANIC AMERICANS

The **HISPANIC** population in the U.S. grew dramatically after immigration reforms were made in 1965, prompted by the civil rights movement. Earlier laws protected immigrants from Europe, who accounted for over 80 percent of

> **HISPANIC**
> of or relating to the heritage, people, culture, and language of Spain and/or Spanish speakers of Latin America

the annual total in 1960. Between 1965 and 2021, almost 59 million immigrants have entered the U.S.; 51 percent of that number were from Latin America, 25 percent were from Asia, and only 12 percent were from Europe. The largest group of Hispanic immigrants was from Mexico, but the Spanish-speaking population of the U.S. also includes immigrants from Puerto Rico (now a U.S. territory), Cuba, and elsewhere.

Many immigrants worked as migrant or seasonal farmworkers, particularly in California. Migrant farm laborers worked under harsh conditions, traveling from one ripe crop to the next. The AGRICULTURAL WORKERS ORGANIZING COMMITTEE (AWOC) was led by DOLORES HUERTA (a Chicana) and LARRY ITLIONG (a Filipino). In 1962, this organization merged with the NATIONAL FARM **A MEXICAN AMERICAN WOMAN** WORKERS ASSOCIATION under the leadership of CESAR CHAVEZ (a Chicano) to form the UNITED FARMWORKERS **A MEXICAN AMERICAN MAN** UNION (UFW). They used nonviolent strategies to gain rights and improved wages for migrant workers. The best-known example was the GRAPE BOYCOTT of 1965 through 1970. The UFW persuaded consumers to stop buying California grapes until the farms recognized the union.

In 1968, Chicano students in Los Angeles led a series of walkouts to protest unequal conditions in Los Angeles public high schools, where 75 percent of students were Mexican American. The students met with the school board and demanded education reform, including bilingual education programs.

In 1970, the organization LA RAZA UNIDA was founded to find better housing and job opportunities for Mexican Americans and help them get elected to public office.

CIVIL RIGHTS for INDIGENOUS AMERICANS

During the 1950s, the federal government still operated on the policy that it was best to assimilate Indigenous Americans into mainstream culture and began to take aggressive measures to achieve this: termination of tribes and treaties (which meant an end to funding and assistance) and relocation to urban areas and off reservations, which resulted in low employment and unemployment as well as loss of culture. Indigenous Americans were one of the lowest-income populations in the country.

DON'T SHOP HERE, UNITED FARM WORKERS STRIKE

CHICANO POWER

EQUALITY NOW

The mid-20th century was a turning point for Indigenous American rights. In 1944, the NATIONAL CONGRESS OF AMERICAN INDIANS (NCAI) was founded to advocate for national autonomy, preservation of languages and cultures, control of ancestral lands, and other civil and legal rights. The INDIAN CIVIL RIGHTS ACT OF 1968 ensured that Indigenous Americans had the same rights shared by all American citizens, as well as tribal autonomy. In addition, the policy of "termination" was replaced by a policy of self-determination.

In 1968, a group of young urban Indians founded the AMERICAN INDIAN MOVEMENT (AIM). The goal of this pan-Indian group was to bring attention to bad government policies and mismanagement; it fostered cultural pride in a group who had been asked for centuries to give up their culture. In 1972, AIM physically seized the Bureau of Indian Affairs headquarters, and in 1973, 300 Indigenous people staged a violent occupation of the town of Wounded Knee, South Dakota. They were surrounded by U.S. Marshals and the National Guard. The two sides fired on each other and the standoff lasted 71 days. Indigenous activists persuaded the government to discuss their demands and raised awareness of the terrible conditions in which so many of them lived.

CIVIL RIGHTS for AMERICAN WOMEN

When WWII ended, women who had taken jobs in fields dominated by men were expected to give up their jobs to returning soldiers. Once given the opportunity to support themselves, many women were unsatisfied with being restricted to domestic labor. This frustration was expressed in BETTY FRIEDAN's 1963 book, *THE FEMININE MYSTIQUE*, which is widely considered to have sparked the second wave of the **FEMINIST** movement (the women's movement of the 1960s and 1970s).

> **FEMINISM**
> the belief that men and women should have equal rights and opportunities

The 1963 EQUAL PAY ACT was a victory for equal rights in employment, and the Civil Rights Act of 1964 addressed some gender discrimination.

In 1966, feminists founded the NATIONAL ORGANIZATION FOR WOMEN (NOW) and campaigned for a complete ban on discrimination on the grounds of gender. NOW's demands would have gone into effect if its 1972 campaign for an EQUAL RIGHTS AMENDMENT (ERA) had been ratified by the states.

THE ERA DATES BACK TO 1923 AND THE PROGRESSIVES.

WOMEN DEMAND EQUALITY

Opponents, led by PHYLLIS SCHLAFLY, convinced people that the ERA would disrupt the structure of American families. The amendment was passed by Congress but was never ratified by enough states for it to become a part of the Constitution.

Feminism made some advances: THE HIGHER EDUCATION ACT of 1972, also called TITLE IX, made it illegal to deny anyone the right to participate in federally funded educational programs or activities on the basis of sex, creating funding for girls' and women's athletic programs in public schools and colleges.

CIVIL RIGHTS for EVERYONE

In the 1950s and 1960s, the first lesbian and gay rights organizations were established. The STONEWALL INN UPRISING of 1969 in New York City's Greenwich Village ignited the LESBIAN, GAY, BISEXUAL, AND TRANSGENDER (LGBT) rights movement. In 1979, an estimated 75,000 people marched on Washington to demand equal civil rights for LGBT individuals.

DISABLED IN ACTION was founded in 1970 to raise awareness about the issues faced by disabled Americans. It wasn't until 1990, with the passage of the AMERICANS WITH DISABILITIES ACT, that it became illegal to discriminate against disabled people.

CHECK YOUR KNOWLEDGE

1. In the middle of the 20th century, where did most Hispanic Americans come from?

2. What job did many immigrants from Latin America work?

3. Why was there a grape boycott in the late '60s?

4. What did the federal government do to force assimilation of Indigenous people in the 1950s?

5. What did the Indian Civil Rights Act of 1968 do?

6. To which movement was the book *The Feminine Mystique* connected?

7. How did Title IX help women athletes?

8. What event ignited the LGBT movement?

ANSWERS ▶ 499

CHECK YOUR ANSWERS

1. Mexico
2. Migrant farmworker
3. The grape farms would not recognize the United Farm Workers union.
4. They terminated tribes and treaties, which ended funding for Indigenous nations and forced people to leave reservations and relocate to urban environments.
5. It granted the rights of citizenship to Indigenous people and protected tribal autonomy, ending the policy of termination.
6. The Feminist movement
7. Title IX required schools to fund women's and men's athletics equally.
8. The Stonewall Inn Uprising

EQUAL RIGHTS FOR ALL

Chapter 44 ☆

The COLD WAR

✭ ★ ✭ ★ ✭ ★ ✭ ★ ✭ ★ ✭

HEATS UP

COLD WAR CRISES

Like Eisenhower, Kennedy invested money to help fight Communism abroad. This caused "cold" conflicts—threats and competitions, espionage and subversions, but usually not all-out war. Each president had to navigate a Cold War crisis, even when they inherited them from their predecessor.

The Bay of Pigs Invasion: In 1959, after Communist dictator Fidel Castro rose to power and began limiting U.S. control of Cuban resources, Eisenhower developed a plan to train exiled Cuban **DISSIDENTS** to overthrow him. Kennedy launched the invasion of Cuba that Eisenhower had planned on April 17, 1961, but it failed.

HAVANA
ATLANTIC OCEAN
CUBA
BAY OF PIGS
CARIBBEAN SEA

> **DISSIDENT**
> a person who disagrees
> with or dissents from the
> belief in question

The Berlin Wall: In August 1961, East Germany built a wall across the center of Berlin to close the border with West Germany. The Berlin Wall symbolized the "Iron Curtain" between Western Europe and Communist Europe.

The Cuban Missile Crisis: In October 1962, an American U-2 SPY PLANE saw potential Soviet nuclear missile sites in Cuba. JFK ordered a naval blockade to prevent Soviet ships from reaching the island. Nuclear war was avoided when the USSR agreed to remove the missiles and the U.S. agreed not to invade Cuba.

The Space Race: YURI GAGARIN of the USSR became the first person to orbit the Earth, in April 1961. JFK set a goal of placing a man on the moon by the end of the decade. It took three sets of missions—Mercury, Gemini, and Apollo— but on July 20, 1969, the U.S.'s NEIL ARMSTRONG and EDWIN "BUZZ" ALDRIN were the first people to walk on the moon. ◄——— THE APOLLO PROJECT

ON the OTHER HAND...

To promote world peace, in 1961, Kennedy created the PEACE CORPS, which sends volunteers to developing countries around the world. In 1963, he helped set up a direct hotline between D.C. and Moscow so leaders could communicate quickly in a crisis. Also in 1963, the U.S., the USSR, and the

U.K. signed the LIMITED NUCLEAR TEST BAN TREATY, which banned nuclear tests except underground.

CONFLICT in VIETNAM: A COLD WAR CRISIS

Vietnam was part of FRENCH INDOCHINA (the present-day nations of Cambodia, Laos, and Vietnam, then colonies of France). Leader HO CHI MINH and his INDOCHINESE COMMUNIST PARTY (ICF) joined other nationalists in 1946 to create the VIET MINH, a military coalition to gain independence from France.

Geneva Accords: In May 1954, the French suffered a decisive defeat at the BATTLE OF DIEN BIEN PHU. Afterward, the French and the Vietnamese met in Geneva, where it was decided that Vietnam would temporarily be divided along the 17th parallel (similar to the tactic that had been tried in Korea); the 1956 elections would decide who would run the whole country. In the meantime, Ho Chi Minh would control the Communist North, and NGO DINH DIEM would control the anti-Communist South.

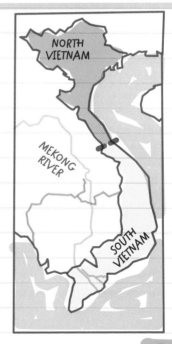

NORTH VIETNAM

MEKONG RIVER

SOUTH VIETNAM

VIETNAM DIVIDED

Eisenhower sent a ton of money and weapons to support Diem's army.

Diem thought he'd lose the national elections, so he canceled them . . . which was not very democratic.

Communists in the south formed the **NATIONAL LIBERATION FRONT**, a group also known as the **VIET CONG**.

The Viet Cong waged guerrilla warfare in South Vietnam and got assistance from northern Communists through a secret network of paths and tunnels called the **HO CHI MINH TRAIL**.

Kennedy sent soldiers from the **SPECIAL FORCES** (known as Green Berets) to help the forces of the south.

In November 1963, Diem's army staged a coup and killed him.

South Vietnam was losing control . . .

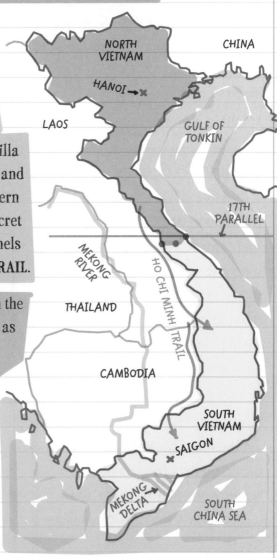

NORTH VIETNAM

CHINA

HANOI → ✗

LAOS

GULF OF TONKIN

17TH PARALLEL

MEKONG RIVER

HO CHI MINH TRAIL

THAILAND

CAMBODIA

SOUTH VIETNAM

SAIGON ✗

MEKONG DELTA

SOUTH CHINA SEA

Eisenhower and the U.S. government believed in the **DOMINO THEORY** about the spread of Communism: If one country "fell" to Communism then its neighbors would fall, too. They used this theory to justify a military presence in Vietnam, despite widespread protests and little progress.

The GULF of TONKIN RESOLUTION

When Lyndon Johnson became president, Secretary of Defense ROBERT McNAMARA told him that he needed to either send more troops to Vietnam or give up the war. In 1964, North Vietnamese patrol boats attacked two U.S. destroyers in international waters. This led Congress to issue the GULF OF TONKIN RESOLUTION, giving the president the power to take military action without declaring war. In March 1965, the U.S. committed combat forces to South Vietnam. U.S. offensive operations in Vietnam ESCALATED, led on the ground by WILLIAM WESTMORELAND.

The USSR was involved in the Vietnam War, but indirectly. The Soviets fought a **PROXY WAR**—they contributed supplies and used a **PROXY**, or stand-in, to do the fighting. The proxies were North Vietnamese Communists. Direct conflict between the U.S. and the USSR would have been too dangerous.

ESCALATION

The U.S. used SEARCH-AND-DESTROY missions to find Viet Cong bases. There was a high rate of civilian casualties because the Viet Cong soldiers took refuge in villages that American troops burned and destroyed.

The U.S. launched a bombing campaign called OPERATION ROLLING THUNDER—which lasted three years and involved dropping hundreds of thousands of bombs on Vietnam, and later, Cambodia.

The U.S. used a fast-burning chemical called NAPALM to burn and destroy forests and villages that lined the Ho Chi Minh Trail.

The herbicide AGENT ORANGE was used to kill the jungle where Vietnamese guerillas took cover. Agent Orange was later shown to cause serious illnesses, including cancer.

Most U.S. soldiers were inexperienced draftees unprepared to fight guerrillas in an unfamiliar tropical climate. The Viet Cong seemed to have an endless reserve of highly motivated soldiers, who infiltrated the south by going through Laos and Cambodia.

The TET OFFENSIVE

On January 31, 1968, during a cease-fire in honor of the Vietnamese New Year celebration of Tet, the Viet Cong and North Vietnam forces ambushed American bases and South Vietnamese villages in attacks called the TET OFFENSIVE. The U.S. had been in Vietnam for years without any territorial gains, and many lives were lost.

THESE ATTACKS RAN ALL ALONG THE HO CHI MINH TRAIL.

The COUNTERCULTURE

Many people thought the U.S. didn't belong in another country's civil war. The DRAFT was controversial: Wealthy individuals and college students could **DEFER**, so those whose incomes were below the poverty threshold were drafted in a larger proportion. Young people turned to the **COUNTERCULTURE**: movements led by HIPPIES and dedicated to peace.

> **DEFER**
> to put off

The MY LAI MASSACRE of March 16, 1968—during which American soldiers murdered hundreds of Vietnamese civilians—drove more people to the antiwar movement.

> **COUNTERCULTURE**
> a culture that is in opposition to (counter to) the mainstream culture

> **CONSCIENTIOUS OBJECTOR**
> someone excluded from military service on the grounds of a moral opposition to war

Some young men declared themselves **CONSCIENTIOUS OBJECTORS**; others burned their DRAFT CARDS or went to Canada to avoid fighting. STUDENTS FOR A DEMOCRATIC SOCIETY led protests on college campuses. They were all accused of being unpatriotic.

> Half a million people attended a counterculture event called the Woodstock Music and Arts Fair, better known as the **WOODSTOCK FESTIVAL**. The August 1969 concert was advertised as "3 Days of Peace & Music."

The ELECTION of 1968

President Johnson announced he wouldn't run for president again because of the stalemate in Vietnam and the unpopularity of the war. Three people were in the running for the Democratic nomination: incumbent vice president HUBERT HUMPHREY; antiwar Minnesota senator EUGENE McCARTHY; and JFK's brother ROBERT F. KENNEDY, a senator from New York. RFK made a strong start, but on June 6, 1968, he was assassinated by a Palestinian, Sirhan Sirhan, because of his support for Israel. Hubert Humphrey won the nomination.

The Republican nominee, RICHARD M. NIXON, won the presidency by appealing to a "SILENT MAJORITY" of patriotic Americans who wanted the war to end but didn't like the counterculture. Nixon promised he'd lead the country out of Vietnam without a shameful retreat. Nixon pledged "Peace with Honor."

> Alabama governor **GEORGE C. WALLACE** ran on a segregationist third-party platform and won over 13 percent of the popular vote. In 1963, Wallace had tried to block desegregation at the University of Alabama. (In his old age, he apologized for his former beliefs.)

NIXON'S VIETNAM

On the advice of National Security Adviser HENRY KISSINGER, Nixon began to withdraw soldiers from Asia and promised to end the draft. Gradually turning over the fighting to the

ARMY OF THE REPUBLIC OF VIETNAM (ARVN) was called the "VIETNAMIZATION" of the war. But at the same time, Nixon secretly bombed Cambodia and sent troops there to cut off the Ho Chi Minh Trail. When Americans found out, there were protests, most of them peaceful. But at KENT STATE UNIVERSITY in Ohio, four students were killed by the National Guard; another protest turned violent at Jackson State University in Mississippi.

NOW CALLED THE "KENT STATE SHOOTINGS" OR THE "KENT STATE MASSACRE"

In 1971, secret documents known as the PENTAGON PAPERS were leaked to the NEW YORK TIMES. They revealed what people suspected: The country had been lied to about how much the U.S. was involved in the war. They also revealed that the U.S. had no idea how to bring about victory in Vietnam.

In the presidential election of 1972, Democrat GEORGE McGOVERN ran on an antiwar platform. But Nixon still won in a landslide of 49 out of 50 states. Nixon had withdrawn almost all American combat troops and drastically reduced American casualties—progress at that point was based on "body counts" and not military objectives.

> **THE TWENTY-SIXTH AMENDMENT (1971)**
> Why was the voting age lowered to 18? Because
> a person could be drafted at 18. The slogan was
> "Old enough to fight, old enough to vote."

OUT of VIETNAM

In the PARIS PEACE ACCORDS of January 27, 1973, the U.S. agreed to withdraw from Vietnam, and North Vietnam agreed to return American prisoners of war. But fighting continued between the North and South Vietnamese. In January 1975, the North launched a full-scale invasion of the South under the belief that the U.S. would not return. Hundreds of thousands of South Vietnamese fled the country; these refugees were called "BOAT PEOPLE" because many escaped by boat. The war finally ended on April 30, 1975, when the Communists captured Saigon, the capital of South Vietnam, and renamed it HO CHI MINH CITY. The nation was united as the SOCIALIST REPUBLIC OF VIETNAM.

VIETNAM AFTERSHOCKS

The war cost 58,000 American lives. Hundreds of thousands were wounded, and others were classified as MIA (missing in action) and were never found. Many soldiers suffered from POST-TRAUMATIC STRESS DISORDER (PTSD). Civilian confidence in the government was low.

Dissatisfaction influenced Congress to pass the WAR POWERS ACT in 1973, limiting how the president could use military force without a declaration of war by Congress.

CHECK YOUR KNOWLEDGE

1. How was the Cuban Missile Crisis resolved?

2. What is the domino theory?

3. What were the terms of the Geneva Accords?

4. What were President Johnson's two choices for how to proceed in Vietnam?

5. Why was the Tet Offensive such a surprise?

6. Why was the draft a subject of protests against the Vietnam War?

7. Under what name was Vietnam reunited?

ANSWERS 511

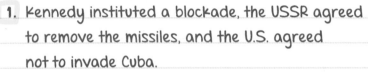

CHECK YOUR ANSWERS

1. Kennedy instituted a blockade, the USSR agreed to remove the missiles, and the U.S. agreed not to invade Cuba.

2. The theory that if one nation becomes Communist, its neighbors will quickly fall to Communism

3. Vietnam would be divided along the 17th parallel until the 1956 elections.

4. He could either pull out or invest fully—he could not continue on a middle path.

5. It came during a cease-fire in honor of the holiday of Tet.

6. Deferments meant that most people who were drafted were living below the poverty threshold.

7. Socialist Republic of Vietnam

☆ Chapter 45 ☆

PRESIDENT RICHARD NIXON

INFLATION

Nixon was elected in 1968 as a socially conservative candidate who promised to end the protest culture of the 1960s. He appointed conservative Supreme Court justices and believed in NEW FEDERALISM, or transferring power from the federal government to the states.

AND MONEY!

He also didn't want to increase taxes.

Between the costs of funding the Vietnam War and the Great Society programs, the U.S. was spending more money than it was bringing in. Nixon's solution was to end inflation by keeping interest rates high (to discourage borrowing) and freezing wages and prices. None of his policies fixed the problem.

"DEFICIT SPENDING"

The OPEC EMBARGO

The economy was also brought to a standstill by the price of oil. The price was so high that some businesses could scarcely function.

In 1973, during the Jewish holiday of Yom Kippur, Egypt and Syria instigated hostilities against Israel in the YOM KIPPUR WAR. The U.S. sent weapons to help Israel. In response, the ORGANIZATION OF PETROLEUM EXPORTING COUNTRIES (OPEC)—a **SYNDICATE** of the Middle Eastern nations that provide most of the world's oil—refused to sell to the U.S. This led to soaring gas prices and massive shortages throughout the U.S. The embargo didn't end until March 1974, when Kissinger helped negotiate a cease-fire between Israel and Egypt.

> **SYNDICATE**
> a group of people or organizations that come together to carry out a specific project, duty, or business

REALPOLITIK

Nixon and Kissinger were believers in REALPOLITIK, the theory that a country should pursue policies that are in its best interest regardless of political or moral ideals. Here are some examples:

In China: Nixon decided that a policy of not recognizing the Communist government just kept the U.S. from doing business with an important world player. In February 1972, Nixon became the first president to make a state visit to China. Nixon's support of China went against the U.S.'s long-standing policy of containment.

In Chile: When **MARXIST** Salvador Allende was elected president in 1970, Nixon feared that Chile would become "another Cuba" and ended economic aid.

MARXISM
the economic theory of Karl Marx, who originated the ideas of modern Socialism and Communism

He helped Allende's political enemies instead. In 1973, when Allende was overthrown by GENERAL AUGUSTO PINOCHET, the U.S. supported Pinochet even though he was a **DESPOT** who committed many human rights violations.

DESPOT
a dictator

DÉTENTE

Nixon went to Moscow to meet with Soviet premier LEONID BREZHNEV. The Soviets were eager to reduce hostilities and keep the U.S. from becoming too close an ally of China. The two nations signed the STRATEGIC ARMS LIMITATION TREATY OF 1972 (SALT I), which called for a reduction of nuclear arsenals and was intended to reduce the fear of nuclear disaster. This led to a DÉTENTE, or a relaxation of international hostilities.

SOCIAL ISSUES

Many major upheavals took place during the Nixon presidency, for example:

In 1973, the Supreme Court ruled in
ROE v. WADE that, on the issue of abortion,
women have the right to choose.

The first EARTH DAY was celebrated on April 22, 1970, and the
ENVIRONMENTAL PROTECTION AGENCY (EPA) was formed amid
rising concerns over pollution and environmental conservation.

AFFIRMATIVE ACTION policies were promoted by
the Nixon administration in an effort to
create opportunities for minorities.

AFFIRMATIVE ACTION
policies that take factors such as race, religion, sex,
and national origin into consideration to encourage
equal access to resources and representation

WATERGATE

Although Nixon won the 1972 presidential election in a landslide, he hadn't expected an easy victory. After all, he hadn't managed to end the Vietnam War, and the U.S. economy was in poor shape. He asked some of his aides (notably JOHN EHRLICHMAN, H. R. HALDEMAN, and JOHN MITCHELL) to help him win. His first goal was to get the FBI and IRS to investigate people he considered his enemies.

On June 17, 1972, five people working for the COMMITTEE TO REELECT THE PRESIDENT broke into a Democratic National Committee office in a Washington, D.C., office-apartment-hotel complex called the WATERGATE to steal campaign secrets; they were caught. Nixon denied any involvement and used his presidential powers to prevent investigations of the burglary.

BOB WOODWARD and CARL BERNSTEIN, two reporters for the WASHINGTON POST, investigated the break-in with the help of a secret inside source called "Deep Throat."

FORMER FBI OFFICIAL MARK FELT FINALLY REVEALED HIMSELF AS DEEP THROAT IN 2005.

In February 1973, a Senate investigation began. JOHN DEAN, one of the president's lawyers, testified that Nixon was involved in a cover-up. The Senate committee found out that Nixon had secretly recorded his conversations with members of the White House staff. Impeachment proceedings began in the House. Knowing the tapes would prove he had committed a criminal abuse of power, on August 9, 1974, Richard Nixon became the first U.S. president in history to resign.

> Americans lost confidence in the honesty of the government.

BUT

> The fact that Nixon was caught and charged showed that the government's system of checks and balances worked.

Nixon, however, disagreed with the concept of checks and balances at the executive level. In a later interview, Nixon defended some of his actions by claiming, "When the president does it, that means that it is not illegal."

CHECK YOUR KNOWLEDGE

1. What are the tenets of "New Federalism"?

2. Why did OPEC stop selling oil to the U.S. in 1973?

3. Why was Nixon's decision to visit China a departure from his predecessors?

4. What is the theory of realpolitik, and how did it influence Nixon's decisions about Chile?

5. What major treaty did Nixon and Brezhnev sign in 1972, and what did it do?

6. What is détente?

7. What was the Watergate scandal?

ANSWERS

1. States would get more power and money, thus reducing the size of the federal government.

2. To protest U.S. support for Israel during the Yom Kippur War

3. He was the first president to visit communist China, going against the previous policy of containment.

4. Realpolitik is a theory that a country should pursue policies that are in its best interest regardless of political or moral ideals. Nixon supported the dictator Pinochet in his revolt against the Marxist president.

5. SALT I shrank nuclear arsenals and led to a détente.

6. A relaxing of tensions

7. Five people working on the committee to reelect President Nixon broke into the Democratic National Committee office at the Watergate apartment-hotel complex. They were caught attempting to steal campaign secrets. Nixon denied involvement, but used his power to block investigation of the crime.

☆ Chapter 46 ☆

PRESIDENT JIMMY CARTER

GERALD FORD and the NIXON PARDON

Nixon's original VP, SPIRO AGNEW, had resigned in 1973 because of a bribery and tax scandal. GERALD FORD was the first—and ONLY—VP to be appointed by Congress instead of being voted in through the Electoral College. When Nixon resigned, Ford became president. Ford's early decisions made him seem a little suspicious as well:

Ford **PARDONED** Nixon for any crimes he may have committed during his presidency. Ford reasoned that it would help the country move on, but Americans couldn't understand why Nixon shouldn't be punished.

> **PARDON**
> release from
> liability of an
> offense

Ford stirred up more controversy by offering **AMNESTY** to people who dodged the draft during Vietnam.

AMNESTY
an official pardon for an offense or group of offenders

Ford was unsuccessful at fixing the poor economy he inherited, even after he froze prices, called on Americans to save money, and cut taxes.

On the plus side, Ford signed the HELSINKI ACCORDS, a step toward détente in the Cold War.

A LIST OF RULES TO FOLLOW TO HELP COMMUNICATION BETWEEN THE COMMUNIST BLOC AND THE WEST

ELECTION of 1976

The Democratic Party nominated JIMMY CARTER, former governor of Georgia. He had an appealing image as an ordinary and honest man. These qualities helped him win but also made it difficult for him to put his plans into action once he arrived in Washington. Here are a few examples:

Carter announced a NATIONAL ENERGY PLAN in 1977 to help solve the energy crisis.

Carter cut and later raised taxes, coming across as indecisive.

The economy suffered from STAGFLATION—high inflation, interest rates, and unemployment—which led to little to no economic growth.

Carter supported **ALTERNATIVE ENERGY SOURCES** but was politically hurt by an incident at the THREE MILE ISLAND nuclear power plant in March 1979, when an overheated reactor released radiation into the environment.

> **ALTERNATIVE ENERGY**
> any energy source that is not a fossil fuel

FOREIGN POLICY

President Carter achieved success in his foreign policy. He rejected realpolitik, saying that he couldn't compromise his ideals regarding equality and human rights.

Carter restricted U.S. relations with South Africa to protest their **APARTHEID** regime.

> **APARTHEID**
> the rigid policy of segregation in South Africa from 1948 to 1994

He signed a treaty with Panama in 1977 to allow the country to gain control of the Panama Canal by the end of 1999 as long as it remained a neutral waterway.

He condemned the USSR's violations of human rights, even though that hurt the Cold War détente.

Carter and the Soviet premier Brezhnev signed the SALT II treaty in June 1979 (but it was never formally ratified by the U.S.).

The CAMP DAVID ACCORDS

Carter's greatest achievement was in 1978, when he invited Muhammad Anwar el-Sadat, the president of Egypt, and Menachem Begin, the prime minister of Israel, to CAMP DAVID, the president's retreat in Maryland. They agreed on the CAMP DAVID ACCORDS, which led to a peace treaty between the two nations—the first-ever Israeli-Arab treaty.

IRAN HOSTAGE CRISIS

A revolution was brewing in IRAN, the U.S.'s other major Middle Eastern ally. The ruler of Iran was SHAH MOHAMMAD REZA PAHLAVI, a pro-American leader who was thought to be corrupt. In early 1979, supporters of AYATOLLAH KHOMEINI, a religious leader, overthrew the shah and instituted fundamentalist religious rules. In November, with the new government's support, students in TEHRAN took over the city's U.S. embassy. Embassy workers were held hostage for more than a year. Carter's inability to resolve the crisis gave him a reputation as an ineffective leader.

CHECK YOUR KNOWLEDGE

1. Why did Ford pardon Nixon?

2. What did American voters find appealing about Jimmy Carter's image?

3. What incident hurt the U.S.'s chances of relying on nuclear power for alternative energy?

4. What is apartheid?

5. What was the effect of Carter's stance on human rights issues on the Cold War?

6. Which two nations were signers of the Camp David Accords and why was the treaty significant?

7. How did the Iran hostage crisis affect Carter's image?

ANSWERS 525

1. He thought it would help the country move on.
2. Americans thought he was an ordinary and honest guy.
3. The Three Mile Island incident
4. The policy of segregation in South Africa from 1948 to 1994
5. He called attention to Soviet human rights violations, which hurt relations between the two powers.
6. Egypt and Israel. It was significant because it was the first Israeli-Arab treaty ever.
7. He seemed ineffectual because he could not get the hostages freed.

☆ Chapter 47 ☆

PRESIDENT RONALD REAGAN

RONALD REAGAN

In the 1980 presidential elections, the Republicans nominated RONALD REAGAN, an actor and the former governor of California. Reagan was a hard-line conservative who believed in

TAX CUTS, **SMALL GOVERNMENT,** and

DEREGULATION OF BUSINESS.

He won by a landslide. Carter spent the remainder of his **LAME-DUCK** presidency working to free the hostages in Iran, who were released on the day of Reagan's inauguration.

> **LAME DUCK**
> refers to a politician in between the time he has been voted out of office and the time he actually leaves office

In March 1981, Reagan was wounded in an assassination attempt by John Hinckley but returned to the Oval Office within a month. He instituted conservative reforms. By dealing harshly with striking air traffic controllers, he established himself as a more decisive president than Carter.

REAGANOMICS

Reagan's conservatism was clear in his economic agenda—dubbed REAGANOMICS. It was based on the idea of SUPPLY-SIDE ECONOMICS: Tax cuts and lenient business regulations would increase investments and business growth, which was supposed to TRICKLE DOWN by providing jobs and then come back to the government in tax revenue.

ALSO CALLED "TRICKLE DOWN" ECONOMICS

Reagan cut taxes and social service programs to spur growth in the private sector, but he also increased military spending. More military spending with lower tax revenues created a big deficit, and the country went into a recession in the early 1980s. In 1983, the economy turned back around when unemployment started to decline and consumers began to spend more money.

> Reagan appointed the first woman Supreme Court justice, Sandra Day O'Connor, in 1981.

The EVIL EMPIRE

Reagan's military spending was based on his belief that the Soviet Union was an "EVIL EMPIRE." He wanted to beat them by outspending them in the arms race. In March 1983, Reagan created an antimissile defense program called the STRATEGIC DEFENSE INITIATIVE (SDI), or its nickname: "Star Wars." It was supposed to shoot missiles out of the sky. It seemed far-fetched, and scientists had difficulty developing the technology.

BZZP!

OOPS!

The ELECTION of 1984

WON 49 OUT OF 50 STATES

As the economy remained strong and Reagan continued to project an image of confidence and optimism, Reagan and the Republicans easily won the election of 1984. The Democratic ticket consisted of WALTER MONDALE (who was vice president under Carter) alongside vice presidential candidate GERALDINE FERRARO, the first woman to be included on a major-party ballot for national office.

The IRAN-CONTRA AFFAIR

Reagan supported revolutions against Communism in Central and South America with money or supplies. When a revolutionary Socialist group called the SANDINISTAS came to power in NICARAGUA in 1979, Reagan supported their opposition, called the CONTRAS (because they were AGAINST the rulers). Congress worried that Reagan was leading the country into another pointless foreign conflict. In 1984, it passed a law banning the president from assisting the Contras.

To get around the ban, members of the White House NATIONAL SECURITY COUNCIL (NSC), notably OLIVER NORTH, sold weapons to Iran in exchange for helping to free hostages in Lebanon and then gave those proceeds to the Contras. By creating alternative funding through arms sales, the NSC bypassed Congress's role in appropriating funds. The IRAN-CONTRA AFFAIR was exposed in 1986. Reagan said he wasn't aware of it, so he wasn't found to have broken any laws.

The COLD WAR THAWS

MIKHAIL GORBACHEV became the Soviet Communist Party's leader in 1985. Gorbachev instituted two policies:

perestroika ("reorganization," or economic reforms)

glasnost ("openness" to freedom of political opinion)

Reagan was encouraged by these moves, and in 1987, Reagan and Gorbachev negotiated and signed the

INTERMEDIATE-RANGE NUCLEAR FORCES (INF) TREATY, reducing the size of their nuclear arsenals.

ELECTION of 1988

In 1988, on the strength of Reagan's popularity, his vice president, GEORGE H. W. BUSH, became president. (The Democratic candidate was MICHAEL DUKAKIS, the governor of Massachusetts.) In 1991, the U.S. and the USSR signed the STRATEGIC ARMS REDUCTION TREATY (START), in which they agreed to destroy many of their nuclear weapons.

The COLD WAR ENDS

Gorbachev meant for his reforms to strengthen and modernize the Soviet Union. Letting people express their dissatisfaction but not fixing the economy led to something he didn't expect: The SOVIET BLOC began to advocate independence. In October 1989, protests forced the leader of East Germany to resign, and the new government agreed to open the border with West Germany. At midnight on November 9, 1989, the gates were opened and people began to tear down the Berlin Wall, the symbol of the Cold War. Soon, Germany was reunited into a single, democratic nation.

OUNTRIES
IN THE
SOVIET
BLOC

On July 1, 1991, the Warsaw Pact was disbanded and the Czech Republic, Hungary, Poland, and more declared independence. Advocates of democracy led by BORIS YELTSIN, who had just been elected president of the Russian Federation, forced the defeat of the Communist Party in the Soviet Union. On December 1, 1991, Yeltsin, along with the presidents of Ukraine and Belarus, declared that the Soviet Union was finished. Gorbachev resigned on December 25. The USSR was dissolved on December 26. The Cold War was over.

Communism was still going strong in China. In 1989, soldiers opened fire on pro-democracy protesters in **TIANANMEN SQUARE**, killing hundreds.

CHECK YOUR KNOWLEDGE

1. How did Reagan think that tax cuts would help the economy?

2. When were the hostages in Tehran released?

3. Who were the Sandinistas?

4. How did the National Security Council get money to help the Contras in Nicaragua?

5. What is the difference between *perestroika* and *glasnost*?

6. How did *perestroika* and *glasnost* influence U.S.–USSR relations?

7. How did *glasnost* hurt Gorbachev's power?

8. When did the Cold War end?

ANSWERS

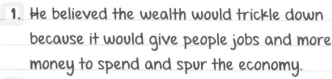

CHECK YOUR ANSWERS

1. He believed the wealth would trickle down because it would give people jobs and more money to spend and spur the economy.

2. The day of Reagan's inauguration

3. A revolutionary Socialist group that came to power in Nicaragua. Reagan supported their opposition.

4. They sold weapons to Iran.

5. *Perestroika* refers to economic reforms, and *glasnost* is a policy of openness.

6. Reagan was encouraged by Gorbachev's new policies and was willing to negotiate the INF treaty.

7. Once dissent was allowed, there were many protests and calls for democracy.

8. The Cold War ended when the USSR dissolved—on December 26, 1991.

Unit 10

American History...
and Current-ish Events!

It's history in the making, and the end is still being written. . . .

Chapter 48

The NINETIES

The PERSIAN GULF WAR

After the Cold War ended, President George H. W. Bush turned to the Middle East. In August 1990, SADDAM HUSSEIN, the dictatorial leader of Iraq, invaded Iraq's oil-rich neighbor KUWAIT and then ignored UN demands that he withdraw.

Under GENERAL NORMAN SCHWARZKOPF JR. and GENERAL COLIN POWELL, the U.S. led a coalition force on a mission called OPERATION DESERT STORM. The PERSIAN GULF WAR began on February 24, 1991, and halted with a cease-fire on February 28.

BUSH LOSES HIS REELECTION BID

President Bush should have been in a strong position for the 1992 presidential election. He had extended environmental protections with the passage of the the CLEAN AIR ACT, he signed the AMERICANS WITH DISABILITIES ACT, making it illegal for the first time to discriminate against people with disabilities, and he had begun the "WAR ON DRUGS." But the economy was weak. The Democratic nominee, Arkansas governor WILLIAM (BILL) CLINTON, defeated Bush and ROSS PEROT, an **INDEPENDENT**.

POPULAR VOTE:
43 PERCENT TO CLINTON
37 PERCENT TO BUSH
19 PERCENT TO PEROT

INDEPENDENTS
voters who choose not to register under either main political party in the U.S.

The CLINTON PRESIDENCY

Clinton's two-term presidency included these achievements:

He persuaded Congress to balance the budget, and the U.S. government had a **SURPLUS** for the first time in 30 years.

SURPLUS
extra (in this context, money), more than is needed

The NORTH AMERICAN FREE TRADE AGREEMENT (NAFTA) opened up trade with Canada and Mexico without tariffs.

He appointed MADELEINE ALBRIGHT as the first woman to serve as secretary of state.

He nominated JANET RENO as the first woman to serve as attorney general.

537

He was part of the 1999 decision by NATO to intervene to end **ETHNIC CLEANSING** in KOSOVO, a region of the former YUGOSLAVIA experiencing civil war.

ETHNIC CLEANSING
removal or killing of an ethnic group in a society

Clinton's two terms in office were also marked by scandal:

The **WHITEWATER** controversy, in which the ethics of a real-estate deal he had been involved with in Arkansas came into question.

He denied (under oath) accusations of an inappropriate relationship with Monica Lewinsky, a White House intern. They were later proved true.

PERJURY
lying under oath

In 1998, Clinton became the second president to be IMPEACHED, for **PERJURY** and OBSTRUCTION OF JUSTICE. The Senate, however, decided not to convict on the grounds that lying about an affair was not a "high crime" (which would qualify for removal from office according to the Constitution).

Step 1: The House of Representatives accuses an official of wrongdoing.

Step 2: The Senate holds a trial of the official and decides to either leave the official in office or remove the official.

A RISE in TERRORISM

The nineties saw an increase in violent political acts called TERRORISM. Terrorism consists of violent and intimidating actions that have a political or ideological purpose, set in motion by individuals or groups not officially backed by a state. Terrorist acts can be initiated by someone on their home country (DOMESTIC terrorism) or by outsiders (FOREIGN terrorism).

Foreign terrorism in the 1990s was primarily the work of **FUNDAMENTALIST** Islamist groups. Examples include the 1993 World Trade Center bombing and the 1998 embassy bombings in

> **FUNDAMENTALISM**
> the strict adherence to a set of basic ideas or principles

multiple African countries. Examples of domestic terrorism in the 1990s include the 1995 Oklahoma Federal Building bombing, and the 1999 Columbine High School shooting.

THE WORLD WIDE WEB

In 1989, a British software consultant named TIM BERNERS-LEE created an open computer network for research purposes, which would become the template for the WORLD WIDE WEB. Following this crucial step, Berners-Lee made key innovations that helped shape the internet we know today:

HTTP (hypertext transfer protocol, which allows you to click on a link and be redirected to that page)

URLs (uniform resource locators, which are web addresses)

HTML (hypertext markup language, which allows you to put links in pages and documents so they connect)

Still, the larger public didn't begin using the internet until the mid-'90s, when companies like Netscape and AOL made browsers and mailed software to people so they could get on the web.

PERSONAL COMPUTERS (PCs) were first mass-marketed in the late 1970s. Before that, people assembled computers from parts themselves. STEVE JOBS and STEVE WOZNIAK sold the first fully assembled Apple computers (Macs) in 1976.

CHECK YOUR KNOWLEDGE

1. What event sparked the Persian Gulf War?

2. What really hurt President Bush's reelection chances?

3. What does it mean to be an independent?

4. What did the North American Free Trade Agreement do?

5. What important jobs did President Clinton give to women for the first time in U.S. history?

6. Why was Bill Clinton impeached?

7. What are the two parts of the impeachment process?

8. What do domestic and foreign terrorism have in common?

9. What do most people call the World Wide Web today?

ANSWERS 541

CHECK YOUR ANSWERS

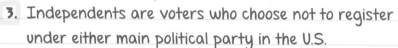

1. Iraq's invasion of Kuwait
2. The weak economy
3. Independents are voters who choose not to register under either main political party in the U.S.
4. The North American Free Trade Agreement (NAFTA) opened up trade with Canada and Mexico without tariffs.
5. Secretary of state and attorney general
6. Perjury and obstruction of justice
7. The House of Representatives accuses, and the Senate holds a trial
8. Both are violent and meant to intimidate, organized by individual people and groups rather than states, based on ideological differences, and hard to prevent.
9. The internet

☆ Chapter 49 ☆

The AUGHTS

2000–2009

BUSH v. GORE

In 2000, Clinton's vice president, AL GORE, ran for president against Republican candidate GEORGE W. BUSH, the governor of Texas and the son of the first President Bush.

The election was a close one. In fact, it was so close that it had no result: Gore won the popular vote, but the electoral result was in question because of disputed vote counts in

> RALPH NADER also ran for president in 2000 as a candidate of the Green Party, which advocates grassroots democracy, social justice, and environmentalism.

Florida. Gore requested that a recount be done by hand in two counties. Bush sued to prevent a recount, and the case went to the Supreme Court.

On December 12, 2000, in the case of BUSH V. GORE, the Supreme Court ruled that hand recounts would not be uniform and would thus be a denial of equal protection of the law. The court also ruled that an alternative recount method could not be established in the time remaining set by Florida law. The original vote count in Florida became official, and Bush became president. The close election led to **PARTISAN** bitterness, made worse by a 50-50 split by party in the Senate.

> **PARTISAN**
> having to do with party politics

STILL CONTINUES TODAY

The PRESIDENCY RESHAPED by 9/11

President Bush followed through on a campaign promise to cut taxes. He also instituted a public education policy, called NO CHILD LEFT BEHIND, to create national testing standards, and he appointed a diverse cabinet. However, his presidency was changed by the events of the morning of SEPTEMBER 11, 2001. On that morning, terrorists hijacked four airplanes in the U.S. Two were flown into the WORLD TRADE CENTER in New York City, toppling the TWIN TOWERS, symbols of American economic power. A third crashed into the PENTAGON, a symbol of American military power, and a fourth was brought down in a Pennsylvania field, by heroic passengers. Thousands

> The **PENTAGON** is a five-sided building in Arlington, Virginia, that serves as the headquarters of the Department of Defense.

of people were killed. The nation experienced a surge of patriotism and was supported by allies all over the world.

WAR on TERROR

The attacks had been orchestrated by al-Qaeda and its leader, OSAMA BIN LADEN. This group consisted of men from various nations who had a shared ideology and were trained in Afghanistan. The fundamentalist party in control there, the TALIBAN, protected them. On October 7, 2001, the U.S. and its allies launched the WAR IN AFGHANISTAN. Initially the Taliban was thrown from power, but their presence remained and attacks and fighting continued for the next 20 years.

President Bush then switched the focus to Iraq. He expressed concern, without proof, that Saddam Hussein had chemical or nuclear WEAPONS OF MASS DESTRUCTION (WMD). Although many allies asked the U.S. to allow UN weapons inspectors more time to look for WMDs, the U.S. (with the help of Britain) began the WAR IN IRAQ in March 2003. The U.S. called the Iraqi campaign OPERATION FREEDOM, but many around the globe considered it an invasion. Baghdad was occupied, and Saddam was ousted. No WMDs were ever found.

HE WAS TRIED AND EXECUTED.

Still, the U.S. continued to occupy both Iraq and Afghanistan. Its process of NATION BUILDING involved maintaining a presence until there was stability in each region—but stability did not come. **INSURGENTS** continued to fight against the U.S. military, and different Muslim sects (notably the SUNNI and SHIA) fought for power.

> **INSURGENT**
> a rebel or a revolutionary

9/11 BRINGS DOMESTIC CHANGE

In October 2001, Bush signed the USA PATRIOT ACT, which increased the capacity of law enforcement to investigate people suspected of terrorism-related acts. Many Americans believed this infringed on their civil liberties. In addition, Congress authorized the creation of the DEPARTMENT OF HOMELAND SECURITY, which began operations in 2003. The mission of the new department was to prevent future terrorist attacks.

Bush won a second presidential term, but as the wars dragged on, he was widely criticized for his handling of a variety of issues,

> During Bush's second term, **CONDOLEEZZA RICE** became the first Black woman secretary of state.

which contributed to his losing control of both houses of Congress to the Democrats in the 2006 midterm elections.

> After the 2006 midterm elections, **NANCY PELOSI** became the first woman to serve as Speaker of the House. She went on to be elected Speaker again after the midterm elections in 2020.

REVOLUTIONARY ELECTION

The 2008 presidential election pitted Republican nominee JOHN McCAIN against a young, Black Democratic senator from Illinois, BARACK OBAMA. Obama ultimately defeated McCain in the general election, becoming the first Black president of the United States. Obama and his running mate, JOSEPH R. BIDEN, campaigned on a platform of "hope" and "change" that focused on:

The **ECONOMY:** After the tech boom of the 1990s ended and a banking crisis in 2008 led to a major recession, Obama promised to boost the weak economy.

HEALTH CARE: Obama called for universal health care for all Americans, signing a bill (the Affordable Care Act, or ACA) into law in March 2010. It is commonly known as Obamacare.

ENDING the **WAR:** This turned out to be even harder than getting health care reform passed.

The **ENVIRONMENT:** Obama promised to engage with the world to find solutions to climate change, a phenomenon that scientists agreed is a big threat.

In 2009, SONIA SOTOMAYOR became the third woman as well as the first person of Hispanic heritage to serve as a justice on the Supreme Court.

MEDIA BECOMES MORE PERSONAL

Two important developments began to transform the daily lives of people around the world, and Americans were no exception. In 2000, there were about 50 cell phones in use per every 100 people in the United States. In dozens of countries today, including the U.S., there are more cell phones in use than there are people!

The AUGHTS were a decade in which people began to use their phones for online banking, sending and answering emails, texting, taking photos and videos, and communicating on SOCIAL MEDIA. FACEBOOK, which initially served the students of Harvard and later all the Ivy League schools, became widely available to the public in 2006, and by 2010 the company boasted 500 million users.

CHECK YOUR KNOWLEDGE

1. What was the Supreme Court's reasoning for its decision in *BUSH v. GORE*?

2. Who was determined to be responsible for the 9/11 attacks?

3. What policies were intended to protect Americans after 9/11?

4. Where is the Pentagon and what happens there?

5. Who was the first woman to serve as Speaker of the House?

6. Why was the presidential election of 2008 considered revolutionary?

7. What was the Affordable Care Act?

8. Which population was the first to gain access to Facebook?

ANSWERS 549

CHECK YOUR ANSWERS

1. Hand recounts could not be uniform and were thus a denial of equal protection of the law.

2. Osama bin Laden, leader of al-Qaeda, had organized the attacks while training his men in Afghanistan, where he was protected by the Taliban government there.

3. The Patriot Act was passed, and the Department of Homeland Security was established.

4. It is located in Arlington, Virginia, and it serves as the headquarters of the Department of Defense.

5. Nancy Pelosi

6. Barack Obama, a Black American, was elected president.

7. Universal health care for all Americans

8. Students at Harvard and other Ivy League schools

☆ Chapter 50 ☆

☆ 2020 VISION ☆

Really recent history is hard to study objectively. Which events will be turning points? Which events will fade? But studying significant political, economic, social, and environmental events of the past decade helps us understand how history is connected to the present and how it may affect the future.

OBAMA WINS REELECTION in 2012

The 2012 presidential election focused on economic recovery and health care. In a contest that pitted Obama against MITT ROMNEY, a Republican businessman and former Massachusetts governor, Americans voted to give Obama another four years. Here are some significant actions he took as president:

- 2009 stimulus package that preceded 10 years of economic growth

- increased regulation of Wall Street

- the DEFERRED ACTION FOR CHILDHOOD ARRIVALS (DACA), which extended residency rights to people brought illegally into the United States by their parents as young children

- the IRAN NUCLEAR DEAL, which required Iran to prove they would use radioactive materials to produce only energy and not weapons

- committed the U.S. to the PARIS CLIMATE ACCORDS, which set worldwide emission standards

- the AFFORDABLE CARE ACT grew to provide 20 million uninsured Americans access to health care

POLITICAL PARTISANSHIP INCREASES

As the 2012 election neared, and Republicans increased their representation in both the House and the Senate, the **PARTISAN** divide got worse and included attacks on Obama's legitimacy. The issue of Obama's birth got little

> **PARTISAN**
> one-sided bias for one's own political party

attention in the 2008 election, but leading up to his reelection campaign, the incorrect argument that he was born on foreign soil and therefore wasn't legally able to be president surged. By 2011, nearly half of Republican voters believed in this argument, which had been nicknamed BIRTHERISM.

MISINFORMATION V. DISINFORMATION: Social media increasingly provides news for many Americans, but these platforms do not require that information be verified. That has led to both **disinformation**, which happens when people deliberately print false or misleading information, and **misinformation**, when people unknowingly believe and repeat disinformation.

There were also power struggles over appointments to the Supreme Court. When conservative Supreme Court justice Antonin Scalia died suddenly in February 2016, MITCH McCONNELL, a Republican senator, refused to hold hearings on Obama's nominee, when the election was more than nine

LATER THE REPUBLICAN MAJORITY LEADER IN THE SENATE

months away. That meant the seat on the Supreme Court was open for over a year. However, when RUTH BADER GINSBURG, an iconic progressive Supreme Court justice, died less than two months before the 2020 presidential election, the same Republican leaders held hearings and confirmed a conservative justice, although voting in the presidential election had already begun.

The ELECTION of 2016

This partisanship lasted into the election of 2016. Both the Democratic Party and the Republican Party had dynamic primary contests. DONALD TRUMP, Republican businessman, reality TV star, and active promoter of birtherism, ultimately defeated a large field of experienced Republican politicians. He ran as a **POPULIST** and appealed to many voters who felt they had been left behind.

> **POPULIST**
> a defender of the rights and power of the people

The Democratic primary also featured a populist candidate, BERNIE SANDERS, whose message was that government needed to be more responsive to the needs of the people. He ran a competitive race against HILLARY CLINTON, which she ultimately won. Clinton went on to face Trump.

TRUMP'S PRESIDENCY

Trump ran as an outsider on the promise that he would shake things up. He continued to be unconventional and took to social media to share his thoughts: TWITTER was his favorite platform. He used Twitter to announce policy decisions, fire people, and criticize his opposition. Here are some significant actions Trump took as president:

- Promoted and signed the TAX CUTS AND JOBS ACT in 2017, which prompted companies to bring a trillion dollars from overseas back into the United States and doubled the child tax credit for families

- Created a sixth branch of the military, the SPACE FORCE, to organize for the defense of U.S. interests in space.

THE OTHER FIVE ARE THE ARMY, THE NAVY, THE AIR FORCE, THE MARINES, AND THE COAST GUARD.

- Led the U.S. to become the world's largest oil-producing nation and negotiated to increase energy exports to Europe

- Worked to reform the criminal justice system and championed the FIRST STEP ACT, intended to help former inmates return to society

UNDOING OBAMA'S 2016 COMMITMENT

- Withdrew the U.S. from the TRANS-PACIFIC PARTNERSHIP trade deal and the Paris Climate Accords

- Moved the U.S. embassy in Israel from Tel Aviv to Jerusalem, recognizing Jerusalem as the capital of Israel

In 2019, Trump faced accusations of improper behavior. He was investigated and ultimately impeached. On December 18, 2019, the House of Representatives, under Democratic Party leadership, officially charged the president with "abuse of power and obstruction of Congress" regarding his dealings with the president of Ukraine. The Senate, under Republican

Party leadership did not call for the release of key documents or call any witnesses, and on February 5, 2020, they voted to acquit the president, who then remained in office.

FOUND TO BE NOT GUILTY

ENVIRONMENTAL EVENTS

Climate activists argued that hurricanes and wildfires, which grew worse during the decade, were signs of the danger posed by global climate change.

In 2012, after devastating the Caribbean islands, Hurricane Sandy made landfall as a tropical storm on the East Coast. Though it impacted 24 states, New York City and the New Jersey coast were especially hard hit.

In a disastrous month in 2017, Hurricane Harvey slammed Texas on August 26, Hurricane Irma hit Florida on September 1, and Hurricane Maria flattened Puerto Rico on September 20.

By December 2020, scientists had identified 30 named tropical storms that season. Having run out of alphabetical names, they began to name the storms for the Greek alphabet.

SOCIAL ACTIVISTS EXERT POLITICAL PRESSURE

Social media is recognized as an effective organizational tool, and many citizens used the internet as well as the streets and the courts to make their voices heard.

Survivors of gun violence worked to change the laws and expose the power of the gun lobby, organizing the MARCH FOR OUR LIVES and promising to vote for change.

The BLACK LIVES MATTER MOVEMENT, first organized in 2013, rose in response to the death of Trayvon Martin and the fact that Black people were increasingly the victims of police and vigilante violence that went unpunished. The deaths of GEORGE FLOYD and BREONNA TAYLOR in 2020 reenergized the movement.

The LGBTQ MOVEMENT began a grassroots campaign for marriage equality that resulted in some state laws allowing same-sex marriage. In 2015, the Supreme Court ruled in OBERGEFELL v. HODGES that all states must allow same-sex marriages.

Indigenous Americans also stood up and blocked the completion of an oil pipeline across the STANDING ROCK Reservation in 2016. The pipeline was finished in April 2017, after an executive order signed by President Trump.

In January 2017, after the inauguration of President Trump, women took to the streets all across the country and around the world to protest in the WOMEN'S MARCH, and, later that year, as film producer Harvey Weinstein's predatory behavior was exposed, women shared their stories of sexual abuse under the slogan #METOO, a phrase that was first used 10 years earlier, but went viral along with the movement.

ECONOMICS: RECESSION, REBOUND, and COVID CRASH

Over the last decade, the U.S. economy has steadily improved. Some low-wage workers saw real increases in wages that resulted in a 17-year low in poverty rates across all **DEMOGRAPHICS**. Single-family home sales jumped over 30 percent from 2018 to 2019. Median household income reached an all-time

> **DEMOGRAPHICS**
> the characteristics of the population, like age, income, or race

high, and the stock market recorded its highest-closing Dow Jones Industrial Average in 2019. But in the last months of 2019, a virus changed all of that.

CORONAVIRUSES had first been identified over 50 years earlier and usually led to coughs and runny noses. The common cold is caused by a coronavirus. But in early December 2019, the first known human infection of a "novel," or new form of, coronavirus, which was a highly contagious and deadly airborne respiratory disease, was identified in Wuhan, China. Based on the year of discovery, it was soon designated as COVID-19. By the end of January 2020, Italy had confirmed its first cases, and Europe had become the epicenter of the disease by the middle of March. By late March, though, the United States had more confirmed cases than either Italy or China. On March 11, 2020, the World Health Organization declared COVID-19 a global pandemic. As 2020 drew to a close, over 70 million people had been infected worldwide and more than 1.5 million had died.

CORONAVIRUS

To fight this global pandemic, many countries closed businesses and schools. Economic activity slowed down as scientists sped up their search for a vaccine. Their research was so ramped up that within a year scientists around the world had developed more than half a dozen vaccines that prevented the worst effects of the virus.

The 2020 ELECTION

In the midst of this pandemic, Donald Trump sought reelection to the presidency. More than 20 Democratic challengers sought the nomination of the Democratic Party. In the end, JOSEPH R. BIDEN, who had been vice president under Obama, captured the nomination. He chose California SENATOR KAMALA HARRIS, the daughter of immigrants from India and Jamaica, who had initially sought a presidential nomination, as his running mate. Running on the strength of the economy, Trump remained popular with the Republican Party and received about 74 million votes. But concerns over his response to Covid-19 and his partisanship disturbed many registered independents. Biden racked up more than 80 million votes in an election that saw the highest voter turnout in over a century. He won the popular vote by more than six million votes and won the Electoral College vote by the same margin that Trump had won in the previous election, 306 to 232. The events of the decade had energized voters, but also left them deeply divided.

Disinformation and misinformation fueled concerns that there was widespread fraud in the election, even though there was no evidence of it. Donald Trump never did concede to Joseph Biden, and for the first time in over 200 years the transfer of power from one president to the next president was not peaceful.

On January 6, 2021, the day that the U.S. Congress was obligated to accept the Electoral College votes as certified by the states casting them, a large group of Trump supporters, believing that there had been voter fraud, stormed the Capitol to prevent the votes from being certified. Ultimately, National Guard troops arrived and helped restore order, and the votes were certified late into the night.

The House of Representatives brought impeachment charges against former president Trump, who had frequently repeated the idea of election fraud and had spoken to the January 6 mob before their attack on the Capitol. On February 13, 2021, 57 senators voted to convict Trump and 43 voted to acquit him. However, an impeachment conviction requires a "supermajority" of 60 votes, and Donald Trump was acquitted in his historic second impeachment.

One defining point of Biden's presidency happened on April 7, 2022—when the Democratic-controlled Senate confirmed his nominee, JUDGE KETANJI BROWN JACKSON, as a Supreme Court justice. Judge Jackson became the first Black woman to serve as justice on the Supreme Court.

JUSTICE KETANJI BROWN JACKSON

As the United States and the rest of the world move further into the 21st century, issues new and old will divide, enrich, and redefine the country.

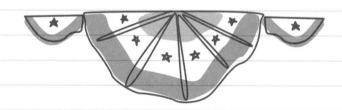

CHECK YOUR KNOWLEDGE

1. How did children of undocumented parents benefit from the executive order known as DACA?

2. What is birtherism?

3. What is a populist?

4. What is the name and goal of the sixth branch of the military as established by President Trump?

5. Why was the Black Lives Matter movement started?

6. What were some of the indicators that the economy was strong by the end of the decade?

7. What was the decision in the case *OBERGEFELL v. HODGES*?

8. What issues were voters most concerned about in the 2020 presidential election?

ANSWERS ▷ 563

CHECK YOUR ANSWERS

1. DACA extended residency rights to people brought to the United States when they were children by parents who entered the country illegally.

2. The incorrect belief that Obama was born on foreign soil, and therefore, not legally able to be president

3. A politician who plans to defend the rights and support the needs of the people first

4. It is the Space Force and is meant to defend U.S. interests in space.

5. To draw attention to the violence committed by law enforcement against Black people that seemed to go unnoticed

6. The U.S. had the lowest poverty rate in years, sales of single-family homes were growing, average or median incomes had risen, and the stock market was strong.

7. That all states must allow same-sex marriages

8. The pandemic, the economy, and partisanship

☆INDEX☆

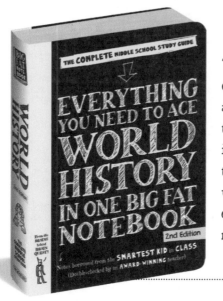